La Moreau

Also by Marianne Gray:

GERARD DEPARDIEU

La  Moreau

A Biography of
Jeanne Moreau

MARIANNE GRAY

DONALD I. FINE BOOKS
NEW YORK

DONALD I. FINE BOOKS
Published by the Penguin Group
Penguin Books USA Inc., 375 Hudson Street,
New York, New York 10014, U.S.A.
Penguin Books Ltd, 27 Wrights Lane,
London W8 5TZ, England
Penguin Books Australia Ltd, Ringwood,
Victoria, Australia
Penguin Books Canada Ltd. 10 Alcorn Avenue,
Toronto, Ontario, Canada M4V 3B2
Penguin Books (N.Z.) Ltd, 182–190 Wairau Road,
Auckland 10, New Zealand

Penguin Books Ltd, Registered Offices:
Harmondsworth, Middlesex, England

First American edition
Published in 1996 by Donald I. Fine Books,
an imprint of Penguin Books USA Inc.

1 3 5 7 9 10 8 6 4 2

Library of Congress Cataloging-in-Publication Data

Gray, Marianne.
La Moreau: a biography of Jeanne Moreau/Marianne Gray.
p.   cm.
ISBN   1-55611-487-7
1. Moreau, Jeanne, 1928–   2. Motion picture actors and actresses—France—
Biography.   I. Title.
PN2638.M636G7   1996
791.43'028'092—dc20
[B]   95-50253
                                           CIP

This book is printed on acid-free paper.
Printed in the United States of America

*For my brother Stephen
who took me to my first Jeanne Moreau film*

INTRODUCTION

When she enters a room with her aura of glamour, a gust of cigarette smoke and the promise of excess, she commands my
attention. As she talks, she punctuates the words with throaty
laughter. At first she looks hard at me with candour, her eyes dark-
ringed, as if searching my face for a reaction, something she wants
to know, something that leaves me unexpectedly swept up. Then I
must have said something disagreeable, for there's a spiky cut-off
made with a pout that leaves me frozen to the core. Somebody
close to her once described it to me as like being 'blasted by
napalm'. She can make you feel wonderful; she can also make you
feel awful.

When I told Jeanne Moreau I was writing her biography, she
sent me an excited – and, for me, exciting – fax, written in her slant-
ing European hand, saying how pleased she was. Then she changed
her mind and decided 'not to interfere' but to continue her own
attempts at writing an autobiography, the guidebook to her life travels, which had been put on ice, frozen out by the demands of *living*
her autobiography.

'It's still too early to write one,' she had said, puffing hard on a long, slim cigarette, her eyes full of experiences we'll probably never know of.

After a further long silence she changed her mind again about co-operating with me. I never asked her why, and we met a few times, for very precise question-and-answer sessions carried out in a strictly businesslike manner. When my time was up, I was dismissed politely but firmly, and referred on to other people in her world.

What is this woman about? She sheds characters like snakeskins. Is she a grand diva still living in some sort of *belle époque*? Is it that she's one of the last of the bohemians with her gap-toothed smile and drifting lifestyle? Maybe she's almost a Bette Davis but with the classic bourgeois elegance that graced the French in the fifties; perhaps just a hard-working woman with a talent for showing a kind of mystery, presence and sexuality.

For most intelligent cinema-going European men over forty she has at some time been a sex symbol, the epitome of sensuality. For many women *d'un certain âge* she has embodied things they aspired to, representing for them the light at the end of the liberation tunnel with her *je m'en foutisme*, lightly shrugged shoulders and the underlying threat that she can be as mad as a hatter.

Her first films came and went, making little impression. The technicians complained that she was not photogenic and at the time she was considered just another chubby young girl doing rather well playing classics on stage as the youngest member of the Comédie Française. Then a chance meeting with director Louis Malle led to him casting her in his film *Ascenseur pour l'Echafaud (Lift to the Scaffold)* and later, in 1958, the film that shocked the world, *Les Amants (The Lovers)*. Aged thirty, she was discovered as the siren of the Nouvelle Vague (New Wave), and became the screen's first woman who knew what it was all about.

Of the three actress icons of French cinema – the kittenish Brigitte Bardot, the glacial Catherine Deneuve and Jeanne Moreau – it is Moreau whose star is still in the ascendant. More than three decades later, her wave is still cresting. There are some human graces that appear to have nothing to do with age and now, in her mid-sixties, Moreau is still stealing the show with an imperishable appeal.

There are many shades to Moreau and she allows herself to be reflected the way the director – or the situation – needs her to be.

There is buoyant Catherine in *Jules et Jim*, balanced by Lysiane, the gravelly bordello proprietress in *Querelle*, or Jeanne Tournier, the adulterous wife in *The Lovers* who caused audiences to gasp in shock when cunnilingus was first implied on screen. At times there is a touch of the nun of *Le Dialogue des Carmélites*, in which she is gentleness itself, or the 'other' nun from *Map of the Human Heart* in which she bristles with the rigidity of religious domination.

In real life Moreau is petite and vital with a persona which seems as fluid and poised as her screen one; this may flash dangerously into impatience or childish point-scoring. She can be very volatile, very capricious, swear like a truck-driver when her temper erupts and is known, friends tell me, to throw terrible tantrums. But the next day, of course, she is plagued by regrets and utterly adorable again. She is funny and wise and flirty, but doesn't begin to suffer fools. She takes her career with professional seriousness, for despite being emotionally dependent on men, she has always had to fend for herself. She worries about illness, loneliness and death, but does not give a damn about ageing and believes passionately in (and seems to have experienced) *grand amour* or rather many *grands amours*.

Her thoughts are so ordered that she can repeat almost verbatim phrases and images used in previous interviews, yet switch to extemporising freely with a flick of the fingers. Always, behind the sharp mind, lies a primal sexuality that tends to put women on their guard and take men off theirs. It is a strange mix of French style from her father's side and Anglo-Saxon pragmatism from her mother's.

Born in Paris to an English Tiller Girl and a French restaurant-owner, Moreau spent her childhood in the Vichy region of central France, from where her father's family came, in wartime Paris, and across the Channel in England on trips with her mother to see relatives. Her English is perfect, spoken in her familiar, scorched voice with French logic. She has performed in English with several British and American directors to build an international body of work over six decades, from the forties, with *Dernier Amour* in 1948, to the present, when she remains busy. By 1965 she had become France's biggest female box-office draw. She can still pull in top money, although for Moreau it is usually the people who count more than the money. She prefers to work on projects that interest her, frequently with young directors in whom she has faith, rather than being involved in stereotypical studio productions.

'I like to have money but I like pleasure more,' she says. 'My greatest passion has always been my work.'

Moreau has directed three films of her own (*Lumière*, *L'Adolescente* and the new *Adieu Bonjour*), made five albums of songs, toured the world with plays and produced her own magazine. She talks of perhaps writing a cookbook and is compiling what she calls a *dictionnaire subjectif*.

In her private life there have been two marriages, one to fellow actor and screenwriter Jean-Louis Richard, the day before their son Jérôme was born; another, briefly, to *Exorcist* director William Friedkin. In between there were many films and quite a few men, including couturier Pierre Cardin.

At her homes, one in Paris and, for some years, another in an old farmhouse in Provence, she has been surrounded by a circle of friends which includes writers, actors, artists, musicians and leading figures in twentieth-century Parisian culture. People like André Gide, Pablo Picasso, Jean Renoir, Henry Miller, Anaïs Nin, Jean Genet and Jean Cocteau were friends at various times although she has never chosen to align herself to any particular group. 'I could never join a group because I walk by myself,' she told me once. 'I never wanted to belong to any organisation which is why I was never a feminist. I don't like labels. I wanted to assert my own difference. Let's just say I'm an isolationist anarchist and thicken the mystery!'

One producer called her 'perversity in the shape of a woman'; another commented that 'she may look like any woman, but she is *every* woman'. Cardin called her 'a simple farming girl'. Truffaut said she had all the attributes of a woman and the best qualities of a man 'without the defects of a man'.

Jeanne herself once said that she loved the lines on her face because they made up the map of her life, etched by the acids of living. As time has gone by her face has seemed to reveal more and more of what may be going on inside her. Whatever this restless, self-possessed woman has done, all of it has made its mark. 'Like any human being I have everything in me – the best and the worst. People who know this about themselves have a deep equilibrium which allows them to see value in everything. I'm not talking in terms of good or bad. It's just that human nature is that way. I was put on this earth to express all these things. The more time goes by, and through what I am discovering about myself, the more I discover about the human race and the rest of the world.'

Jeanne Moreau has been on some interesting travels, both exotic and banal. Her face shows perversity and purity, tragedy and comedy, simplicity and impossible complexity. In repose, her features droop and suggest resentment, danger. When she smiles they light up like a beacon.

To get behind the public face of La Moreau I spoke to friends, family, colleagues and associates in France and in Britain. I visited her birthplace in Montmartre and homes in France to get the feel of her life and spent countless days in dark rooms watching about two-thirds of her films. I have seen her working, watched her at ease, witnessed her whimsical changes of mind.

What follows is a fair observation of the strange life and good times of this untypecast one-woman icon of our times.

Marianne Gray
April 1994

1

M

'Had my mother left my father sooner I would have been an English actress.'

Montmartre in the late twenties still resembled the Paris of the turn-of-century paintings of Toulouse-Lautrec and Matisse. Full of dancers, writers, artists, pimps, prostitutes, people who woke up at sunset and went to bed at dawn, it was a part of the city which still managed to be colourfully seedy.

Chez Moreau was a tiny tenement flat on Place Blanche, an insalubrious and dusty square in the ninth *arrondissement*, a step away from Pigalle, just round the corner from the Moulin Rouge and within a shout of Clichy, where Henry Miller, a friend of Jeanne's in later life, spent his 'quiet days'. The Roaring Twenties were in full swing to the rhythms of Mistinguett and Maurice Chevalier and although post-Great War Paris was still putting back on her pretty face, the decadent early thirties had almost arrived.

These historical vagaries would not have affected the bright brown-eyed baby in Place Blanche, but they could have raised her parents' hopes for Montmartre's glittering revival and their future as a family.

Her father, Anatole Désiré Moreau, a young man from country stock, had left the Allier in central France after the war, hoping to make good in the capital. He was to succeed by running a café-restaurant with his brother Arsène in Rue Mansart. La Cloche d'Or was perched on the gentle slopes of Montmartre, just south of the Sacré-Coeur. They'd bought it as a *tabac* and turned it into one of the 'in' bistros of café bohemia where artistic folk recreated a little of the atmosphere of pre-war Montmartre. Certainly Miller, Anaïs Nin and Josephine Baker could have taken their coffee there.

Among Anatole Moreau's clients one rainy evening in 1927 was a group of English dancers, young Tiller Girls, who lived around the corner in a hotel in Rue Duperré but had supper after the show at La Cloche d'Or. One of them summoned the rakish chef to complain about the food. She said it was too rich, which it probably was for someone used to school dinners.

This was the last time the petite English girl was to complain about his cooking. Two months later, after the young Protestant had taken her first Catholic communion, they married. By the time Kathleen Sarah Buckley Moreau from Oldham started her new job, just down the road in the chorus of the Folies Bergères, she was obviously pregnant. 'It was a big scandal,' recalls Jeanne Moreau, 'because, of course, it was known she was pregnant and, worse than that, my father had been engaged to the daughter of the *boulangère* across the road. I know my Uncle Arsène paid for a wedding because my mother was desperate. My mother never spoke openly about it to me, but through a cousin of mine I learned that my French grandmother, who was supposed to be so close to the Church, asked my mother to try to have a miscarriage.'

On 23 January 1928 Madame Kathleen Moreau had her first child. 'My arrival was not a miracle in the family,' relates Moreau. 'I was unplanned and they wanted a boy. My father got so depressed because I was a girl that he got drunk and had to be taken by friends to the town hall to register my birth.'

The name Pierre had already been chosen. They considered changing it to Pierrette, the female diminutive for Pierre, but the registrar that day was sane enough to protest. 'What a terrible name. Why should you treat a baby that way! Why not call her Jeanne?' So, according to Moreau, she became Jeanne instead – Jeannette to most, Nanette to some close to her.

Madame Moreau suddenly found herself, aged twenty, at the end of her career almost before it had really begun. Half English, half Irish, she had come from Lancashire to Paris at seventeen as a Tiller Girl to dance at the Folies Bergères. Her mother was a Lancashire cotton-mill girl, her father a fisherman who nicknamed his French granddaughter Chatterbox. She grappled with her new life and for years she mourned the death of her career. She never spoke about it to Jeanne, except on one occasion, about three or four years before she died, when she told her daughter that she had once been asked to go and dance in the States. 'I could have had a career,' she'd cried as an old lady, silently, as she had done years before in the cold, unlit dining-room of La Cloche d'Or, so that she didn't wake her baby.

Anatole Moreau's origins were even more rural than Kathleen's. The Moreau family were neither workers nor peasants, but *forains*, itinerant middlemen who handled harvest produce, milled oil, traded delicatessen goods and made farming implements. Deeply traditional, they never quite accepted their foreign dancing daughter-in-law into the fold. Showbusiness people were not to be trusted.

Like her father, Jeanne grew up loving the country and viewing the big city with the eyes of a provincial. From the very early days it seems that, in spite of radical differences in later life, the authoritarian Anatole and his daughter bonded in an unspoken, if fractious, closeness. She sympathised with her mother but she was her father's child. After all, they were both French.

When Jeanne was a year and a half old, her father and his brother split, selling La Cloche d'Or. The restaurant is still there, plastered with rusting signs of recommendation and with a menu that boasts, I was told, the best *lapin* in Paris. Arsène opened another brasserie in Paris, and Anatole moved with his family to Vichy in the Allier to open a small hotel with a restaurant and café, l'Hôtel de l'Entente. His family came from Mazirat, a village close to Vichy, where Moreaux had lived for generations and still do. 'When the brothers parted my grandmother came with us and I had the impression, even at that young age, that things went wrong as soon as they were separated,' Moreau told me years later in Paris.

Vichy, a decorous spa town with a chequered wartime reputation as Pétain's collaborationist government headquarters, is in the Bourbonnais region of central France, 345 kilometres south of Paris, surrounded by oak forests and mountains. Time seems to have stood still in this elegant gamblers' paradise since about 1930, when Jeanne was reaching her first school years.

Today, outside the strictly religious school she went to, giggling little girls in blue and white uniforms still tell jokes behind their hands as they run to their dancing lessons, as she must once have done. Under the *catalpa* trees in the square, tall handsome gentlemen from *départements outre mer* still promenade after drinking of the five different spa waters to clear their systems of anti-malarial pills, and shrunken old ladies wearing original Chanel suits and two-tone shoes sip tea outside Le Rabelaisian *thé dansant*, awaiting the cocktail hour. Nostalgia for the last days of the British Empire has nothing on Vichy's remembrance of things colonial.

During my visit there in 1993 Claude Chabrol's version of *Madame Bovary*, starring Isabelle Huppert, was playing at the main cinema. Chabrol's controversial documentary *L'Oeil de Vichy*, comprising collected official newsreels and short feature films made by the Vichy government from 1940 to 1944, might not get a screening there, however, as Vichy remains very bourgeois. It seems doubtful that there will be a Jeanne Moreau season in Vichy either as nobody questioned by me seemed to be aware that she had spent a little of her childhood in 'the place where the water comes from'.

Probably her happiest times during the Vichy days were passed in isolated, forgotten Mazirat, a hamlet of about two dozen honey-grey stone houses set between the Loire and the Cher, where the Sioule flows along the valley leading to the Auvergne. The cemetery is full of tombstones bearing the name Moreau. Childhood holiday snaps show her sitting happily in the hills nearby with her father, both smiling identically, although she says she does not resemble her father.

According to Jeanne she had a lively childhood in Vichy. She charmed people, telling them interminably long, inventive stories, taking all the roles in various accents. She grew up a tomboy, a real Pierrette, collecting poisonous snakes to sell to the chemist, climbing trees, falling off the white bicycle which had arrived from the city one day on the roof of a rickety country bus. 'When I was a little girl I was built like a tomboy. I was always running wild, always had big scabs on both knees.'

Her first real shock came when, despite the mineral waters running freely in the town, her best friend died of the respiratory disease croup at the age of eight. Going to school without her became hell and Jeannette started to slip into her own world. For her *l'âge de raison* arrived when she was about seven, the age she says she began to feel exiled from life. 'I started to feel there was an incredible sadness to things around me. That was the period when I wanted to become a nun. As a child at a Catholic school, going to church every Sunday, the life of a nun seemed like an enchanted world when I saw what went on outside and the problems of grown-ups.'

She was already aware that the women around her were accepting a life that tended to be violent and sombre, that the men became bitter and unfulfilled. Her parents, unhappy together, would bicker behind closed doors, shutting out their daughter. Aged about eight she decided, as do many children, that she was unwanted. She stole some of the household money and fled from the house on her bike. Six or seven hours later she was caught.

Some time later her mother took her to her breast and whispered, 'You must be courageous, you and I are leaving all this.' Jeanne recalls how she built up her pride at being 'a conspirator' with her mother, planning for the two of them to run away together. But fairly soon after that incident her sister, Michelle, was born. 'I felt betrayed. I knew my mother had given in to my father. Suddenly there was the late birth of my sister. For almost ten years I had been an only child and I'd liked it that way. My sister's birth was a horror to me. I became more secretive and my father couldn't reach me any more. In fact, I came to dislike him profoundly. Then he started adoring my younger sister.'

Michelle was born nine years and nine months after Jeanne. The attention given to the new baby obviously hurt the elder child and she tells a dreadful story about how she plotted to kill the baby by trapping her in the glass-fronted clock on the wall. However, later, when her mother had to go out and find work, it was Jeanne who stayed at home washing, feeding and tending the baby. Gradually an attachment based on Jeanne's powerful protectiveness developed between them. As a result the two sisters have remained the closest of friends and allies.

There were several trips to England to enable Kathleen's family to see the children. She first took Jeanne there as a baby, and returned a few years later when, in Oldham, the child uttered her first words, reputedly in Lancashire-accented English. Moreau's English links, although fewer than her French, apparently remain. Although she is deeply French, the English parts of her past come through, constantly – she drinks cups of tea with milk and sugar all day, loves crumpets and butter, has a teddy bear and all these years later is still able to sing BBC Radio's 1930s *Children's Hour* theme, 'Goodnight Children', as sung by Uncle Mac.

'People are so related to things in childhood,' she remarks. 'I still long for a sort of soup my mother made with Lancashire cheese in milk. I can still smell a certain detergent my English grandmother used to scrub the house. I remember when I was very small crossing the river at Littlehampton with my grandfather in a small boat called *The Wagtail*. We went across to a yacht called *Windswept*, which he used to rent out to others for trips. Sixty years later all this is still so clear in my mind.

'I love so many things about Britain – the food, the tea, the manners, the gardening programmes on TV. And, of course, the tradition – it gives one something to push against. When it goes well for the UK I'm proud. When it goes wrong, I don't like it. I'm very proud of being half English and I think that as time passes my best English qualities are more and more visible. I'm pleased I can be outrageous as only the English can be!'

In 1938, when Jeanne was ten, the family was obliged to move from Vichy back to Paris. It was, she remarks, a few days before King George VI and Queen Elizabeth visited the capital. 'My father had lost everything in the 1936 economic crisis and we were in a state not of actual beggary, but indisputable poverty. He was back to square one and found work in the brasserie on the corner, but this time as a servant. We lived in Rue Mansart again, but in one room in an *hôtel meublé*, with whores and so on. Our room was on the fifth floor. I remember it was very hot. I slept on a little mattress on the floor and when in my sleep my leg or hand fell on to the floor it would become all black with fleas, or with those terrible *punaises* – flat, smelly bedbugs. I thought my mother would go crazy. My sister was still very young and somehow the family had exploded. My grandmother wasn't there any more; my uncle wasn't there. Our ties with this part of France were very loose.'

Jeanne went to the school round the corner in Rue Chaptal, but she was a sickly child and spent more time as an absentee, in bed suffering from a variety of childhood illnesses. To persuade her to eat, her mother used to dance for her – a high kick for each spoonful. These lonely, dreary periods of convalescence were eased only by reading, until she 'wore out' her eyes. When too ill to read, she lay counting the flowers on the patterned wallpaper and listening to the soundtracks of the movies playing at the cinema next door. She had to imagine the images that went with them.

For her mother there was less immediate relief. Realising she'd made the wrong marriage, the dancer-turned-housewife increasingly found herself trapped in an unsuitable life in Paris with two small children, a heavy-drinking husband who refused to learn English and very little money. It was not what she'd been prepared for at dancing school. 'Life must have been very difficult for her,' Jeanne says. 'She didn't speak a word of French at the beginning – later she spoke it fluently, but always kept a lovely English accent. Some of the family liked her very much, but others on my father's side didn't. She was a stranger, she was a foreigner, she was a dancer.'

Kathleen Moreau tried to make another go of life in Paris but, finally defeated, in an attempt to sort out a solution, she decided to take her daughters back home to her parents in England. By the time France and Britain declared war on Germany on 3 September 1939, the three female Moreaux were staying with the Buckleys, now living in the seaside resort of Southwick, near Brighton in Sussex.

On the news of the declaration Madame Moreau decided she must return to France immediately, but the onset of war prevented this and in the end she spent the next four months with her daughters bobbing around on a yacht off the beaches of the English south coast with her mother and father. The yacht belonged to an uncle from the Isle of Wight; unable to find a house to rent, the entire family lived in it together.

During her months spent off Littlehampton, Hove and Southwick, Jeanne managed to attend a school near Brighton. Locals remember her as the prettiest Bumble Bee in her Brownie pack and had she stayed she would have become a Girl Guide. But on New

Year's Day 1940, the three Moreaux, two on foot, one in a pram, left from Newhaven to return home to Paris. Because of the war the journey, which should have taken two days, took almost two months.

On 14 June, a few months after they arrived in Paris, the Germans occupied the capital. They saw the Nazi swastika flying from the Eiffel Tower and the Arc de Triomphe and the victorious German troops marching along the Champs Elysées. Under the ceasefire regulations, France was to be divided into the northern occupied zone and the southern zone under Pétain. As the Germans had just launched a large-scale offensive against Britain, the British were now considered aliens in France. Although she and her daughters had to stay in Paris, Madame Moreau was refused a work permit. Neither was she allowed, as an enemy alien, to leave the occupied zone. Anatole Moreau, meanwhile, had been called up in his native region of Vichy and was not permitted to leave the 'free' southern zone.

Kathleen Moreau had to register daily with the Gestapo. Usually her elder daughter went along with her and Jeanne still recalls going off from their room in a grubby Montmartre hotel, an *hôtel de passe*, where once again most of the inhabitants were prostitutes. Jeanne would run along corridors that stank of cooking, down the stairs and along the street past long queues of German soldiers waiting to be served by the girls. To her it was a world filled with 'people greedy for money and sex'.

'I knew nothing of sexuality. We'd lived, the four of us, in one room together. My mother told me nothing about sex. I was lucky to have grown up in the Allier and spent much of my time outside. I was aware of sensuality, things like changing seasons, hot and cold, beautiful and ugly. But about sex I knew nothing.'

She says her late childhood during the Occupation made her afraid of people. Still too young to follow fully what was going on and not really understanding where her father was, she was aware of an overriding feeling of 'disharmony' in her attitude to people. She now feels that, in a way, she has spent the rest of her life trying to learn how to build up trust and love for other people. 'I suppose I already knew, at the age of about twelve, that I did not like the way people were or what life was about. I didn't like adults at all. I was determined to escape from this world of sex, greed, the black market and prostitution. Everyone knows that in the German Occupation lots of people weren't heroes.' Jeanne went on to draw from these years in the second film she scripted and directed, *L'Adolescente* (1978), which was about a girl growing up in the country during the war.

The war and the daily struggle of mother and daughters to survive with no man around to help taught Jeanne to toughen up at an early age. 'I was still at school and it was a terrible blow when I discovered that some girls were missing after a bombing, and then later some came to school with yellow Jewish stars on their sleeves. There were some girls who were in the Resistance or the Communist Youth, but I always hated being part of an organisation. I later briefly distributed Communist Party leaflets and my father found out and became so angry he boxed my ears. But I was not, and am not, a militant. It is not part of my character.

'Maybe if I'd been older I might have been, but when you're twelve years old you don't really understand much. I feel very nostalgic about my childhood, but it wasn't privileged. I suppose I was happy enough. The war was fun for children in some ways, particularly as the rule-making fathers were away fighting. Everything was suspended, you had a sort of freedom. But I think I was a miserable brat.' She exemplified this on Henry Chapier's popular French chat show *Le Divan* when she laughingly recalled how she once brought charges against her parents for slapping her.

Jeanne recalls how her mother, without money or work, decided to take off with the two girls and escape Paris to join her husband. With Michelle still in a pram, Jeanne by her side and one suitcase, she managed to get them across France, walking one hundred miles under fire as far as Orléans; there they crossed the bridge just before it was blown up. It had taken them three days. Then they were arrested by the Germans and returned to Paris.

'At the Liberation we went to the Place Vendôme, where the English staff officers were headquartered at the Ritz. We were trailing around and suddenly somebody screamed out in amazement. It was my cousin – my mother's nephew from Oldham. It was so strange that we were on either side of the line.'

During the war Jeanne had managed to leave reality behind. She had grown tired of being herself in a hard world. She felt the need to escape, to get out of the dark into a life that would be totally different from her own and her parents' life. She decided that she wanted to become somebody of quality. 'Like my mother, who became a dancer to get out of Lancashire, I've always wanted to be somebody. I knew early on that I didn't want to be like the rest of my schoolfriends and do the usual things kids do. I wanted to be a ballet dancer. Margot Fonteyn's life is something I would love to have had. My Uncle Arsène paid for my ballet lessons. When he died, a few months before my sister was born, they stopped. So instead I read, voraciously, too many books, too soon. That's why I've got these great things under my eyes!

'I'd learn whole texts for fun. By thirteen I'd read Zola and Gide, fascinated but terrified by the darkness of their novels, convinced that life was a dark, solitary place.'

Post-war family life remained almost as solitary for Jeanne as it had been under the Germans. Now reunited with his family, Anatole Moreau was a very strict father who became increasingly tyrannical towards them, hating it when he heard his daughters speak to their mother in English and becoming totally incensed when he caught Jeannette reading novels or newspapers. He mistrusted a young woman developing a will of her own.

She was not allowed to go to the theatre or the cinema. He had banned that because he reckoned he knew about acting folk. To a simple person like him a profession such as acting was to be considered scandalous – performing, like prostitution, was not real work. Jeanne remembers her father taking her to the cinema only once, to see a film by Jean Renoir, someone who was to become a friend many years later. The film was *La Bête Humaine*, (aka *The Human Beast; Judas Was a Woman*) based on Emile Zola's novel about life on the railways, starring Jean Gabin. It was banned by the censors at the start of the war as 'depressing, morbid and immoral'. At the beginning of the film Anatole Moreau fell asleep, but his daughter was entranced by it.

But of course, because she had previously lived next door to a cinema, films were no mystery to Jeanne. When she was a child her father had sent her there with a bowl of soup for the projectionist. In his little box she would watch countless films through the 'port' while the old man slurped down his *soupe de légumes* and munched on his baguette. A ray of light shone back at her from somewhere up on the big screen.

Then, one autumn day in 1943, led on by schoolfriends at the Lycée Edgar-Quinet who talked of nothing but the theatre, she skipped a Latin class. With three friends who were permitted to go to the theatre, she went to a performance of Jean Anouilh's *Antigone*. 'I was amazed because in *Antigone* the girl rebels. She resists authority. She is not afraid of time. I wanted to be like her.' The fifteen-year-old came out of the theatre enraptured. Two days later she spent an afternoon at the Comédie Française watching Marie Bell in a production of Racine's *Phèdre*.

'That was passion. Being in the audience I felt, even the first time, that my place wasn't there in the dark. I didn't feel like being the one who just watches. I wasn't born for obscurity. It was the *coup de foudre*, Paul on the way to Damascus. I knew at once I wanted to be an actress. It was not a money or a fame thing, but an escape from real life. In the theatre I found purity and reality existing together. I lost all interest in school. While my parents thought I was attending class, I was actually at the theatre.'

A couple of days later she saw another play, *Le Voyage de Thésée* (The Voyage of Theseus) by Georges Neveux, starring the great Maria Casarès. The experience was a turning point. Afterwards, completely stagestruck, she went home and announced that she wanted to become an actress. 'My father was drunk and the first word that came out of his mouth was *putain*, "whore". To be an actress was to be a whore.' He slapped her hard across the face and said he never wanted to hear her talk rubbish like that again. *His* daughter was to take up a profession, to be respectable, have a proper job – as a post office employee or a teacher of English.

'He actually wanted me to marry a man who owned a restaurant. I probably would have been behind the cash desk with babies at my feet. I would have ended up in jail because I would have killed the guy!'

Her mother understood her feelings better, but nevertheless worried, confiding in a neighbour the scandalous secret that her daughter wanted to become an actress. The neighbour, a Monsieur Laurençon, himself an actor at the Odéon, was later to recommend a drama teacher for Jeanne. Madame Moreau, against her husband's wishes, sided with her daughter.

After leaving school, having passed the first part of her *baccalauréat* (France's school leaving certificate), and undertaken a brief training to prepare her, in October 1946, Jeanne auditioned at the Conservatoire d'Art Dramatique (France's RADA) with a piece from Daudet's *Le Curé de St Cucugnan* (The Priest of St Cucugnan). She was accepted for the preparatory drama course run by one of Paris's top drama coaches, Denis d'Inès. 'When the Conservatory said yes to me my mother was delighted but my father reacted violently. He was furious. He couldn't understand how I could do this when there was a whole life waiting for me as a woman with a proper career. Not once in my career did he ever compliment me, although I did everything to try to please him and make him proud. Even when I was given the *Légion d'honneur* he said, "But why did they give that to you? What have you been doing?"

'He spent his last ten years at my house in the south of France and my relationship with him was very close and very emotionally violent. It kept me going. Right to the end there was an aggression between us. He never understood what I did. When he saw me in the house cooking and getting things ready for my guests, to him that was real work. That meant something. The rest was just air.'

Anatole Moreau died in 1975, unreconciled to his daughter's profession. She admits that she still feels his presence, somehow spurring her on in rebellion. 'He was, in a strange way, ultimately helpful to me because of his reaction and his obstruction. For him, having me was always like a hen having a duck.'

2

M

'Acting is not a profession, it's a way of life. One completes the other.'

According to fellow student Jean-Louis Richard, the new girl in class at the Conservatory may have been sixteen, but she looked fourteen. When she climbed up on stage she seemed still like a child. But her classmates could already see that somehow she was beginning to express herself in a special way.

'They recognised the core spirit in this free, strong girl with apparently astounding strength concealed beneath a certain gentleness. She was not very centred, but was already extraordinary. I had no doubt about her future as an actress,' comments Richard of those early days. 'She just got up on stage and was transformed. Even then she had the decisive factor – the dividing line between effectiveness and the lack of it – with her tenebrous face and eyes with almost too much happening behind them.'

Richard was to fall in love with Jeanne and later marry her, but before that there was a lot of progress to be made in her transition from young hopeful to somebody.

Her sister, who was seven at the time, remembers her pacing up and down the tiny apartment reciting the lines she had to learn for her classes. Sometimes Michelle was lumbered with the other part to read. She does not recall being overly impressed by the talent of her sister until the first end-of-term production, when Jeanne became the shining discovery. 'Seeing Jeanne on stage was exciting stuff for a little sister,' Michelle Moreau recounts. 'I loved the grandeur of the theatre, but best of all was her crinoline, a vast creation of black and white taffeta which certainly beat the lace curtains I used to dress up in.'

It was clear that she would pursue acting as a career. The Conservatory had given her a path to follow: she was old enough to make up her own mind and take it.

Her decision made, her parents finally parted, Jeanne elected to stay with her father in Paris, living in the maid's room of the hotel where he worked. Her mother, after twenty-four difficult years in France, finally returned to England with Michelle. Although husband and wife were never to see each other again, Jeanne and Michelle remained close and saw both parents regularly until their deaths.

'When I speak to my sister about my mother and father and their friends, she doesn't know the same people I do. Being born so many years before, I knew them when they were still full of pep and optimism. When she arrived their relationship was difficult, the financial situation was terrible and very soon the war arrived. She can't possibly have the same impressions as I do. She became an Englishwoman, grew up with her English stepfather, married an Englishman, had English children.

'Only years later did I learn that when my mother went home before the war, she had planned to leave my father and not return. But the war brought them back together again. Had she left my father sooner, I could easily have become an English actress. Equally, if I'd failed the entrance exam to the Conservatory I would undoubtedly have left France with my mother and sister.'

As a student Moreau became deeply absorbed in classical texts, rehearsals that lasted late into the night, preparations that went on for weeks for scenes in which she perhaps had only a couple of words to say. Already her sense of endurance and determination, which Jean Cocteau was later to compare with a metal wire, was keenly developed. Although d'Inès was not as strict as his predecessor, Louis Jouvet, the lion of French theatre, his classes were not an easy option. Pupils were expected to bury themselves entirely in their work. There was no time to cross the Seine to the Latin Quarter and sit in the cafés and *caves* of Saint-Germain-des-Prés, where post-Liberation intellectual and artistic life was renewing itself. The ferment of the Left Bank, led by Jean-Paul Sartre, passed Jeanne by.

While the rest of her lively circle were listening to *chansonniers* like Juliette Greco and discussing burgeoning existentialist movement over too many cigarettes and much black coffee, Jeanne studied. Sartre, Camus, Prévert and Freud would come to her in the fullness of time. Later she became aware of existentialism and decided she did not like it, even though Sartre, who apparently liked her, used to toss compliments at her from his table in cafés.

'I did not reply that I had "adored" his last book; I had not read his last book,' she commented. She was too busy reading Molière, Racine and de Musset. She seemed to understand their imagery as second nature and gloried in the verse instinctively. She wallowed in texts, her near-photographic memory consuming them eagerly.

Just as she was finishing her first year at the Conservatory, in June 1947, she was approached by Jean Vilar, then an almost unknown actor who later became a mainstay in training young performers. He was looking for a young actress to whom he could give a theatre debut. It was early days for the man who was shaping himself as a revolutionary of the theatre, but when they met they found they shared a common spirit.

Vilar was organising the Avignon Theatre Festival, France's first open-air festival set in the town's great white stone mediaeval Palace of the Popes, and chose Moreau to play in Maurice Clavel's *La Terrasse du Midi*. Her role was small, but hugely important for her – not only was she seen performing on stage in the Grand Courtyard, but she also got to know Vilar well. His concept of the theatre was diametrically opposed to that of more classical organisations such as Comédie Française and the Conservatory, and his attitude was to influence her decisions in her future career. Vilar's Festival d'Avignon is still a flourishing annual summer event in Provence, staging up to a dozen productions ranging from French classics to Edward Bond and Tom Stoppard plays.

A few months later the Comédie Française, France's version of the National Theatre and as venerable an institution as the Royal Shakespeare Company, approached her with an invitation to join them. Of course she was delighted. Not surprisingly, when she went off to join a troupe of periodically travelling players without even finishing her studies at the Conservatory, her father was not. He was even less pleased when he discovered that her first job was playing the part of Veroushka in a complicated Russian play (Turgenev's *A Month in the Country*), directed by Jean Meyer. This was the first time the work of a Russian author had been performed by the Française, and it was all a bit foreign – not only to Monsieur Moreau, but to *le tout Paris*.

Her first real break was in fact quite by chance. The company had tested everybody available for the role except her. Somebody suddenly remembered *la petite Moreau*, and in due course she was chosen for the female lead. She did not let them down; in fact she triumphed as Veroushka, and the play stirred up huge interest both in the press and among the public.

'I was a great success on the opening night but all I could think of was that my parents could not be there; I felt so alone,' Jeanne remembers. When she returned home that night, her father actually scolded her for coming in after midnight. 'The first thing he knew about any of it was when my face appeared on the front page of the evening paper,' she recalls with a crooked grin.

The play was to run and run, until the end of 1948 to be precise. Pierre-Aimé Touchard, the Française's director, then offered her a four-year contract, something that had never happened before to a student who had not yet even graduated from drama school. The one stipulation was an extra clause added to her contract that she finish her drama training.

As she had a strong streak of idealism buried deep in her, cared about security, feared poverty and the destructiveness of failure, she accepted the contract. She determined that nothing should prevent her from succeeding. On her twentieth birthday, in January 1948, she signed the contract and hurtled into an actor's life as the youngest permanently employed *pensionnaire* in the long history of the company.

Welcoming her, Jouvet told her: 'If you want to be a success on the stage you've got to be ready to take a few kicks in the pants.'

'*D'accord*,' answered Jeanne, 'provided I can choose who does the kicking.'

On the day she began she set her own timetable for success: ten years to achieve fame, ten years to exploit it.

At the Française things started out well. In her four years there she was to handle twenty-two parts, and she was cast in virtually every production. She handled roles that spanned Bianca in Meyer's production of *Othello* through to an appearance in Jean-Louis Barrault's version of *Ces Mal Aimés* and in André Gide's *Caves du Vatican* – Gide himself, by then aged eighty, guided the cast through rehearsals of the latter. She particularly shone in farces like Feydeau's *Le Dindon* (The Turkey) where, cast as the maid in an apron, she worked her audience into near hysterical laughter.

While employed at the Française she fell in love with the friend she had had since she was sixteen – tall, good-looking Jean-Louis Richard. She had known him at the Conservatory where he first made a name for himself before he switched to acting with a group headed by Louis Jouvet. Then, while rehearsing for the Française's 1949 production of *Othello*, she found that she was inconveniently pregnant.

'I didn't know it until one day I felt a weakness in my body,' recalls Moreau. 'I was completely unprepared for having a child. My father didn't want me to stay with him and so I moved to a small hotel. I didn't want to marry and we put off marrying till the last moment, and then rushed to the registry office.'

So despite her wish to defy convention, she and Jean-Louis married, on 27 September that year. The next morning at six o'clock their son Jérôme was born. 'We were living together happily unmarried and now I look back and think of all those poor wretches who get married to avoid a scandal. It was so stupid to be pushed into it. Even the obstetrician at the hospital would say things like: "What name will he have?" and "He will be mocked at school for not having his father's name." My only concern was that the baby should look like his father, and when he was born, he did. But then he changed and looked like all other babies.'

Motherhood did not constitute much of an interruption to her work, although it is quite hard to imagine Moreau even at that tender age changing nappies and boiling a baby's bottles. Such mundane activities do not fit with her screen image. Unlike her mother, she would not be confined by her baby. She became even more involved in her acting and was back on stage within a month, leaving Jérôme to be brought up by her mother-in-law. 'I had no disposition at all to be a mother. We all lived together in a small flat in Rue de Richelieu, my husband, my son and my in-laws. We were poor. It was not very easy, but the baby was well looked after.'

Two years later their married life together ended when Jean-Louis Richard left them. He and Jeanne had fallen in love during difficult times, brought closer by constant work and a shared passion for the theatre and their common profession. But they were both too young and, on the surface, life was too exciting for the marriage to work. Moreau feels that, deep down, her marital instability may be pinned directly to her being too involved with her career, but it may also be traced back to her own family and her parents' unhappy marriage. 'All my bad ideas about marriage came from my parents and their disharmony. But all the men I have ever loved, I will love forever.'

Her ex-husband expands: 'I went on long tours round the world with Jouvet's company, and Jeanne, for her part, was always consumed with work at the Comédie Française. Our lives were always bursting apart and dispersing. Acting couples generally don't stay together because of this element of separation. I remember once coming home after a four-month tour and Jeanne leaving the next day for a play in Scandinavia. We separated quickly, but it was evident that we'd be very attached forever. We've made two films together since then. She is still a very important person in my life.'

At about the same time as they separated, Jeanne decided to move on professionally too. The offer of a twenty-year contract with the Comédie Française sounded to her like a rope with which to hang herself. Initially she loved the idea of working for them and concentrated her energies exclusively on the company, but by the time she had spent a couple of years in repertory with them, the paternalistic attitudes of the management had begun to irritate her. To have her spirit hemmed in by such authority on a more or less permanent basis was not what she wanted. Furthermore, she had developed a fiercely hostile relationship with one of the company's leading ladies, Micheline Boudet, and Marie Bell, the *grande dame du théâtre* (and Moreau's teenage idol) had become sour towards her, envious of the younger actress's youth and energy.

So in 1952 Moreau quit the Française. She had had a very good run there and was already a recognised new face. Her voice had become well known on the radio as well. *Paris Match* had run a cover story on her; the American producer Walter Wanger had offered her a seven-year contract with Paramount, which she refused; she had played several of the big stage roles and had a stash of great reviews; she had done a tour to Scandinavia with *Le Dindon*. She had even been mobbed by fans at the station in Copenhagen when the Danish government had invited Jouvet to bring an actress to play in a Hans Christian Andersen homage at Odense, and fans in Paris queued nightly at the stage door for her autograph.

'Everyone thought I was mad to leave, but it had become a prison for me. I was disgusted by the immorality of the company. Everyone had been very sweet to me because I was the youngest, but the situation there was terrible. The established actors would take roles they didn't want just to keep others from having them.

'But more than that, the functioning operation essential for the existence of a company doesn't suit me. It's the death of enthusiasm, and without enthusiasm I'm in a permanent state of inner revolt.'

By the time she left, in June 1951, Jeanne had several feelers out in different directions. She decided to try her luck in the more lucrative vineyards of the popular theatre, and joined the Théâtre Nationale Populaire (TNP), France's most important post-war repertory company. This was an exceptional organisation, started in 1920 by the actor Firmin Gémier. It had a drama school attached to its own 2,600-seater theatre in the Palais Chaillot (it is now called the Théâtre National de Chaillot), and is generally considered to be the company which transformed French theatre. Designed as a touring company, it took all kinds of productions around France, training young performers as it went.

When Jeanne joined the TNP, her old friend Jean Vilar was already one of their directors, mounting open-air productions and more experimental shows. For Moreau this was a fresh start. She was a young girl at heart and everything was still an adventure. She left traditional acting behind and now leaped into contemporary drama in new plays which critics would all too often hate and the public would frequently fail to comprehend.

For Moreau the move was a case of being in the right place at the right time, as 'happenings' in Paris were stripping away bourgeois conventions and moralities. Everyone at the TNP, on her own evidence, ate, drank and slept theatre, drama and performance. She found herself swept into daring roles opposite performers like Gérard Philipe, the dark, dashing leading man of the day. She was involved in Vilar's fifth Avignon Festival, alongside Philipe in Corneille's *Le Cid* and Kleist's *Prince of Hamburg*. She made her TV debut in the documentary made on the festival – *Avignon, Bastion de la Provence* – and was clearly in her element, thriving in a new kind of paradise where she was discovering new areas of experience. She felt she was achieving recognition not only as an actress, but also as a woman and as a person with a life-consuming mission.

'If a war or some other unforeseeable event had prevented me from being an actress, I could have seen myself probably working in the fields, on a farm. But early on I discovered that I could be and would remain an actress, and that acting is not a profession, but a way of living,' she comments on the effect of the TNP's approach. 'One completes the other. What an actor needs is a sense of involvement, an unconscious familiarity with his role, nothing more than that. There's no point in pursuing the character's real-life experience. It's absurd to think you can truly enter it for a week. How annoyed I get to hear people speak of "the profession of acting". The only thing worse is when they say, "You're a real pro."'

But, whether she likes it or not, Moreau has always been 'a real pro'. Under the honing eye of Philipe, a man six years her senior, she progressed in leaps and bounds as an increasingly well-versed actress. On his advice she took her next daring step into the unknown, deciding to go freelance into the Paris stage world.

Samuel Beckett's *Waiting for Godot* had just had its world première in Paris when, in January 1953, the curtain first went up on Moreau, the independent actress, in one of the two leading roles in a new play. This was a boulevard comedy by Anna Bonacci called

L'Heure Eblouissante (The Dazzling Hour), directed by Fernand Ledoux; her role was that of a tart.

On the opening night apparently all went like a dream. Before the second night, however, the other lead, Suzanne Flon, who played the 'wife' role, fell ill. Jeanne was asked if she would like to play the role – as well as, not instead of: the two characters were never on stage together. Amazed, she accepted the challenge, and went home to learn her new lines.

Her father, by now slightly more reconciled to her way of earning a living, stayed up with her all night, helping her memorise the new role, playing the husband to his daughter's wife and mistress. Moreau remembers that they watched the sun come up over Sacré-Coeur. Exhausted, the next evening she appeared in both roles, alternating between ' an honest woman who feels like a streetwalker and a streetwalker who feels like an honest woman'. It was no less than a *tour de force* and ran for two years, almost 500 performances.

Paris had truly discovered Jeanne Moreau. She moved on to other shows. Jean Cocteau, the poet, dramatist and film-maker, called her his 'immortal sphinx' when she appeared in *La Machine Infernale* (*The Infernal Machine*) as his leading lady, hair dusted with silver powder, hands in clawed gloves and body covered in flesh-coloured net. Jean Marais, who had once asked her what her perfect role would be, mounted a production for her in the role she chose – Eliza in Shaw's *Pygmalion*. He also signed up Jean Wall as director, but after three days of rehearsals Moreau said, 'It's him or me.' Marais fired Wall and directed the show himself.

'Jeanne Moreau was more important to me than anything else,' he wrote in his book, *Reflection of my Memories. Pygmalion* ran to full houses until 1957. For her it was another *succès fou*, although it was not a time of easy self-discovery. She remembers herself off stage as being troubled, sad and lonely: 'I was still shy, totally diffident. I felt as if I had started talking only a short while earlier. All those war years had been for me an epoch of silence.

'For years on stage I was ashamed of what I was, perhaps because of my father. I worried about physical defects. Actors told me I was ugly. Then, when I was doing Cocteau's *Machine Infernale* with Jean [Marais], I realised I had a certain magnetism in the theatre. After *Pygmalion* I was more certain of it.'

But it took the controversial British stage director Peter Brook to really push her into her element. Brook had transplanted himself from London's Old Vic to Paris, where he still lives and runs the Théâtre des Bouffes du Nord at Place de la Chapelle. He had seen her a couple of years before in *L'Heure Eblouissante*, thought she was riveting and wanted her for Maggie the Cat in his upcoming production at the Théâtre d'Antoine of Tennessee Williams' steamy Southern melodrama *Cat on a Hot Tin Roof*. American director Richard Brooks brought out his film version of the play two years later with Elizabeth Taylor in the same role.

Brook sent Moreau the manuscript of the play, but she sent it back to him, saying that she could not imagine herself suitable for the sex-hungry Maggie. Brook continued to coax her to take the role seriously, finally managing to persuade her to accept.

Brook did not disappoint her. With Paul Guers as Brick, Big Daddy's neurotic, sexually ambivalent son, and Moreau as the wife he refuses to sleep with, the production proved a stage triumph for her. In her diaphanously flowery frock and spiky stilettos, she floored the audience with her smouldering, frustrated Maggie.

When, as Maggie, she asked: 'What is the victory of a cat on a hot tin roof?" and Brick replied: 'Just staying on it, I guess,' a friend who saw the production remembers a frisson of tangible sensuality vibrating through an audience as yet unused to such raw emotion and searing earthiness. *The New York Times* wrote of her performance: 'Jeanne Moreau now belongs in the forefront of the young generation of French actors. Her incredible fervour and her attractive appearance have brought her a resounding personal triumph.'

But for Moreau the biggest triumph of all was to be the reaction of one Louis Malle. While watching the production he decided to offer her the leading role in a ground-breaking film. 'Contrary to legend, it was not her first film. It was my first film,' he told me. 'Jeanne was already a star in her own right, the greatest stage actress of her generation. By then she'd made about a dozen films, but they didn't know how to use her in film and she was not yet a big movie star.

'I had optioned a thriller called *Ascenseur pour l'Echafaud* (*Lift to the Scaffold*) and with a novelist I admired, Roger Nimier, had adapted it for the screen. I offered the part to Moreau and luckily for us she accepted, because we probably would never have got it made without her. The people putting up the money were thrilled to get her. They wouldn't have given that much if we hadn't had Jeanne.'

This was the start of a long-standing professional relationship and also the beginning of a tempestuous and productive personal one.

3

ℳ

**'If I hadn't been an actress
I might have been an hysteric.'**

Theatre, really, was what Jeanne Moreau did as her night job.

From 1948 her day job was acting in films, shooting all day in studios in and around Paris before racing to the theatre in the evening for the show. She first became involved in this double life to raise money towards her mother's divorce costs, but even without that spur the film work would surely have come as a natural progression from stage work.

Among the film-producer set, however, it was generally held that she was not quite right for the time. She was not an elegant blonde; her face, they said, was asymmetrical, and her mouth would not pout properly. She did not look like Michèle Morgan or Grace Kelly. Technicians had difficulty with her nose, which was too small, and her mouth, which was too big. The word among cameramen was that she was not photogenic. For a woman who managed to hide her insecurity successfully, it could not have been easy to work knowing that the professionals considered her unattractive.

This stereotyping of Moreau persisted right up to the mid-sixties when, for example, American *Cosmopolitan* coverlined her as 'Sexy, smouldering, yet "plain" Jeanne Moreau'. She shrugs this off now, saying that a woman 'always seeks her beauty and is never sure how she looks'.

'From childhood the moment of beauty can come, but we never know when,' she told me in Paris, aged sixty-five and still fascinating to watch. But the constant reminder that she did not look like a star must have chafed away inside her.

'In the old days,' said François Truffaut, 'she had quite a different face. She was just a nice girl, rather saucy, rather chubby. She could have been the Edwige Feuillère [France's version of, say, Anna Neagle] of low-budget B pictures.' Certainly, if you watch those early films now, she appears girlishly full-cheeked with the wrong sort of beauty, not the provocative *jolie-laide* that she would grow into as she found her true face from film to film.

Whatever her looks, however, the young Moreau was well enough known and audiences wanted her to play 'the girl' in their movies, designed as crowd-pleasers and made with known directors and known actors. Film-making in France in the fifties was by no means a cauldron of innovation; actresses were usually there to enhance the images of leading men in their middle years. Jeanne Moreau was no exception.

Her first film was made not long after she joined the Comédie Française when, in 1948, she was offered third billing in Jean Stelli's romantic thriller, *Dernier Amour* (Last Love). Second billing was Suzanne Flon, the actress whose bout of 'flu a few years later gave Moreau the extraordinary break she needed on stage in *L'Heure Eblouissante*. *Dernier Amour* was a reasonable work in which she played the ingenue vamp who came between a husband and wife. She was billed as '*pensionnaire de la Comédie Française*'. The film is now a rare, delicious classic of manners.

'I think I received about three hundred dollars as salary for the entire film. In those days at the Comédie it was *la misère*, or almost, for all of us, and my chums and I almost literally ate what was left of that first pay cheque at a little restaurant in Pigalle. We ate there every night for a week. I lived on my favourite dishes, *bécasse* (woodcock) and *bananes flambées*.'

Dernier Amour was made at the famed studio in the Bois de Boulogne which at the time was threatened with closure as the French film industry was being crushed by the flood of post-war

American films. Thousands of film actors, including notables like Jean Marais and Simone Signoret, had marched through Paris demonstrating for import restrictions on American films. For the novice film actor, the demonstration was an eye-opener and the first time she had started to be concerned about political issues. Although she has consistently resisted getting involved in political causes and says she has never signed any petition apart from the one to prevent the stopping of abortion on demand, this was for Moreau a timely showdown which alerted public attention to the fact that there was a body of serious stage actors working in film.

A year later, in 1949, when the French government unexpectedly took drastic steps towards supporting the home film industry, she realised that films were indeed the required extension of her stage work. The demand was there and audiences were increasing: in 1952 35.6 million people in France went to the movies; five years later this had grown to 41.5 million. The place was right for Moreau to make a career move – she was ready for the different values that come with movie-making – but, in a way, the late forties was the wrong time.

The new so-called Quality Premium backed by the government, there to assist the local industry, resulted in a glut of French films aping the American product. Moreau entered a marketplace heavily preoccupied with gangster movies. Like many other actors, she found that she was accepting roles which were beneath her and she was to spend her cinematic apprenticeship in no fewer than 'nine years of bad films'.

In the twenty time-serving potboilers she made before *Lift to the Scaffold* she was usually cast as a mistress or a tart, and few such parts did her much credit. Some of them were released in Britain as second features on double bills, but mainly they were retained in France for local consumption. Be that as it may, these unmemorable films indubitably taught her all the ropes of working in front of the camera; they also made her a bit of extra cash, and through them she met extraordinary entertainers of the day such as the comic Fernandel and the heavies Jean Gabin and Lino Ventura.

'These pictures were badly treated by the critics, those men who became the directors of the New Wave, but they helped me be what I am, especially as the men who criticised them saw me and later asked me to be in their films. Now there's no such thing as saying, "I prefer this film to that one," because they're all part of my life, part of my experience. One or two I didn't like, but so what?

'Yet in those days I never felt at ease on the screen because I was aware that I was far from beautiful. People who wanted to be nice about my looks would say, "You remind me so much of Bette Davis." Very nice, wonderful in fact, except I can't stand Bette Davis.'

She describes her early insecurity as a film actress as feeling "like a butterfly pinned to a piece of paper". This possibly could have been caused by her so often having been cast as the underdog female. Often she was just badly cast, frequently the work was badly scripted and usually she was stuck with a role in which, as an inexperienced actress, she had to struggle alongside seasoned professionals.

'They taught me plenty but I hated going to the rushes of the day's shoot. They said it wasn't professional if I didn't go to them, so I went, but as I was working hard shooting during the day and acting on stage at night, I just closed my eyes and went to sleep. I was physically present, but I didn't watch! I still don't watch rushes, or the finished film if I can help it. I hate to see my films when other people are around.'

The films she made between 1950 and 1958 (when *Lift to the Scaffold* was released) were all fairly mediocre genre films. Viewed today they are enormous fun nevertheless, and provide an interesting glimpse into the style and period of this era of French showbiz history.

For the record: after *Dernier Amour* came the ingenue role in *Meurtres* with Fernandel for Richard Pottier, followed by a gangster musical called *Pigalle-Saint-Germain-des-Prés*, directed by André Berthomieu, in which she played another ingenue called Pâquerette. Next there was *L'Homme de Ma Vie* (The Man in My Life), in which she played a whore's daughter for Guy Lefranc; and then as a rather plain nurse she was armed with a hypodermic syringe and in love with the famous doctor in André Haguet's allegory of colonial 'goodness', *Il est Minuit, Docteur Schweitzer* (It's Midnight, Dr Schweitzer) – somewhat eclipsed by Pierre Fresnay, she was very sombre but at least not a tart.

In 1953, while she was wowing them as the double lead in *L'Heure Eblouissante*, she had a small part as the pert, almost slapstick waitress in a delicious comedy thriller, *Dortoir des Grandes* (Big Girls' Dormitory) with Jean Marais, directed by First World War flyer and sports author Henri Decoin. That year she worked again with Marais in Marc Allégret's comedy *Julietta*, playing what *Variety* called 'a sharp-tongued and bewildered fiancée'. The film was based on the popular novel by Louise de Vilmorin, then the queen of the Paris literary world and later to become a symbol of women's writing in France. Moreau and de Vilmorin in fact developed a close friendship and were to work together years later on the script of *Les Amants* (*The Lovers*). De Vilmorin also created a musical spectacle called *Migraine* especially for Moreau.

The same year there was another film which was to bring together three of the most important survivors in post-war French cinema: Moreau, Lino Ventura and Jean Gabin. The gangster classic *Touchez Pas au Grisbi* (*Honour Among Thieves*, aka *Hands Off the Loot*) was directed by the great Jacques Becker, himself half Scottish, half French. In a way this film was the start of Moreau being seriously noticed on screen. *Honour Among Thieves* is a genuinely witty, engrossing study of underworld life in which she is almost unrecognisable as Josy, the callgirl dancer in a seedy cabaret who gets marginally involved with the gangsters. Although we watch her dance only briefly, clearly the dancing lessons Uncle Arsène had funded were finally starting to pay off. While it is unlikely that the young Moreau would ever have made the *Josephine Baker Show*, with her neat legs and high heels she gets by in the studio.

The film has stood the test of time and is one of the best of France's imitations of popular American cinema. It is also a prototype of what were known as *série noire* films, now better known as *films noirs*, which are deeply entrenched in film-making in France. With the post-war underworld supplying a conventional setting for later films that were to be less about crime and punishment, more about loyalty, solidarity and friendship, this picture still solidly holds its own as an influence on period pieces and modern remakes.

Moreau could not have found herself a better teacher than the burly, tight-lipped Jean Gabin and, likewise, Gabin could not have found a better pupil. He influenced her screen technique enormously, teaching her about minute gestures and ways of hinting at actions, traits in her acting we still may watch – the slightly raised left eyebrow, the slanted head angle, the seemingly spontaneous use of her hands.

As soon as Moreau wrapped on that film she went into two more for Decoin. The first was a melodrama made in 1953 by four different directors, each on a twenty-minute 'bed' theme, called *Secrets d'Alcove* (Secrets of the Bedroom). She played a pregnant woman in the episode called *Le Lit* (The Bed), with Richard Todd. Todd remembers the film, made when he was a keen young British leading man who had worked in a couple of French films after spending much of his war service in France, as 'a funny, funny picture, full of giggles and jokes'.

'I play a British officer driving by jeep through France and billeted for the night to sleep on a farm,' he recounts. 'I arrive and find the wife, Jeanne, very pregnant. I fall exhausted into the bed of the title, to be woken by the shriek of her having her baby in the kitchen. I help deliver it and carry on my way. It was, in fact, an episode I'd encountered in France during the war, which added to the pleasure of making this film with Decoin, and with Jeanne, who was a very attractive person. She didn't mind at all being made to look very pregnant and very plain and we got on terribly well.'

Todd did not make another film with Decoin, but Moreau did, the following year. In *Les Intrigantes* (*The Parasites*) she plays the scheming wife of a theatre director in a story set on the seamy side of Paris after dark, co-starring Louis de Funès and an old friend from plays at the Française, Robert Hirsch.

When the film eventually opened in London at the Paris-Pullman two years later, the press came out for the first time to greet the woman they had now discovered as a golden-haired and sultry 'English Girl-Paris Star'. Much copy was made of what they called the 'star of French films' really being British. The *Daily Mirror* claimed that she had gone to Paris five years before to appear in a play and, being such a success in France, had decided to stay. Much, too, was made of the reviews of her *Pygmalion* and of the fact that (apparently) in Paris she was called *La Sexe Bombe*.

The tabloid press revelled in her visit to her mother, then living in Southwick; delighted in her sister having joined a troupe of acrobatic dancers and went gooey over her six-year-old son for whom she was going shopping in London for winter woollies. 'My mother will advise me what to buy,' she cooed. They also mentioned with fifties demureness that she was in town with her co-star, dishy Philippe Lemaire, until the *Evening News* grew bolder and reported outright in May 1956: 'French Stars to Wed'. (They did not; they merely romanced.)

Even in France she was trivialised in the press. Unifrance, the government-backed organisation to promote French films abroad, would put out press releases headlined 'A Star', and then spend paragraphs describing how superstitious she apparently was, relating how she worried about every little omen, tried to avoid bad luck, and so on. Serving this kind of apprenticeship better geared to a dizzy blonde must have taught her a lot early on about the nature of the industry which was publicising her. I imagine it all amused her, for she is a woman of quick wit and sharp humour. Indeed, today *The Parasites* is not remembered for much else.

Much as she loved the magic of black and white films, Moreau, like the industry in which she was becoming a figurehead, needed to switch to colour. In 1954 she accepted a film designed as a vehicle to make her as big on screen as she was on stage, taking the title role in the Technicolor film of Dumas' sixteenth-century Huguenot war drama, *La Reine Margot*. This was directed by Jean Dréville from a script by the wide screen pioneer, Abel Gance, who also wrote the script for the 1927 film *Napoléon*.

As the libertine Queen Margot, she looked like Anne Boleyn on a bad day, corseted to the gunwales in an orgy of ruffles and flounces, garish paste jewellery and boned waists. She was being offered to the public as a popular-style sex queen, unbuttoning her robe, showing her breasts. (Moreau has never had any objection to nudity but came away from the project saying she would not care to play in films like *Margot* again.)

It should have been a triumph, what with the flurry of Unifrance publicity featuring kooky pictures of Moreau in costume pointing to a château, with the caption 'La Reine Margot invites you to visit the château of her loves'. But as Louis Malle comments: 'She was brutally lit and you could scrape the make-up off her face with a trowel.' The week this monster came out coincided with the release of *Richard the Lionheart* and *Romeo and Juliet*, and Moreau in high period costume was swamped out of the picture. Further insult was added to injury when the critics who bothered to take it seriously concentrated on the lighter scenes, which had been done by a double, rather than on Moreau's acting in the intimate ones. The only advantage the film had in advancing her career was that she was talked about in the gossip columns as a result, although that was hardly the sort of coverage she sought. In the recent remake Isabelle Adjani plays Queen Margot with far less fuss and bother.

Moreau's stock, meanwhile, had risen in her night job, due to her extraordinary work on stage in *The Infernal Machine*. This was followed by a second run of *Pygmalion*, which now became an anglophone favourite, and Britons flocked in to hear her using a French guttersnipe accent, with '*pauvre fille que je suis*' coming out as '*pauv fille que j'sis*'.

By day she returned to the safety of black and white film for *Les Hommes en Blanc* (Men in White), playing another devoted nurse but this time in a village hospital drama with Raymond Pellegrin. Then she appeared as a *poule* of Pigalle in *M'sieur la Caille* (translated as *The Pigeon*, although *caille* is actually quail). Co-starring Lemaire, whom she was still romancing both on and off the screen, it was described as an 'empty shocker' full of sensation.

The third film that year, 1955, was a sort of early road movie, called *Gas-Oil*, with Jean Gabin playing a lorry driver and Moreau the village teacher who falls in love with him. Yet if the truth be told none of these efforts amounted to much. Neither did the clutch of mainly gangster films with the usual ingredients which followed in 1956 and 1957, although some of these did eventually cross the Channel to be screened at the faithfully Francophile Paris-Pullman.

The hint of far wider recognition first came for Moreau when she made *Le Salaire du Péché* (*Wages of Sin*) for director Denys de la Patellière. Based on Nancy Routledge's novel *Emily Will Know*, this one managed to compete at the 1956 Berlin Film Festival. Although here Moreau's role was secondary to that of Danielle Darrieux, this tasteful nerve-tingler stirred up the first signs of ripples for her in the international pool.

My favourite of the Moreau films of this epoch has to be *Jusqu'au Dernier* (Until the Last), a seductive *film noir* directed by Pierre Billon.

Again with Raymond Pellegrin, Moreau was definitely the female lead this time – as the dancer in a circus, teetering around the ring *en pointe* in black tutu, fishnet tights and a diamanté tiara. Naturally she leaves the circus to follow tradition by running away with a crook, and with her hawkishly striking face and wave of blonde hair she could well have proved an inspiration to the young Faye Dunaway.

Moreau finished shooting *Les Louves* (The She-Wolves) – a rather better class melodrama about a soldier (François Perier) who escapes from German imprisonment and is seduced by the heroine (Moreau) – as she was about to go on stage as the sexy lead in *Cat on a Hot Tin Roof.* While scandal raged through Paris over the raunchiness of Moreau's performance, she quietly continued her morning routine of going down to the film studios. There she shot *L'Etrange Monsieur Steve*, playing the temptress to Lemaire once again, and two more gangster films for Gilles Grangier, the director with whom she had made *Gas-Oil.* In *Trois Jours à Vivre* she is part of a couple (with Daniel Gelin) hounded by a crook and in *Echec au Porteur* she is the fiancée of a gangster who, for love of her, wants to leave the business. The latter turned out to be a rather appropriate theme for the actress, for she was about to 'leave the business' of the films of that old guard and start making a new sort of film.

Until this point her screen presence had represented a robust Gallic national stereotype. But, as mentioned previously, she was about to meet Louis Malle, the director who allowed her to move into the role of a woman rather than a girl, and a woman who had lived intensely and intelligently. Almost overnight their first film together made her the emblematic new woman of European cinema, a woman who could express universal emotions just through her face looking into the camera. Whatever he may say, it was Malle who started the real Moreau legend.

When they met Moreau was twenty-nine. Malle four years her junior. He had noticed her on stage in *Cat on a Hot Tin Roof*, when he was still a director of 'somewhat random' shorts. He felt immediately, he says, that there was something deep, strange and strong about her, something that carried an extraordinary dramatic weight. With Roger Nimier and Prince Napoléon Murat, a producer, he went backstage very shyly after a show at the Théâtre Antoine-Simone Berriau.

He describes her at their first meeting as 'hiding behind black glasses'. 'Of course, she was brilliant in *Cat*, but she must have been in a difficult period; she had some trouble following the conversation, and it seemed as if she was in a very complicated world of her own. But we immediately knew she had to play the part we offered,' he recalls. 'We invited her for dinner that night and after she'd read the book we met for lunch. She was very late, not in great shape and sopping wet because there was a huge storm. We met in the Relais Saint-Germain in Boulevard Saint-Germain and for the first time I had a chance to observe her. I had an intuition that she was an extraordinary *coup de foudre*, especially in the literal sense, for there was a lot of *foudre* outside! Both Roger and I had seen her in *Grisbi* and a couple of other films with Gabin and we thought she was perfect for our film. Her greatness is, of course, that in the space of a few seconds, you can see changes of mood on her face.'

Moreau herself has this to say of their meeting: 'When I first met Louis I knew nothing about him. I knew Roger and I was attracted by what they said. There was something different in their approach to cinema. I loved their enthusiasm and said yes immediately when they asked me to be in their film.'

Moreau said yes, but it was against the advice of her agent, at the time an important man in her career. The director was unknown and they were working without adequate funds or salary, so the agent gave her an ultimatum: it was them or him. She chose to go with the new team. For the first time she felt she had a sort of special relationship with her future director.

Louis Malle was born into a family of great wealth and privilege and they expected him to go into their Béghin sugar business. Educated at conservative Catholic schools, he studied political science at the Sorbonne and then went on to IDHEC, the French government's film school in Paris, despite his family's disapproval. He left after a year when he got the opportunity to join oceanographer Jacques Cousteau as his underwater cameraman aboard the *Calypso*. The resulting documentary, *Le Monde du Silence*, won the Palme d'Or at the 1956 Cannes Film Festival. Malle, who was credited as joint director with Cousteau, was just twenty-four. He then returned to Paris to work, briefly, as an assistant to Robert Bresson on *A Condemned Man Escapes*.

In the fifties Malle had not mixed with the *Cahiers du Cinéma* critics who were forming the core of the so-called *Nouvelle Vague*, but followed his own fairly rosy path. Indeed there is nobody in the French New Wave to whom he can easily be compared. He was a man whose eye saw human experience as others saw landscapes, whose spirit has always been that of an explorer. He would take his camera and go where he was curious to look at something. His films are always full of tiny background tales – the doorman's story, the cab-driver's, the waitress's, the cleaner's, evidence of lives bubbling away behind the scenes. His characters always have inner feelings that need no explaining.

Nurtured and encouraged by him, Moreau felt she had at last found home, a place where reality and art could meet and grow. Swept up in their own interchange, it came as no surprise to anybody in the know when, while making their first film, *Lift to the Scaffold*, they very noticeably fell in love. *Lift* was based on a thriller written by Noël Calef. The complicated plot deals with a woman who spends much of the film wandering around Paris looking for her lover (Maurice Ronet). He has just murdered his boss, her rich, powerful husband (Jean Wall). She is his accomplice, ready to flee with him, but he is trapped, Hitchcock-style, in the elevator back at the office.

Lino Ventura and Moreau's long-standing friend Jean-Claude Brialy also featured, and after Malle met Miles Davis in a jazz club in Saint-Germain, he decided to score his menacing film with 'the inner voice of a quick jazz soundtrack' duly provided by Davis.

'We shot the film using TriX fast black and white film and available natural light, which was interesting for us as TriX had been around a long time but it was so grainy that traditional film-makers didn't use it,' explains Malle. 'We didn't hide Jeanne's face in cosmetics but allowed her to be herself. After years of having make-up artists covering up her looks in a desperate attempt to force her to conform, suddenly she became a real woman. I think she looks particularly beautiful in the night scenes going down the Champs Elysées, when we used only the light from the shop windows. You can see her soul in those shots.

'At the dailies the producers were horrified. They attacked our brilliant cameraman, Henri Decaë. "You can't photograph a famous actress like that!" they shouted at him.'

But *Lift* represented, for the first time, true cinematic reality and it marked the first of the new directors making an *auteur* film in what was to become the *Nouvelle Vague*.

This landmark film opened in 1958 in Paris, a few days after the release of Moreau's *Echec au Porteur*, and two other high-profile *policiers* starring the top box-office stars Jean Gabin and Eddie Constantine. Those who saw *Lift*, unaccustomed to the changed face of *La Sexe Bombe*, wondered what Moreau had done with her mouth and her provocative eyes until then.

As Malle had another project to move on to, he and Moreau had to wait a few months to make their next film together. On Malle's advice she took a role in another director's debut film, this time for Edouard Molinaro, a former technical film director. It was a very black thriller called *Le Dos au Mur* (*Back to the Wall*), a film highly praised by the great André Bazin for its overwhelming technical mastery. Moreau was the lead, again cast as the rich, adulterous wife powered by passion and criminal leanings to murder her husband. The role had been originally destined for Michèle Morgan, but her appeal, it was felt, was too straight for such an evil role.

Moreau gave an ice-cold performance in *Le Dos au Mur*. Once again people raised their eyebrows at such visceral acting. Only slightly prepared for what was still to come from this Jeanne Moreau, with this film they thought they had seen it all.

4

ℳ

**'The public sees me too much as they see me in films where
I'm always playing unorthodox characters.'**

For Alain Siritzky, producer of all seven *Emmanuelle* films, *Les Amants*
(*The Lovers*) was the great erotic classic of his youth. 'I was a kid at
the time, I shouldn't have even seen it,' he says, 'but my father ran
Parfrance Cinemas and so . . .' He shrugs, smiling. 'I still remember
the huge "Oooh!" from the entire audience when Jean-Marc Bory's
head went down Jeanne Moreau's nude body and disappeared off the
screen.'

Louis Malle's film about the upper-class *ennui* of a housewife who
abandons herself into an achingly sensual affair had the same effect on
Siritzky as it did on most of the future members of the erotic New
Wave that was to break; young directors like Francis Leroi, François
Jouffa and Frédéric Lanzac. Seeing the first suggestion of cunnilingus
on screen in a mainstream feature film changed all the rules of the
game. Audiences would henceforth be able to make their 'ooohs'
against the traditional whistles of loud disapproval from moralists.

The Lovers is a fascinating film. As François Truffaut wrote when
it came out, it is done with 'absolute tact and perfect taste'. There are
no scenes of silhouettes cut off by a light or insinuating jokes. Love
is simply presented truthfully. Whereas Roger Vadim's *Et Dieu Créa*

la Femme (*And God Created Woman*) stressed eroticism to put over its message, Malle's film showed love in familiar, almost banal terms.

Written for Moreau by Malle and Louis de Vilmorin, whom Malle had met at the première of *Lift*, from Dominique Vivant's eighteenth-century novel, *Point de Lendemain*, the idea of *The Lovers* was to show the strength and the power of love. Moreau plays Jeanne Tournier, the wife of an ageing newspaper publisher (Alain Cluny). They live with their child in a grand country house surrounded by servants. To stave off death by boredom, Jeanne socialises among the rich and chic in Paris, where she has a debonair polo-playing lover. Basically she is a frustrated provincial who wants to shine and seduce. One weekend her husband persuades her to invite her friends home. She does so, albeit reluctantly. Among the house guests is an unexpected visitor, a young man, played by Bory, who helped when her car broke down on her way home.

After dinner they meet by chance in the garden while separately taking the air, an encounter that results in a night of unpremeditated love. At dawn she goes off with him without a qualm.

'I started shooting the film without an actor to play the lover role,' says Malle. 'I had wanted Jean-Louis Trintignant, but he was doing his military service and as this was during the French-Algerian War days, they would not release him. He was *the* one actor I wanted for the part. I worked like mad to get him released but at the time there was a scandal because some pop singers had been let off their army service and they absolutely refused to budge on Jean-Louis.

'It must have been very hard for Jean-Marc Bory to do the role as Jeanne and I were in the middle of a great love affair, living together, arriving on set and leaving together. She had a house in Versailles, which she'd moved into between *Lift* and *The Lovers*, but mainly we were living in my apartment in the sixteenth, near the Trocadéro.

'The whole thing of doing the love scenes must have been very tough for Bory. That's probably why we didn't see much of him. The love scenes were difficult for all of us. They were improvised. They weren't in Louise's script and she disapproved of them − "I don't want to have anything to do with this," she said. With scenes like these, one had to understand that something was happening to this woman, Jeanne Tournier, that had never happened to her before.'

The scenes in question begin when the Moreau and Bory

characters fall in love, graciously flirting in the moonlight, romancing according to accepted levels of screen morality. Then Malle lets his camera follow the lovers back inside to the bedroom, to bed, to the bathtub and back to bed again, something most audiences now expect in a filmed love scene, but which then had never before been witnessed on celluloid. Holding her world-weary yet childlike face on camera while Bory is almost an off-screen shadow, Malle simply filmed Moreau in close-ups – a hand gripping the sheet, eyes half shut, lips half open – holding the camera as she sensuously slithers her arched body across the sheet, zeroing in on the moment of rapture. In the background the soundtrack picks up her gravelly whisper, sighing, 'Mon amour.' Even now it is a heart-stopping scene. Then it was shocking.

Jean-Marc Bory says he has now forgotten the love scene that changed the world of cinema. In a letter to me he simply remarks that since making the film he has lost touch with his co-star. Moreau reinforces his diffidence: 'He doesn't remember that scene and I don't remember, sometimes, being with him, because he was not there. He appeared on set when he was called. The rest of the time he was sleeping or sunbathing.'

'The scene I was actually most tense about was the one when I had to laugh, when I come back to the house with Bory and start laughing at the idea of my husband and guests as big, furry, disgruntled bears. I see my husband standing there in black and say, "*Je vois un ours*" [I see a bear].'

'For Jeanne,' says Malle, 'it was a very difficult scene because she had to start laughing in the car, come out of it laughing, and go up the stairs to her room, a scene which was shot way afterwards in a studio, still laughing. I was pretty new to this sort of thing and didn't know how to help her. I knew everything about film-making but had no experience of actors. We had to do take after take until, finally, she said, "*Vous croyez c'est facile à faire ça avec tous les deux*" – myself and Henri Decaë, – *avec vos regards sinistres derrière la caméra?*" [Do you think it's easy to do this with you two and your sinister looks behind the camera?]'

The film ran headlong into censorship problems. John Trevelyan, then head of the British Board of Censors, found it a major headache as it was an intelligent and well-made film yet, with its clear implication of cunnilingus, it was regarded as censorable. He describes the dilemma in his book *What the Censor Saw*: 'The problem arose from the music-track. The scene was shot like a ballet to the music of the opening theme of the Brahms String Sextet No.1 in B flat played at half the normal tempo for erotic effect. Visually the scene could easily be cut, but this would involve cutting sections from a well-known piece of music, and this was obviously undesirable.

'Fortunately, Louis Malle, with whom I discussed the problem, was able to use extra film material to fill the gaps, so we were able to pass a modified scene and keep the music intact. Whenever I hear this music I am reminded of *The Lovers*.'

The film was released in Britain with an X certificate but the poster, featuring a photograph of Rodin's 'Le Baiser', the sculpture of a nude couple in a tender embrace, was banned by London Transport. Instead the film was promoted by a floridly painted poster of a fully clad blonde woman on a bed grappling and laughing with a fully clad man.

In France, the Minister of Cultural Affairs, André Malraux, (later Louise de Vilmorin's companion until her death in 1969) refused the film a permit. The cause of the dispute came down to the scene of Moreau's reaction to physical love. Malle said he would not alter the scene, contending that it was essential to his theme. He won, and after a long wrangle – and the attendant clamour of publicity – the film was released uncut. Thousands queued nightly round the block and hundreds were turned away from cinemas all over the country. The naked scene sparked a hot newspaper controversy which even French academics joined, and the press revelled in how Moreau had made Brigitte Bardot, as they said, look like a Girl Guide playing ring-a-roses.

In Germany the film was shortened by fifteen minutes. The cuts included the scene where Jeanne hugs her daughter, as it was not acceptable for a married mother to have an affair. Luckily Hitler's decree that a woman unfaithful to her husband must die before the end of the film had lapsed! America accepted the film, despite its 'perverse' roles, with only one cut, applauding Moreau's talent for suggesting the unsuspected inner passions beneath an external composure, reluctantly accepting it and attributing it to her being a European actress.

Moreau says she found the nude scene quite normal, even in the moral climate then prevailing in France. At the time she was passionately in love with Louis Malle, the mother of a nine-year-old son and still married, though separated from Jean-Louis Richard. The taboos broken in *The Lovers* were ones she had personally left behind a long time before in her private life. 'I would have refused to have done it if I had thought it would be seen in a salacious light,' she said at the time. 'I do not regard myself as a sexy actress. The physical expression wasn't meant to be sexy, but after all, in love there is sex.'

That year the film won a special prize at the Venice Film Festival after much of the 'too revealing' footage had once again been removed. It nevertheless caused a scandal in Venice and there were near-riots and much censure from the Catholic Church. (Pope Pius XII suffered a stroke and died a month later!)

'The Archbishop of Venice more or less said it was a mortal sin to see the film,' remembers Malle, laughing. 'Perhaps it was because of this scandal that Jeanne didn't win the Best Actress – that went to Sophia Loren for a mediocre film [*The Key*]. Jeanne was very depressed by that. We stayed on after the festival but it was sad for both of us. It was Jeanne's film. She was so deeply linked to it. The fact that she didn't get what she deserved was sad.'

The film nevertheless won Moreau a devoted group of serious fans who were to remain loyal thereafter. It took her from the espresso-drinking art-house circuit into the international arena. She had become the epitome of the great screen lover, way beyond local boundaries. In short, after twenty-two films, one scene had made her a star. She became celebrated as the Brave New Woman, the Joan of Arc of the bedroom.

But at the same time her relationship with Malle foundered. 'He could no longer stand to see me as others then saw me – and as only he had seen me until then,' Moreau has said. 'I knew that if I played the love scenes just as Louis wanted, he would love me as an actress but hate me as a woman. I could not play them without betraying him. When I am standing in front of the camera I am an actress through and through.'

She told her friend, author Marguerite Duras: 'I was both ashamed and in love. I couldn't refuse to act as he wanted me to because I loved him. But I also knew it would mean the end of our love. There was never any bitterness or animosity between us. There was grief on my side, but with the passing of time I understood many things. If you have had a very deep relationship in terms of creation on a set, then you have touched a certain intimacy that has to do with creativity. If your communion has been in daily life, as well as in bed, you may lose that intimacy – but the creative intimacy is something divine.'

Malle is perhaps less spiritual about it. 'I was very put off balance by the success of *The Lovers*. I was not sure it deserved such a scandalous success. I was not happy with that. I suppose I was very young and afterwards I ran away to a film festival in Mexico and wanted to make a film in the Caribbean. I came back to Paris but couldn't stand the talk about *The Lovers* so I went back to Mexico. I was always leaving Paris. I didn't like Paris. I was trying to escape. I don't know what I was escaping from – the film's success, the Venice scandal. Whatever it was, I just wanted to be left alone.

'Now I would have a simplistic enjoyment of the success but then anything to do with *The Lovers* and I just freaked. Jeanne and I sort of lost each other. We drifted apart. There was a difficult moment, for about a year, in our private lives, and then we became very good friends for the rest of our lives.'

In spite of her career taking her in the direction of further film-making, Moreau decided to take a break from filming and spend some time in the theatre. She was frightened of being trapped by her role in *The Lovers*. In fact, she was terrified by the crowds which were packing in to see it and she never watched the film again. She was wary of the fact that success is helped by publicity, which she detested. She knew too many actors who had ruined their whole existence in pursuit of success. The temptation 'to be done with it', as she says – not to do any more films, not to have her private life intruded on – is still with her, especially at the end of making a film.

'I think the public sees me too much as they see me in films where I'm always playing unorthodox characters,' she told Oriana Fallaci in the book *Limelighters*. 'My private life is rather different. My private life . . . no, I never talk about my private life. Not that I like to cloak myself in mystery – besides there's very little mystery about me – but it's already so very difficult to sort out one's own problems when there's nobody knowing and watching. Imagine what it would be like with the world knowing and watching.'

Moreau still does not open up easily about her private life. Her son, Jérôme, who has always been kept in the background, is a forbidden subject. There are a few snaps of the mother and her little boy on the beach or gambolling in the sea together, but even in those days he was the mystery man in Moreau's life, living with her when she was not away working, living with his father when she was, living with his grandparents when both were away.

In an attempt to be more private she resumed a lower profile and took a stage job. Her role was a tart named Marie Paule under the direction of André Barsacq in Félicien Marceau's comedy *La Bonne Soupe* (The Good Soup), at the Théâtre du Gymnase. It goes almost without saying that the production was a triumph and that performing with her childhood heroine, Marie Bell, playing Bell's character as a young woman in equal but different roles, must have marked some sort of new psychological headland in Moreau's voyage of discovery.

That year she had moved from her old apartment in Saint-Germain in the Latin Quarter, with Jérôme and housekeeper and confidante Anna Pradella, to a house in a small residential section in the Rue des Missionaires in Versailles. According to friends, she was moping in seclusion and directionless for months. But distanced from Paris, forty-five kilometres south-west of the capital in elegant Versailles, where the National Assembly had resolved great national issues at the palace in 1789, she had time and space to think. A very subtle, rather eccentric Aquarian, she has always taken time off to go into seclusion and ponder. She believes in looking into herself to find the answer and seems always to have done so. She believes in astrology, believes in herself. There is an aura around her of a sort of cosmic insecurity which prevents her from letting things slide.

'I have found astrology can be very helpful,' she says. 'The stars don't tell you who you are or what you are going to experience. People think that to follow astrology is to admit that one's life is a fatality – it is not. The stars are just the print of your own map, the knowledge of what you can use in yourself. What we think is negative can be very positive. Everything is energy. Of course, you succumb to fear when negative and it becomes totally painful and terrible. But fear is just the lack of knowledge of oneself. Every human being knows confusion and confusion is born from fear. I have always followed a philosophy of life that is one of holistic astrology. A very important man in my life was Dane Rudyar, a Frenchman who lived in America, who wrote his philosophy of holistic astrology. His books helped me to get to know myself.' Sister Michelle adds that they sometimes go and consult at the feet of astrologer Patric Walker.

At that time of internal reflection she considered giving up films altogether and staying with the tried and trusted stage. During this time she was supported emotionally and spiritually by Florence Malraux, the charming and pretty daughter of novelist and Minister of Cultural Affairs André, who is still a very close friend, while her career was turned over to a new agent, Micheline Rozan, a friend since her TNP days. Geared to making films, with no other career option that appealed apart from theatre work, Moreau remained almost becalmed in her inner troubled waters. She was thirty years old and the toast of theatrical Paris, brooding and waiting for the wind to fill her sails and show her the shore.

The landfall that was to appear came in the form of François Truffaut. They had met when she and Malle were in Cannes after *Lift to the Scaffold*. As they walked down one of the corridors of the old Palais du Festival, a tiny young man with charcoal eyes came towards them. Malle recognised him as the film journalist François Truffaut, and they stopped to talk. At the time Truffaut, in Cannes as a critic, was the sternest voice on *Cahiers du Cinéma*. *Cahiers*, the trumpet and bible of the New Wave, was a monthly publication in which writers stressed especially the importance of personal expression in the cinema, so forming the basis of *auteur* cinema theory. For the new generation of actors it was vital reading, particularly as so many of the critics of the 1950s became the *Nouvelle Vague* filmmakers of the 1960s. Moreau knew of Truffaut, having read his articles.

She did not recall Truffaut even looking at her at the meeting but later, back in Paris, she received a letter from him inviting her to lunch in a restaurant in Rue Marbeuf. She joined him eagerly, and was surprised when the meal passed in virtual silence, but not too concerned about it. Truffaut had snails and spinach, Moreau had salad and steak. Like her, Truffaut had bunked off school to go to the theatre and spent his formative years in wartime Paris, deeply affected by certain aspects of it, such as collaboration, hustling, black-marketeering and cynicism in general. His 1980 film *Le Dernier Métro* (*The Last Metro*), named after the last tube home within the eleven p.m. Nazi curfew, was about theatre people during the Occupation.

In his book *The Films in My Life*, he describes how he saw his first 200 films 'on the sly, playing hooky and slipping into the movie house without paying, through the emergency exit or the washroom window'. Moreau was already coming to terms with *auteur* film-making; Truffaut as yet had not felt the tremendous need to enter the film world at all.

After the first one, these silent lunches continued on a regular basis, always with the same menu, once a week for all of six months . . . until one day there was no lunch. Truffaut was ill. Too many snails, declares Moreau gleefully, adding, à propos of nothing, that Truffaut did not know the difference between chicken and lamb. But there was an express letter from him that contained all the things he had wanted to tell her, but had not managed to get out. Then he rang to say he was making his first film, *Les Quatre Cents Coups* (*The Four Hundred Blows*), and would she like to be in it? He told me he invited her to join them to bring them luck.

'He wanted me to appear as myself in a small scene,' says Moreau. 'Because I was still doing *La Bonne Soupe*, we had to do it after the performance late at night.'

'She came along with her friend Jean-Claude [Brialy], to film a short improvised scene in the street,' remembered Truffaut. 'She asks Jean-Pierre [Léaud] to help her catch her dog but Brialy turns up and gets rid of Léaud. He then accosts Jeanne and leaves her to look for her little dog alone.'

The Four Hundred Blows is said to be based on Truffaut's own childhood. It is a beautifully observed picture of a twelve-year-old boy (Jean-Pierre Léaud) who is unhappy at home and lives rough in Paris, only to be sent to a detainment centre from which he escapes and keeps running. Truffaut himself, the overlooked son of eccentric parents, spent time in a reform centre after being arrested for unpaid bills at the Movie-Mania Club he had started at the age of fifteen. Producer André Bazin, then running a successful film club, got him released and took over as his guardian. Truffaut dedicated the film, which won him the best director award at Cannes, to Bazin.

After *The Four Hundred Blows*, Moreau and Truffaut continued to meet for lunch. 'He was a very nice gentleman, a good friend and a very talented director. He introduced me to his friends. I found myself among people I understood, people I wanted to know, people I admired,' commented Moreau in a *Time* cover story in 1965. 'The cinema began meaning something beyond simply being an actress.'

The New Wave brought her a new life. She was spiritually hungry for it and went back to work with a passion. She thrived on the excitement of working with small camera crews, shooting in the street, wearing no make-up, working with directors with whom she had been up all night talking about script changes and who let her appear on film as herself. 'Before, they used to coat me with make-up to hide all the black shadows under my eyes. Now make-up was just make-up – a base and powder, like any woman in the street would wear. These new people let me look tired.' Even, at times, haggard, worn out, showing herself cut back to the fibres of her soul.

When she talks about how her approach to acting was allowed to change with the New Wave, she always emphasises that she tried – and still tries – to do it in only one take, never more than two, relying on the director and moving by instinct. 'I rarely talk about a film before starting it. In a way it is like giving birth, because you don't know what will come out. The director might ask you to do a scene not yet scripted or say new lines but if you're confident and ready to live the life of the person you represent, you can do anything.'

Not for Moreau alone was the New Wave a release of latent talent: with her were Jean-Paul Belmondo, Catherine Deneuve, Anna Karina, Jean-Claude Brialy, Alain Delon, Maurice Ronet and many others, bringing the art movie into its great days. For the cinemagoer coming of age in the sixties in France, there were few pleasures as challenging as watching the curtains part on a new film by a real *auteur*.

The scandal of *The Lovers* had hardly died down when Moreau, lured back to the screen by Roger Vadim, emerged in another morally controversial role as Madame de Merteuil in an updated adaptation of Cholderlos de Laclos' elegant and lustful novel, *Les Liaisons Dangereuses*, released in 1960. As the vicious socialite La Merteuil, she taunts her husband, Vicomte de Valmont, played by Gérard Philipe, into abandoning a young mistress (Annette Vadim, née Stroyberg) who consequently goes insane. In the 1988 version, *Dangerous Liaisons*, Glenn Close and John Malkovich took the Moreau/Philipe roles.

Although Vadim's film has dated badly, in its day, with its dodgy morality and moody jazz soundtrack by Thelonius Monk and Art Blakey, it certainly ruffled the sternness of the bourgeois infrastructure. The French government refused to give it an export licence and a long legal process started. Of course this prompted endless and welcome publicity, so that when the film was released, censored by some municipalities, it was an instant hit. In fact, it became the highest grossing French production of its time. See it for the curiosity value of Jean-Louis Trintignant, aged twenty-nine, as Danceny and Boris Vian as Prévan.

Moreau saw La Merteuil as a treacherous and malicious woman, faithless and amoral, but nevertheless completely emancipated. Vadim saw her as a 'cold, blasé beauty'. 'As far as anyone can tell at the very beginning of life on this earth there was only one sex, which was the best of all possible worlds,' he says in his strongly accented French, by way of presenting his film. 'Today, as far as I can tell, there exist two sexes – male and female. Of course, I know that the problem has never been as acute or universal as today. We are all beginning to encounter this new species of liberated young girl who has abandoned the restraint usually imposed on her sex like overripe fruit.'

Vadim tended to draw this type of character on screen in the form of Brigitte Bardot, his first wife. The character of La Merteuil, a woman who operates behind a mask and uses different weapons, he decided to portray through Jeanne Moreau, the essential *femme fatale*.

'I don't want you to think that in France all my women behave like La Merteuil,' continues Vadim. 'Obviously she's an exception. However she does exist – the woman who wants to prove to herself, at any price, that she is equal. But this woman knows that any man around her with a great many mistresses is known as a Don Juan. She also knows that any woman with a great many lovers is known as a trollop. And it is this fact she cannot accept. I've tried to show her here without her mask.'

This is a charming introduction to a film which, Moreau reflects, should have been set, not in immoral Paris, but in some provincial town where sexual relationships are kept secret and their revelation would provoke a scandal. Or, as she told the *New York Times*, 'in New York, where immorality is entirely in the open and is taken for granted'.

Once again her private life came under scrutiny and headlines gloated in catchy lines like 'Gallic Star Pairing Brains and Beauty'. Indeed, at times she seemed to ask for controversy by making provocative, mischievous statements. She once told an interviewer: 'There are men one goes through like a country,' which inevitably prompted the riposte that she must be a well-travelled woman, and so on. Cuttings on her are littered with indiscreet gems, for example: 'My life is strewn with emotional obstacles that trip me over and end up becoming films.' One can hardly blame the public for assuming that La Moreau on screen was the same woman off it. *Les Liaisons Dangereuses* certainly helped to foment that image.

Almost as if to clear the air, however, the next role she took was as a nun in the Rev. René-Léopold Bruckberger's film of Georges Bernanos's story set in the Revolution, *Dialogue des Carmélites*. With Madeleine Renaud as the mother superior, Moreau plays Mother Marie of the Incarnation, the nun at last saved from the guillotine. A picture of piety, her hair cropped and hands clasped in deep reverence, she managed to utterly break the public's simplistic image of her as the woman who walked on the wild side.

As if by divine intervention, the film won the international cinema's Catholic Grand Prix de l'Office for 1960. The Archbishop of Venice could, at last, see her films again.

5

**'I know what I don't want to do; the problem is I don't
always know what I want to do.'**

By now the world had forgotten about other famous Moreaux: the
celebrated Symbolist painter Gustave Moreau who taught Rouault
and lived in Montmartre, just around the corner from where
Jeanne Moreau grew up; and H.G. Wells' mad mutant-making scientist Dr Moreau. Everybody wanted this Moreau.

American actor Kirk Douglas apparently realised that she would
be box-office dynamite, and wanted her to play his slave girl in
Stanley Kubrick's Roman epic *Spartacus*. 'She exudes sexuality without trying,' he said. But when he approached her agent, he found the
actress was in a play for another month and wouldn't leave. Even
when he offered to buy it out, she still refused. Douglas says that the
reason she rejected his offer was because she was in the middle of a
love affair. 'French actresses fall in love and that takes precedence
over everything. I admire that,' said the actor, who eventually gave
the role to Jean Simmons.

Moreau told me: 'I was actually at the end of the love affair with
Louis Malle and I should have done Kirk Douglas's film. I should
have accepted it. I also refused the Mrs Robinson role in *The*

Graduate, which Mike Nichols offered me, because I didn't like the part. I was silly. I should have done it.'

Instead Moreau made her Hollywood debut in the disastrous *Five Branded Women* for Martin Ritt. It is one of the few films of nearly a hundred she has appeared in that she'll go as far as to say she dislikes. 'I agreed to do it in order to pay back taxes,' she admits with spirit, clearly having written off this misjudgement years ago. 'I hate dealing with money and am not good with books and figures and the taxes had mounted up. I accepted the film only to pay my taxes and not because I liked it. I was justly punished for it. But I'm pleased I did it. I became friends with Silvana [Mangano] and it was fun to work with Martin and I learned Italian. I still have some beautiful pictures of the film somewhere.'

She was cruelly miscast as a cropped-headed, sub-machine-gun-swinging character in Ritt's bizarre war adventure about five Yugoslav girls – Moreau, Mangano, Vera Miles, Barbara Bel Geddes and Carla Gravina – who first associate with German soldiers and then variously join the partisans. Most of the film is guerilla gunshot, blood, mud and the whole damn thing, from childbirth to death. Moreau looks like a displaced refugee throughout, 'action' in a true Moreau role being something usually confined to a more cerebral and emotional level. Expression with a spitting tommy-gun is not her style.

Shot in Yugoslavia, the film should have been better as Ritt, the man who taught Paul Newman how to act, has a track record of fine popular successes, such as *The Spy Who Came in from the Cold* and good emotive cinema like *Norma Rae*. But this film, as Moreau says, paid her taxes. Although actually shot before *Dialogue des Carmélites*, *Five Branded Women* came out some months after the award-winning nun's story, much to the horror of those faithful fans who, after *Dialogue*, had voted Moreau French Film Actress of the Year. In this *Figaro/Cinémonde* readers' competition, she polled twice as many votes as Simone Signoret, with Emmanuelle Rova in third place and Bardot fourth.

But the fans were not to be disappointed for long as Moreau was about to start a series of films, classics of the *Nouvelle Vague*, which remain stamped on the memory, constituting her finest body of work to date. These are the films that constantly crop up in Jeanne

Moreau seasons and in the repertory. While researching this book, I saw dozens of them in London, always at matinées among audiences of senior citizens, homesick au pairs and UB40s killing time, but also with a hard core of true Moreau devotees – French bankers bunking off work, Eastern Europeans who had long ago caught her films at underground cine clubs in Prague and Warsaw, and middle-aged professionals who had ridden the New Wave vicariously first time round through her films. Perhaps the most stubborn Moreau fans I noted were ladies *d'un certain âge* who had originally been egged on to shed the shackles of up-tight middle-classdom when they first saw their spokeswoman for the twentieth century at the Everyman Cinema in Hampstead, say, or in the salacious reaches of Drayton Gardens at the Paris-Pullman, and had gone on to some nearby coffee shop like the Café des Artistes to sip too many espressos before catching the train back to the home counties, their husbands, their children and their dogs.

The first of these touchy, edgy films was *Moderato Cantabile* (*Seven Days, Seven Nights*), from Marguerite Duras' novel, directed by Peter Brook. With Duras, one of France's most esteemed exponents of the *nouveau roman*, who had made her name in films with the screenplay for *Hiroshima Mon Amour*, and with Brook, the director Moreau found strong and sympathetic, it was a tightly knit film, based deeply on the emotions of the group.

The story is a married woman's fixation for one of her husband's employees and their ultimate renunciation of their affair. As Anne Desbaresdes, Moreau plays the bored wife of a rich foundries chief. Trapped in a rigid social position, she pours her wayward emotion into her young son (Didier Haudepin). While taking him for a piano lesson in a rough neighbourhood, she hears the dying screams of a woman strangled by her lover. Returning later to the same place, she meets labourer Chauvin (Jean-Paul Belmondo), who will become her lover.

Not much happens in the conventional sense in this slow-burning drama, driven by Moreau's brilliance at small, precisely judged details. Although it was knocked for being too *moderato cantabile* and not *allegro furioso* enough, it won Moreau a Best Foreign Actress award in Germany, and the 1960 Cannes Best Actress Award. This latter prize she shared with Melina Mercouri for *Never on Sunday*, and it came as a surprise because audiences at the Cannes Festival public screening had walked out hissing after barely fifteen minutes. At the time, controversial as ever, Brook said he did not care who disliked the film; he had made it to please just two people – Moreau and Duras.

Moderato Cantabile is still compellingly beautiful to watch, perhaps even more so now than when it was first released. In contrast to *The Lovers*, which used the premise of elopement with a handsome stranger, Duras' script presents the antithesis – an extraordinarily intimate view of a woman's mind which perhaps only those who can cope with deep inner turmoil may sit through happily.

The film also stands out as a good example of Moreau's similar approach to work and life, of her need to live through a role and emerge at the end, usually half dead, to convalesce morally and physically back to her off-screen self. One bears in mind her ability to transform herself into character while shooting, for according to producer Raoul Lévy she duplicated the troubling habits of Madame Desbaresdes, even going as far as to take to drinking wine in the morning. Duras says she totally 'interiorised' her role; Brook says that she developed a telepathic relationship with her character, down to the last flicker of an eyelash. Two of Moreau's friends have told me that she will have the astrological chart of the character she is playing drawn up to get closer to the fictitious person.

Just before shooting began, during the critical period when she prefers to be alone, she went to live in Blaye, the little town on the banks of the Gironde where the film was to be shot. For a week she walked about the town 'until it had permeated not only my brain but my feet, while I gradually became a native'.

But her most perfect of preparations were to be horribly disrupted. With her on location she took her son Jérôme, then aged ten. During filming he was invited by Belmondo to ride in his sports car. They crashed and the boy was rushed to a clinic in Bordeaux, where he lay comatose for sixteen days. Both his mother and his father grieved round the clock at his bedside until he regained consciousness and finally recovered. Although her performance seemed unaffected by this disaster, it became a time of great introspection for the actress. Having witnessed life gravely threatened she abruptly learned to value it more. A few years earlier her close friend Roger Nimier had been killed driving home one night, something she still cites as one of two particularly important moments of her life which contributed to a change in her attitude to living. 'The taste of death makes you feel very deeply,' she said. The trauma of Jérôme's threatened life stayed with her for a long time.

The guilt-stricken Belmondo, who had escaped with a broken wrist, also took the accident very badly. 'Jeanne was wonderful,' he said. 'She never reproached me in the least. She always acted as if I had not been responsible.' Less forgiving were some members of the public who wrote to Moreau saying that she was now reaping a bad harvest in punishment for all the scandals she had caused with her films.

While making *Moderato Cantabile*, Moreau saw Michelangelo Antonioni's *L'Avventura* and loved it. She wrote to the director to offer her services should he ever have need of her. His reply was almost instant, and asked her if she would like to be in the second of his trilogy, *La Notte*. He had first noticed her one evening in Paris with Louis Malle at a screening of *Lift to the Scaffold* and was very taken with the way she walked. He had told Malle then that he would like to use her in one of his films.

La Notte went into production in Milan with Moreau as Lidia, the wife of Marcello Mastroianni's novelist, Giovanni. Antonioni's then constant companion Monica Vitti co-starred.

The film went on to win the Berlin Golden Bear, but Moreau disliked the whole project: Antonioni, her character and the story, a beautiful but unbearably pessimistic study of conjugal boredom set over one night. She hated working all night, loathed the film's bleak point of view and never sympathised with the spiritually anaesthetised character she played. As the sulky-faced, lifeless-eyed Lidia, trying to escape a disintegrating marriage, she became deeply depressed. She was living on sedatives and sleeping pills and felt she had never looked as ugly.

'I hated acting the wife in that film,' she told a friend, the novelist Penelope Gilliatt. 'There are people like that poor woman, of course, but not for me. That is not what love is like.'

Further, according to Moreau, Antonioni was in pain, a pain she never asked him about but something they all had to suffer with him. 'There was no communication between Antonioni and me. He's a very shy man and he has problems with communication. I had the impression during the film that it was hard for him to deal with everything. Every day I felt morbid, near to suicide. I only knew what was going on from Mastroianni, who was charming, but not from Antonioni. This was not done on purpose. I'm sure, although my mood of depression may have shown on the screen and fitted the film.' On top of everything else the producer went bankrupt during the third week of shooting and she was never paid.

Mastroianni, however, fell in love with her. 'Many people fall in love with her. I did,' he has said. 'And she loves you in return but just till the end of the film. She is always searching for love, and she leaves victims along the roadside.'

The Moreau road might be littered with such as Mastroianni, but those found lying there are not necessarily true victims. During my researches I found some 'old loves' who had since cropped up as friends and colleagues, still part of her life. When I met her in Paris for our interviews she gave me some of their telephone numbers and they chatted easily enough with me about her. It all seemed so civilised. What she had once said about having a really big house where she could live with all the men she had ever loved did not seem quite so whimsical. In later years she modified this to a house where all the people she had loved – men, women and children – could live. I suppose, in a way, she has achieved this, if one considers one's life to be one's home. I am not sure how happy this attitude has made her, but certainly love, people keep telling me, has continued to come to her.

La Notte rounded off the 'chic, bored wife' trio which The Lovers and Moderato Cantabile had begun.

Perhaps exhausted by the emotional grilling of it all, Moreau chose as her next job the narration of a film on Matisse by Marcel Ophüls, the son of a friend, the director Max Ophüls. Then she slid into a cameo in Jean-Luc Godard's Une Femme est Une Femme. Drifting through as herself among friends Belmondo, Brialy and Godard's then wife Anna Karina, she looks refreshed and vital, after the morose style she had shown in recent films. Finally, as if all the foregoing had been mere preparation, the time came for her to ride the New Wave into immortality with *Jules et Jim*. When it opened in Paris on her thirty-fourth birthday, she was in her prime.

Jules and Jim, a German and a Frenchman, are friends in Paris. They once visited a Greek island and fell in love with the statue of a woman with a mysterious smile. In Paris they encounter Catherine, who has the same smile, and she falls in love with both of them. They form an inseparable trio. Catherine marries the short, plump Jim (Oskar Werner) after fatefully missing a rendezvous with the tall, thin Jules (Henri Serre). The Great War comes and Jules and Jim have to leave their youthful idyll to fight in separate trenches for their opposed countries.

Catherine and her child by Jim live through the war in Germany. Later, after Armistice Day, Jules visits them. Despite the resumed idyll of domestic life, Jules tells Jim that he has been unable to hold Catherine emotionally. With her husband's approval, she returns to France with Jules, but now they are unable to recapture the past. Based on the first novel of a man of seventy-three, Henri-Pierre Roché, the film is an audacious tale of Bohemian Paris and beyond. Truffaut told me in an interview in London, before he died in 1984: 'The idea motivated me but I knew the moralising side of Roché had to be preserved, so the actors had to act against the situation, and nature constantly had to be fitted in, hence all those three-hundred-and-sixty-degree panoramas. The passing of time, twenty years in all, we depicted through newsreel inserts and successive stages of Picasso's printing style used for posters. The actors wore no make-up, no period costumes and had to work against sets indeterminate of time and place.

'I wrote to Henri-Pierre Roché, sending him several photos of Jeanne. He replied: " Many thanks for the photos. She pleases me. I am happy that she likes Kate. I hope to know her some day." It was four days after writing me that letter that he died.'

Roché's Kate – Moreau's Catherine – was, says Moreau, 'a criminal, but we are helpless to condemn her. She is not especially beautiful or sincere but she is a real woman.' With her sudden laugh, little-girl pout and funny walk with hands turned palms up,

Moreau makes Catherine mercurial and mischievous, a spellbinder, even though she is egocentric, unreliable and for the most part completely unaware of the torment through which she puts her men.

With her ever-ready bottle of vitriol 'for lying eyes', she was the first truly 'modern' screen woman, the first female free spirit we had seen on film. She affected countless people in their formative years and liberated a generation of women a decade before it was fashionable. In France, when the film was released, a wife still had to obtain her husband's permission to open a bank account.

Said Truffaut: 'When I wrote the screenplay for *Jules et Jim* the danger was the character of Catherine, who could become an exquisite pain in the neck, a first-class self-willed bitch who gets away with everything. In Jeanne's face her fragile, charismatic beauty can disintegrate quickly into hardness, into a savage sensuality. She's exactly what men love and women hate.

'During the shooting I had these dangers well in mind, and part of the work consisted of preventing the film from falling into them. I liked the idea of showing that sometimes nobody's right, that a woman can love two men and that the two men might get along with each other. I don't consider that I ever direct an actor. I simply try to switch him or her on to the things I like. I try to keep them on the rails that are my own but which are not necessarily indicated in the script. That's what I did here with Jeanne and the rest came easily.'

According to some reports it came more easily to some than to others. Oskar Werner later asserted in a *New York Times* interview that he had written a large section of the script. Truffaut, who had already pilloried Werner in his published diaries of the shooting of *Fahrenheit 451*, said the claim was absurd. 'He could hardly speak French – he had to read some of his lines from a board we'd hold up. Half the time he was saying words he didn't understand.'

But such wrangles apart, the decisive factor always was that Truffaut would not have made the film without Jeanne Moreau because she was the only actress he knew 'mad enough to do a project with no money, no script and no perks'.

With Godard's cameraman, Raoul Coutard, *Jules et Jim* was shot on a shoestring. On location in Alsace Moreau would cook daily lunches for a cast and crew of twenty-two (estranged husband Jean-Louis Richard was also part of the team). Moreau insists she cooked because she wanted to rather than because there was no money for catering. 'I co-produced the film with Truffaut and we put all our own money into the project,' she told me thirty years later. 'I only received the first cheque for this film two days after opening in *Zerline* [the play *Le Récit de la Servante Zerline*] in 1986. Now I receive thirty-three per cent of the profits each year!

'Towards the end of shooting we ran out of money and had to find more. We made all our own clothes, or found them. We shot it all without sound, just made up the words as we went along, then later we dubbed it in ten days. It was fun and I'm very grateful to François for making me a *femme fatale*.' She chuckles her nicotine-stained laugh. 'Of course, I don't see myself as one.'

Truffaut clearly did. Obviously he adored her. Some say they were lovers, she says it was a mutual fascination. They were both Aquarians and they developed their relationship as though, it seemed to them both, they were 'twin brothers'.

'We didn't live a love story,' she says. 'It was a very different relationship. We were fascinated by one another in terms of craft and intelligence and sensitivity. He was so involved with his film and so passionately attracted to all his characters, including the men. I felt the flow of passion that was also very demanding and I wanted to be up to it. I wanted his dream as a film director to be fulfilled. That's the feeling I always have when I'm filming.'

In his book Truffaut went as far as to write an ode to Moreau, entitled 'A Luminous Memory', and there are enchanting photos of them together on location. Both look like kids, eyes wide with excitement as they race through their film-making together. He has committed her letters to him to a safe until the year 2000 and she has said she will never release his letters to her, so the secrets they shared will remain, for now, the kind of material great movie scripts are made of – mystery, passion and provocation.

Jules et Jim took numerous prizes worldwide. Perhaps the one with the best social comment on the times and the state of the cinema was the French Academy's Crystal Star for Best Actress for Moreau, a prize she accepted on a stage shared with Albert Finney. He won the

Best Foreign Actor award for *Saturday Night and Sunday Morning*, the title which marked the start of Britain's own New Wave of sixties 'kitchen sink' films.

Between finishing *Jules et Jim* and starting work on her next film, Jeanne Moreau met boyish dress-designer Pierre Cardin, two years her senior and classically good-looking, when she was trying on one of his outfits in a fitting booth at one of his collections. It was love at first sight. 'It was instantaneous. I wanted to see him again right away so I went back on the pretext of looking at some clothes. I used to get my clothes from Chanel, but if I'd had the means I would have kept going back until I'd bought out every dress in the Cardin collection – just so I could go on seeing him!

'I was aware of the reputation he had in Paris [that he was homosexual]. I knew all about it and I didn't care. Quite the contrary. All the obstacles I knew were there only made him more attractive.'

Moreau told Duras: 'I wanted Pierre to love me. I knew he was capable of loving a woman. I had to be patient and gentle, not frighten him with the dreadful phantoms a sadistic society flourishes with such pleasure. I had to make him understand that I could understand, could admit everything – and that he should too.'

By all accounts she was successful in spreading this understanding. They had five years together, their relationship slavishly captured by the press: on holiday in Greece, at home in Paris in his apartment, escaping to Tahiti or the Canary Islands or Brittany, on location on the Riviera. She became his best-known model and he became the man behind her looks. He designed an entire collection for her, which must have put quite a strain on his in-house models, expected not only to look like Mademoiselle Moreau but also to imitate that Catherine-esque walk of hers. Always clad in Cardin, she was the ultimate elegant Parisienne. (Her sister Michelle, the one who inherited all the hand-me-downs, gave their relationship wholehearted approval!)

The press made a banquet of the Cardin-Moreau union. At his July 1962 fashion launch she stole the show 'with the discretion of a pickpocket' when he brushed aside his rich fashion worshippers to seize her in what was described as a 'private, exclusive passion'. Forget about dropping hemlines: he'd made thirty outfits for her alone and he clearly did not give a damn whether they suited the rest of the social sirens in the world of *haute couture*.

That year Cardin hemlines stayed the shortest in Paris due, no doubt, to Moreau having rather good legs. In the city, at that time, next to guessing who would be President de Gaulle's successor, the favourite café game was deciding whether or not Pierre Cardin and Jeanne Moreau would marry.

6

'She could be elemental or elegant, warm or astringent.'
Orson Welles

American director Joseph Losey had first seen Jeanne Moreau in *The Lovers*. He was devoted to French cinema and knew he wanted to use her in one of his pictures.

The film was *Eva*, based on James Hadley Chase's novel about a high-class prostitute who comes to destroy the life of her leading client. Moreau had first got to know the book when Cocteau brought it backstage to her while she was doing *The Infernal Machine* and told her that, when she became a star, she would have to do this role in a film version. When the time came for her to be involved, she asked for Jean-Luc Godard as director, but when he told the producers how he would like to do the story they vetoed him. She suggested Losey, who was delighted to accept.

Losey had fallen foul of Hollywood – he was on the McCarthy black-list because of his background studying acting in Russia under the legendary film-maker Sergei Eisenstein and early features with the accent on problems of social conscience. He had re-established himself from a British base, had just made *The Damned* and was looking for another project.

When he went to speak to Moreau about the planned film of *Eva*, he found her spending the summer in Brittany. She had rented a small, rather strange old château in this remote part of north-west France. He was met by her driver in the large grey 1958 Rolls-Royce she had bought after *Jules et Jim* ('It was only an old one,' she said defensively when accused of buying a status symbol) and taken through country roads for more than an hour before reaching her hide-out. There he found her sitting in a small room with a fire, surrounded by stacks and stacks of Billie Holiday records. For Losey, who had known the singer when she was sixteen, that sealed their relationship. So passionate were they both about Holiday that they decided that in the stylish park scene in *Eva* Moreau would wander off reading the singer's autobiography.

Losey liked the way Moreau seemed to be handling her personal life and asked her for some input on the character of Eva. Although a courtesan, Eva is essentially a middle-class woman with taste and style, and many of her accoutrements came directly from the life of Jeanne Moreau. He noted that Moreau had a fine collection of ornamental eggs, and so Eva was endowed with a collection of ornamental eggs. Moreau loved the idea of Cardin designing her costumes, and so Eva became designer-dressed. It comes as no surprise, either, that Truffaut named one of his daughters Eva after Jeanne's role in the film.

On set for support Moreau had her current agent Micheline Rozan, and her best friend, Florence Malraux. 'There was a group of us who were all working together in the cinema,' recounts Malraux, who was married to the director Alain Resnais. 'Jeanne and I had been introduced by Marguerite [Duras] at dinner one night, before she made *Moderato Cantabile*. Peter [Brook] was a friend of mine and I was doing some assistant directing work on the film with them. Jeanne introduced me to Truffaut and I later worked with them on *Jules et Jim* and then on *Eva*. We were all good friends and we had a lot of fun.'

When they started shooting, however, the film was by all accounts not a lot of fun. In both Rome and Venice they had to shoot external sequences in temperatures of at least ten degrees below, and for some reason interior shots were frozen out by mysterious clashes between the director and his Italian team, who either could not understand Losey or could not understand English. Losey was eventually to renounce his rights to the film and it was later recut by the producers, Robert and Raymond Hakim, who according to co-star Stanley Baker, 'couldn't produce a fart out of a can of beans'.

The Italian crew was confused by Moreau and her Rolls; puzzled as to how an actress who, in their terms, lacked the glamour of Lollobrigida or Loren, could play this sort of sexy role. As one critic wrote: 'She is not beautiful but imposes by her presence and acting ability.' Another was not so kind: 'Her lips are too thick, her nose is not straight, her ears are too small and her legs are too thin. But,' he added, 'men have tried to commit suicide over her.' Moreau has since commented that the suicide bit was not true, but this Italian critic had undoubtedly picked up on a report that Raoul Lévy, Brigitte Bardot's ex-producer and something of a French Mike Todd, had apparently tried to take his life for love of Jeanne.

According to Roger Vadim, in his book *The Memoirs of Roger Vadim*, Lévy had fallen 'madly in love' with Moreau, who was apparently briefly infatuated with him and then ended the affair. 'Raoul took sleeping pills, slashed his wrists, turned on the gas, took his revolver out of a drawer,' writes Vadim. Lévy also phoned some friends, and was consequently rescued. The incident went down in showbiz folklore as Lévy attempting suicide over Jeanne Moreau.

Moreau's co-star, Stanley Baker, claimed that Losey was the only person in the world for whom he would 'drop everything at a moment's notice'. He played Tyvian Jones, one of Venice's expatriate characters, the man Eva would break. Virna Lisi, the popular Italian star, her voice dubbed into English, also starred and cameos were provided by Peggy Guggenheimer, Vittorio de Sica and Losey himself.

In an interview published in the American magazine *Cinema*, Moreau is quoted as saying she found Losey 'a very strange man'. On a colour-count of the directors she had worked with, she lists him as 'black and white' (Truffaut gets 'something blue, green', Antonioni 'yellow', Orson Welles 'red' and Luís Buñuel 'purple'.) But as with her previous directors, there was something special between them, special enough for them to make another two films together.

In the 1967 book *Losey on Losey*, the director says: 'I was in love with her as an actress – very much attracted to her, but nothing happened between us, just in case that needs to be made clear. There was a period after *Eva* when I felt a bit betrayed by Jeanne' – she had been party to Tony Richardson acquiring the rights of *Mademoiselle*, which Losey had been very keen to film – 'but she and I have a kind of permanent love which came out of that film. Moreau haunts you. She has the gift of intensity. From the moment you first see her face, you can never forget it.' His widow, Patricia Losey, told me she felt that Joe, although bedazzled by his leading lady, would have been positively scared to get involved with her, because it was not 'professional'.

'He had come into films through the theatre and was stagestruck. Actors were so special to him. His relationships with actors were very intense but totally professional. I remember during the shooting of *The Trout*, twenty years after they made *Eva*, he told Moreau how enthralled he had been with her on Eva and her answer was: "Oh, why didn't you tell me?", as if it would have been so simple.'

Talking about a director's feeling for his leading lady, Moreau has said that she does not think any leading actress can make a film without the director falling in love with her in one way or another. 'He knows so much about you, watches you so closely, he's got to understand every hidden spring of your personality. He needs, if he's a great director, to make the best use of you. His fascination with you inevitably becomes a sort of "love" relationship.

'For me, to be an actress, to make films is a way of love, and I was so lucky that the most extraordinary people I could have wished to work with were attracted to me.'

In its time *Eva* was another shocker. The French distributors planned to bill it as *Eva, The Devil's Woman* and it was advertised there as offering '*Le rôle de ma vie* – Jeanne Moreau'.

'I was really angry about that because every film is the *rôle de ma vie*,' she says. 'But what I contested was the editing. It made Joe so unhappy. When the producers came on set in Rome and tried to stop the sequences that Joe wanted, I waited with a kitchen knife, big as this,' she holds her hands a foot apart, 'and I said: "If you come further, I'll open you up like a purse."'

Having seen *Eva*, as I did only once, on a tiny screen with guillotined edges, Finnish subtitles and somewhat laterally compressed views of Moreau and Baker, it would be unfair to comment on the film other than to say it seemed sublimely sixties. For Moreau it was the first film in which people actively compared her with Brigitte Bardot. All the stretching around nude in towels looking like a lithe, beautiful cat, and a very capricious bath scene, had crossed the line into B.B. country.

At that time, however, professionally, things were up and down for Moreau. A film of Genet's *Les Bonnes* (The Maids) with Nico Papatakis had fallen through and so had one with Ingmar Bergman, *L'Amour Monstre* written by Louis Pauwels, over which they had been corresponding for years. Sophia Loren had got the role in *El Cid* that might have gone to Moreau and a film with Federico Fellini, *Three Rooms in Manhattan*, based on a Georges Simenon story about another prostitute who destroys the life of her leading man, did not materialise either.

Luckily Moreau had always kept in touch with Orson Welles, whom she had met in Paris as early as 1950, while she was still at the Comédie Française. Whenever he passed through Paris he would telephone her. She was devoted to him because, in the early days after she'd been rejected for some films for being unphotogenic, he had been the only person who had backed her. Welles himself was on the verge of being rediscovered after *Citizen Kane* had been selected by a 1962 poll of international film critics as the best film in motion picture history. (Antonioni's *L'Avventura* was placed second and Jean Renoir's 1939 *La Règle du Jeu* (*The Rules of the Game*) was third.) He was planning to film Kafka's nightmare novel *The Trial*, which, although written in 1923, was very suited to the anxiety-ridden sixties. In order to secure funding capital from many countries, his studio decided he would shoot it with an international cast. Anthony Perkins was signed up as Josef K., along with Romy Schneider, Katina Paxinou, Elsa Martinelli, Akim Tamiroff and then Moreau. Most of them accepted a fraction of their regular salaries simply because they wanted to work with Welles. He had written the script and was going to direct the film without taking an acting role too, but failing to find anybody suitable – and inexpensive enough – to play the part of the smooth-tongued, tormented advocate, he ended up doing that as well.

'Out of admiration for Orson, I gladly accepted the role of Miss Bürstner – a completely episodic character, a drunk, flirtatious striptease girl who has no existence of her own other than as a brief early-morning event in the life of the hero Josef K.,' said Moreau. 'When Orson owns the screen he owns us. Flowing sequences, close-ups, words, camera movements; the eye of Orson Welles's camera, looking, staring, gazing, glaring, creates the magic spell that breaks the bad one. We watch. We know we won't be misled.'

Talking about Welles at the time of his death in 1985, she explained: 'I loved and detested him; he's Kane, he's Othello, he's Falstaff, he's rarely himself. He would play any puny part to stay solvent, because he never had any money, yet when he was in the middle of shooting a film it was as if he were on an island away from worries, and he'd order a dozen pairs of silk underclothes and meals from Fortnum and Mason or wherever. Orson was a child, a fragile man, very vulnerable. When you get to know that huge strong man, you know that he's very easily loved so you'd love and want to protect him. And if he called and said "I need you," then you say, "Orson needs me and it's something important," and you'd go.

'With Orson, you never knew where he was. He'd disappear and it'd be nearly impossible to find him because his life was always complicated. And then, suddenly, you'd find yourself face to face with him, or else he'd call you from somewhere. And, like all men, of course, he wants you immediately . . . Whatever you are doing, or whatever your plans are, you drop them.

'I loved his enormous gusts of laughter, his enormous rages, his enormous enjoyment in living, his enormous interest in everything, in women, men, anger, drunkenness, light, darkness. I particularly loved his hands, so small and white and manicured, rather like Jean Gabin's.'

The Trial turned out to be a truly Kafkaesque experience. The shoot was one of those nightmare ones – under-funded, over-active and all over the place. Cast and crew spent three weeks in a huge exhibition hall outside Zagreb, Yugoslavia, which it was felt most audiences would find difficult to place. 'The faces in the crowd had a Kafka look to them, and the hideous blockhouse, soul-destroying buildings were somehow typical of modern Iron Curtain architecture,' Welles commented.

A couple of weeks before they embarked for the location they received the news that they would not be able to build a single set because the producer had already filmed there once before and had not yet paid his debts. They had to use the existing sets, which radically changed the look Welles had in mind for the film. Working under extreme duress, he managed against all the odds to create the famous scene of 850 desks, 850 typewriters and 850 secretaries behind them in the massive office where Josef K. worked as a bank clerk.

They also filmed in Dubrovnik, Rome, Milan and Paris, where, owing to insufficient funds, instead of the Bois de Boulogne Studios the abandoned Belle Epoque railway station of the Gare d'Orsay (now a splendid museum) was used for interiors. This location was found while Welles and Moreau were having a drink one evening at his hotel, Le Meurice. The window was open, overlooking the labyrinthine station with its large round clock, and Moreau said, 'Look at the full moon, so close.'

Welles replied: 'That's not the moon, that's the clock at the Gare d'Orsay, let's go and have a look at it.'

The result of all this is undoubtedly one of the classics of serious cinema and remains the only screen effort which captures Kafka's sinister message. Anthony Perkins, as a frail-looking Josef K., was thirty at the time. He found the filming quite overwhelming, especially as he had just become famous for *Psycho* and was not quite sure he was suited to the role, though it was one he wanted passionately to play.

'Everything was going for it, the role, working with the great Orson Welles, having a love scene with Europe's *femme fatale* Jeanne Moreau, but I was terrified by it,' he told me in 1978, while he was shooting *Les Misérables* in the Dordogne. 'Despite being a production from Alexander Salkind, a mainstream Hollywood guy, it was a very European picture and I struggled quite a bit. It made *Psycho* seem easy!'

After the stringencies of *The Trial*, Moreau and Cardin took a summer holiday on the Greek island of Paros, to relax, but also to escape the constant speculation in the press that they were about to marry. She had at last started proceedings to divorce her estranged husband and this had sent Paris into a frenzy. Word was that she had invested a large amount of money in her companion's company ('I wish I did have money to invest in the House of Cardin!') and that she had an unofficial job as adviser to Cardin on what the modern woman wanted from her fashion garments. He had got her to slim down and together they were considered the best-looking couple in Paris.

I found very few examples of Cardin quoted on Moreau in print, but in one, in a 'Jeanne Moreau as seen by . . .' spread in a French magazine, he caught her in a couple of paragraphs: 'One hundred per cent woman,' said Cardin, 'she can go from moments of weakness to moments of strength, changing all the time, from sweet to tough, from authoritarian to easily influenced. She is physically vulnerable, with that fragile skin on which every experience leaves a mark, but she is psychologically spontaneous, with an immediate opinion which she can change voluntarily.'

At the end of the summer of 1962, Jeanne Moreau left Paris for London to work on Carl Foreman's film *The Victors* at Shepperton Studios. Once again the hacks descended on her as she arrived at Heathrow, carrying her hatbox with 'Pierre Cardin' printed on the band and dressed in one of his inimitably chic outfits. This time the press reported her as half French, half English instead of the other way round. Wasting no time, she floored the collective masses with outspoken diatribes in perfect English on life, love and everything in between.

'To the French and Italian film-makers I represent the new woman who lives singularly, who represents adult love, who preserves her dignity and understands the problems of living and loving; a woman who has a will of her own. Perhaps this can only happen to a Frenchwoman living in Paris,' she is reported to have said with aplomb. For someone who calls her private life private, she has always been unconventionally open about her affairs, all of which have been well enough publicised in any case.

She has always been what the French call a *grande amoureuse*. I quote one of her views on love that was used as part of the publicity material for *The Victors* because I think it says more about her than I could: 'Love is the most difficult affair in life. Besides, I am not a young girl. I have been married and I have a child. Now, when modern women are emancipated, it is more difficult for them to find men who are right for them. Socially, men no longer have superiority over women. Women used to be bred by their mothers to give in to men – it was the conspiracy of the kitchen. Now men are on the run, frightened, concerned to show how virile and how masculine they are. Many of them are not the sort of men who can take love on. They're too busy, too involved, their private life just has to go by the board.

'The most difficult thing in love is jealousy. Things are all right in the periods of passion when all you want is to be alone together. But then there are the periods of work, especially creative work, when the person you love is preoccupied and has secrets, and words are not enough to explain what the secrets are. You are used to seeing them face to face and suddenly you see them across the street, and they are different.

'Pierre Cardin understands this, not because of what he does. He would be the same if he were a scientist or a factory worker. To marry Pierre Cardin is not important. What is important is to keep love alive. In a few years I will be able to tell you if I have done that.'

The Victors was her first film in England. It was a Second World War adventure, told in vignettes with newsreel footage, about an American infantry platoon in northern France. In it she is a shell-shocked French widow who returns to her blitzed home to recover her husband's art treasures. Albert Finney co-stars as a Russian soldier, with George Hamilton, whom she would romance in *Viva Maria!*, George Peppard, Peter Fonda, Eli Wallach, Melina Mercouri and Elke Sommer. In the background Romy Schneider, from time to time, enigmatically plays a violin.

The film was designed to show her off to a full international audience and she accepted the part because of Carl Foreman, who had produced *The Guns of Navarone*. He thought she was 'peerless in films today' and gave her the female lead role. But even challenged by grime, laddered stockings and with haunted eyes, she lacked the fire that had always burned in her women. There were no dark and secret whirlpools of desire in the soul of her sad war widow. It proved not to be a great movie at the box office ('War has revealed Mr Foreman as a pompous bore,' wrote one critic), but in America today it is one of the favourite war epics on late-night television.

Moreau's other bid for international recognition came a couple of years later in *The Train*, another Second World War story, starring Burt Lancaster and Paul Scofield. When she took the role Arthur

Penn was signed to direct the picture, but two days later after he and Lancaster had had a disagreement, he was replaced by John Frankenheimer.

The film is about an attempt by the French Resistance to prevent a German general (Scofield) from taking art treasures back to Germany on a special train. Moreau plays the war-weary station hotel-keeper who finds the road to recovery in the fleeting embrace of Burt Lancaster. Off screen perhaps there was less embracing. She tells a withering story about working with the Method-trained actor whose concern, in her opinion, seemed to exceed his craft.

'He'd discuss his motivation for picking up an ashtray for an hour. You'd want to say to him, "Just pick up the ashtray and shut up." To me it was exasperating. The Method preparation for concentration is some actors' way of doing what I try to do in a totally different way. I went once to the Actors' Studio in New York to watch how it was done and I was appalled and left. Intellect has got nothing to do with acting. Thought can go on beforehand. Then you just have to be there, present and functioning.'

She got on better with Scofield with whom she planned to return to the stage, in London, in *Antony and Cleopatra* with Peter Brook directing. It never happened. Scofield, who had hardly any scenes with her in *The Train*, remembers her arriving on set at exactly the same time each day, 'an extremely charming and tiny woman in a brown dress and travelling in a grey Rolls-Royce'.

The Train, a gritty thriller and very good in parts, did well when it was released. Frankenheimer was one of the most exciting directors working in the States in the early sixties, and had turned out hit films like *The Manchurian Candidate*. But, to be honest, these 'international' pictures were thoroughly mediocre compared with other smaller-scale movies on which she had previously worked. Yet they did enough for Moreau's reputation outside France for her to become considered by the mainstream audience to be more than just another foreign actress.

Watching her in them now, things do not always gel in the English language with her American-toned accent and blatantly French ambiance. That wonderful look of hers, showing the trace of time and desire, which someone has said gave the impression that she was carrying 'an abiding hermetic mystery', somehow does not come through in these more anonymous films made with sprawling crews who were not 'family', by directors who didn't immediately touch the 'love pulse' in her. Moreau is a person filled with signs you look for knowing that some people will never see them.

Maybe this is where the problem lay with the big studio pictures; too big a budget, too many technicians, too many stars, too much fuss, too few buddies, too few sessions around the table discussing how to cut loose the spirit of the film.

Louis Malle puts it succinctly: 'We were used to shooting two films a year, perhaps two films in ten months, as we did with *Lift* and *The Lovers*. Films were cheaper, with less risk, more spontaneous. Then we moved to the American way of making films and it took millions of bucks and years in production. Nowadays I spend two, two and a half years making a film.'

7

'You're like a feather going where the wind blows it.'
Cardin to Moreau

In 1963, under pressure from Pierre Cardin, Jeanne Moreau bought an old orchard farm and house in the hills of the Var above St Tropez. Two hundred yards down a steep private road shadowed by pines and cork oaks, the house – called Le Préverger – was a sun-baked Provençal cream-coloured farmhouse. Its shutters were the blue they call Mistral blue after the colour of sky when the purifying Mistral has blown. It was rather like a scene in a painting by Cézanne, with a stream in a valley of fruit trees and terraced vineyard. The nearest village, La Garde-Freinet, was perched on the yellow gorse foothills of the Maritime Alps where centuries before conquering Saracens had built fortresses and walled towns.

'I bought the house after Pierre Cardin told me that it was for sale and I had to buy it.' Moreau told me. '"You're like a feather going where the wind blows," he said. "You earn money and you spend it. You should think about old age."'

Unless you count the house, the finest in Mazirat, she had bought for her father, this was the first house of her own. She saw it as a place to which she could withdraw in times of stress, to recharge and recuperate. 'I bought the house on borrowed money, for my old age.

OM

It was the first place I ever owned and it was the place I most loved for walking and swimming, the only exercise I do. But as time passed, I was spending less and less time there and I felt like looking around more to see what was going on in the world.

'As for old age, a friend of mine told me a French saying, "You never see a safe following a corpse or a coffin at a funeral", and I thought yes, she's right. So, as long as I earn money, I spend it. If I don't earn much, I won't spend much. That's the way I live.'

We were sitting taking tea at the Savoy. It was winter 1985 and Moreau was in London to promote the controversial Fassbinder film *Querelle*. This was our first encounter and it still remains with me vividly. Her blue fox coat was slung over the arm of her chair and her perfectly cut suit was short enough to show shapely legs and neat knees. She was tanned from a trip to Marrakesh, where she was working as a director on a TV film. Her lustrous bronze eyes probed through the smokescreen she made, never missing a trick. Charming and warm, she had the manner of one eager to help me get to grips with her. Underneath the warmth and charm, I sensed her alert mind, formidable tensile strength and an indomitable will. And also human frailty. She had time to reminisce.

'Yes,' she sighed, inhaling deeply, 'I did own that house, which was my refuge for twenty-two years, and last year I sold it to the Laura Ashley family. I loved it thoroughly, but when I sold it I was really relieved. A house is like a man – when it is finished between you, you will find another one somewhere; you do not know where, or when, but one will be waiting. I had the impression I was beginning a new life when it went. I couldn't afford it and didn't have enough time to use it. So now I have the pleasure of enjoying friends' houses. I don't have to worry any more about leaking roofs or forest fires when you have to batten yourself down and douse the house with water from the swimming pool and pray – even if you don't believe in the Church.'

Going back now to the neat, clearly affluent, brownstone mountain village of La Garde-Freinet, I found that Moreau is well remembered by the older residents, like the butcher, the baker and the garage-owner, who have probably never seen her in a movie. Nobody was particularly impressed by having a film personality living locally. She was known rather for being a canny shopper who bought only the freshest greens and the finest cuts in the market. Her sister remembers trailing through markets with her, doing weekend shopping for Le Préverger in La Garde-Freinet, St Tropez and Cannes.

'Going to the market with Jeanne, each time it is memorable,' says Michelle. 'She marches ahead, empty shopping bags flapping off her arms, while I bring up the rear with yet more. It's not easy to keep up with her. Of course she's recognised, which means that her progress is somewhat royal; but she so obviously appreciates all the produce on sale that it creates quite a bond between her and all the market people. On quality she can't be fooled and they know they can't sell her a dud avocado.'

During her time at Le Préverger Jeanne restored the property and had a pool built. Several magazines did lavish house-and-garden spreads on it, savouring the atmosphere, showing it as a place full of charm, filled with a rustic Gallic ambiance created by knick-knacks, quirky pieces of furniture she had picked up in local *brocantes*, mantelpieces filled with her favourite *objets* such as ornamental eggs and exquisite little boxes given to her by Cardin. Walls were lined with her collections of beloved books and with signed sketches by Picasso and paintings. Plain flagstone floors were covered with carpets brought back from film locations in Mexico and Greece. In the double-height *salon* was a wooden gallery, filled with music.

It was, says her old friend Joan Juliet Buck, luxurious but in a grounded way. 'It was one of those wonderful French country houses you see in films like *La Belle Noiseuse*, sensual, simple, a nostalgic ideal one longs for.'

Every room, said Moreau, ended up resembling her – meticulously, eccentrically filled with the things she loved. Naturally, it was intensely feminine. Wardrobes were full of Cardin – but less so after she'd packed all her Cardin dresses into trunks and sent them back to Pierre with instructions to let them go at a bargain price so that she would have room for lots of new ones. She created her country home with her housekeeper and confidante, Anna Pradella. They had met a few years before in her dressing-room when Moreau was in *La Bonne Soupe*, just after she had divorced Jean-Louis Richard. Anna, in a way, was to become her missing mother. She and Anna's husband, Louis, had worked the rambling garden into lush, peaceful greenery which smelled of fruit and herbs. There was the sound of water and birds and the criss-crossing tracks of wild boars, deer, Niok the deaf cat, and her Alsatians, Nemo and Manon. There is a tale of how the dogs once kept a neighbour up a tree for so long that a case was filed against Moreau in court in St Tropez.

Moreau and her father themselves attended to the *vendange* of the vineyard, pruning the vines and harvesting the grapes. For a time she even made her own perfume from her garden, a blend of the Guerlain essences, vetiver, jasmine, rose and heliotrope. Friends recall glorious, informal meals served on a colourful mix of odd plates on a wooden trestle table beneath the sweet chestnut and the oleanders. Elaborate dishes emerged from the great big Provençal kitchen, with its shelves full of home-grown produce preserved in chunky jars and sideboards laden with fruit and vegetables fresh with bloom.

Moreau has always treated food as the great aesthetic experience it should be. The quality of the food she eats and its careful preparation and cooking are standards she will never let slide. She made her first mayonnaise in her father's kitchen in Vichy when she was five. Uncle Arsène had once been a chef at the court of Austria, after all, and Uncle Marcel had owned a *charcuterie*. It is in her blood to provide delicious meals and to enjoy eating them.

'She is a perfectionist,' says Florence Malraux. 'She does things to the end. When Jérôme was in hospital as a little boy she was the best nurse there, with all the appearances of a trained nurse who had been there ten years. In the kitchen she is amazing to watch. The meals she made at Le Préverger were the best in the world and people would stay around the table for hours. Now it's a little different. When I go to have dinner with her we start early and end early. We are older, we are no longer at Le Préverger. But the food is still sublime.'

Her greatest pleasure during those days at Le Préverger, Moreau told me, was on a Saturday or a Sunday to cook classic dishes like *coq au vin*, a *blanquette* or *pot-au-feu* for a lot of friends and then go off quietly to bed with Plain French, her English teddy bear, and a good book. She organises her reading in themes: all of Nabokov perhaps, followed by Proust, Diderot or Céline. Around the house are volumes of history, the weightier modern novels, the odd psychological study. After a burst of reading, she loves to analyse and discuss with friends what she has read.

She has always read intensely, with a driving need to feed herself through words. 'With me,' says Moreau, 'it's not like those people who eat but they cannot remember what they ate the day before. I remember all of it. I feed myself with books, reading is my food.'

Strangely enough, for one so insistent about maintaining her privacy – on set she tends not to do interviews at all – Moreau invited several journalists up to Le Préverger to meet her at home. Some of them noted how, while they were there, she would speak on the telephone to Brigitte Bardot, who lived down the hill in St Tropez. This was almost the set piece of her promotional tableau. One remembered being offered for a country walk with boots that had been left in the hall by Cardin or her ex-husband. Another recalled driving her mini-moke into a ditch. Other journalists conducted interviews with her lying by the pool while she sunbathed topless. The dividing line between letting it all hang out and keeping to the constraints of a formal interview seemed to have become hazy. Indeed, with François Reichenbach she made a documentary on her life there and let the camera probe without scruple behind all the screens of privacy.

Artist Adrian George, who went there in 1983 to draw Moreau for *The Sunday Times*, found her totally open. 'She was dressed in a little gingham pinafore dress, dancing round the garden in pigtails and bare feet. It was childlike and charming and very unexpected,' he says. 'She was very *gamine* and surprisingly girlish for her age. The whole sensation was very Colette-ish, full of flowers and fruit and a certain feel for the afternoon. It was sheer *joie de vivre.*'

When Moreau bought Le Préverger she seriously needed a safe haven to which to escape. When in Paris she lived in and worked from Cardin's opulent apartment on the Seine, but between films she would go into seclusion on her rolling fifty-seven-acre *domaine*, to walk, to read, to sleep – sometimes for days – and to wake to the birdsong. 'All serious actors are terribly vulnerable,' she said in an interview conducted shortly after she bought the house. 'We're exposing ourselves constantly in all ways, as if we are peeled down to the bare nerves. We have to *give*. It's the exigence, the personal demand, that is so devastating. Success is very dangerous – and failure is dreadful.'

At Le Préverger she savoured her successes with close friends, inevitably cooking for them. Her son often visited as did old lovers; Jean-Louis Richard and his second wife (her nearest neighbours); old friends such as Truffaut, Duras, Malraux, the Loseys, de Vilmorin; neighbour Tony Richardson, who had a *domaine* at nearby Nid du Duc; Claude Berri and his wife; Jean-Luc Godard and Anna Karina. It was there, she said, that she also weathered her failures in private, and where the breeze laden with the aroma of thyme and rosemary soothed the soul a little.

What particular failures she was smarting over at the time of this interview is not clear. She had just part-funded and played the lead in *La Baie des Anges* (*Bay of Angels*) for Jacques Demy, which probably did more for her reputation abroad than *The Victors* had. On this project she surprised even herself at how far she would let a director push her into doing things she had not done before on screen. Demy, who died in 1990, was in 1962 still a young unknown, about to become one of France's most lyrical directors with films like *Les Parapluies de Cherbourg* (*The Umbrellas of Cherbourg*) and *Les Demoiselles de Rochefort* (*The Young Girls of Rochefort*), the film that made him and the actress sisters Françoise Dorléac and Catherine Deneuve.

Bay of Angels is a whirling little masterpiece of a film about a highly strung, raddled gambler who does not care what happens to her as long as she has a chip to start her on the roulette tables. The role of Jackie was written for Moreau by Demy, based on his own first experience at a casino. Cardin, who was Moreau's constant companion on set, designed Jackie's hyper-sixties, all-white costumes. Wearing a rumpled platinum Marilyn Monroe wig and complete with a beauty spot on her right cheek, Moreau plays the obsessed Jackie rather like a derailed Liz Taylor, crossed with a deadbeat Jayne Mansfield.

She meets a young bank clerk (Claude Mann) at the roulette table. He is an innocent at gambling, who has suddenly been intoxicated by the chance of winning large amounts of money; he is infected by her with the gambling fever. Together they win enough to lead, briefly, the millionaire's life on the glittering Riviera, but when he tries to persuade her to give up gambling and go off with him to find a beach in the sun, she refuses. Gambling is the only compulsion she has. She returns, quivering, to the casino with her fatalistic belief in luck, saying, 'I don't love money, if I did I wouldn't waste it'.

The film was released in France at a time when the country was in the throes of a gambling fever of its own and it seems to have hit a sore spot, sadly winning no prizes.

At this time Jeanne Moreau undertook another gamble of her own in the form of an alternative career as a *chanteuse*. She had always had friends who were singers and musicians and had held *soirées* with guests of honour like the gypsy guitarist Manitas de Plata. Her *Jules et Jim* theme song, '*Tourbillion de la Vie*' (Whirlpool of Life), had been a big radio hit. Riding on the back of it, she made her first album of a dozen songs by songwriter Cyrus Bassiak (in real life the painter and writer Serge Rezvani, a friend from La Garde-Freinet).

The album won her the Charles-Cros Award. She was invited to sing at the Swiss jazz festival on the shores of Lake Léman at Montreux. Directors started asking her to sing theme songs for their films – examples are *Peau de Banane* (*Banana Peel*), *Viva Maria!*, *L'Humeur Vagabonde* and *Querelle*. Truffaut used one of her discs on the soundtrack of *La Peau Douce* (*Silken Skin*). She was later to make another four albums.

Moreau is not a traditional Juliette Greco or Cora Vaucaire-style *chansonnière* from the cabarets of Saint-Germain-des-Prés. Although her lilting soprano has the necessary huskiness of a life of wine dregs and cigarette smoke, she is no torch singer; she sings quite gushy songs, often with a jazz piano plus elaborate orchestral backing. Mainly European cocktail jazz, the songs are usually about love and making love. One of the most revealing is '*Le célébrité, la publicité*' with its boulevardière shoulder-shrugging words which express her absorption in her art:

> La célébrité, la publicité
> Photographiée ou interviewée
> Mais quel effet cela vous fait?
> Moi, j'aime faire du cinéma
> Bien isolée dans les lumières
> Le monde alors n'existe pas
> Je m'abandonne toute entière.

This she sings in what is a well-established tradition of French actors moonlighting in music. Movie stars seem to make records relatively anonymously. Deneuve and Depardieu have done so, as have others, with varying degrees of success – Michel Blanc, Isabelle Adjani, Marie Laforet and even Bardot. In France it seems normal for acting to be enhanced with singing. As actors always claim to be frustrated by their vehicles, to sing and take risks on one's own is perhaps a new and stimulating way for them to communicate.

'The age of specialisation, when you did only one thing, is over,' Moreau once commented. 'Nowadays people do everything they can – act, sing, dance, write, direct. I don't think you should neglect any talent, however small. It's another person in me who sings. I love singing and people do buy my records.'

At the time of her first album, her name was being bandied around Los Angeles as an appealing financial proposition. American fans were breathless for her first Hollywood film and the studio chaps were casting around for a role for her. There was talk about Moreau for the Russian role in *55 Days at Peking*, but Charlton Heston insisted that there had to be no better Russian countess than the all-American Ava Gardner. No Hollywood picture gelled for a while and, instead, Moreau returned to France's favourite genre, the gangster send-up movie, with *Banana Peel*. She did it mainly to help her friend Marcel Ophüls to get his debut film off the ground. She had met him through Truffaut, narrated his short on Matisse and she thought he had talent.

Banana Peel, a pre-war Hollywood comedy imitation, based on Charles Williams' police novel *Nothing in Her Way*, was scripted in part by Claude Sautet, now the director of conformist films like *Un Coeur en Hiver* (A Heart in Winter). The film concerns a daughter trying to avenge her father, who has been ruined by his associates. She engages some rough types to do the job, including her ex-husband (Jean-Paul Belmondo). Costumes were, as usual, by Cardin, and the music was a rhythmic jazz score by Ward Swingle.

Banana Peel, with its alternative humour years ahead of its time, hit the jackpot, with audiences in Paris alone reaching nearly half a million. Not the sort of film to go down in the annals of film history as great, it was nevertheless the right film at the right time for Moreau. It also brought her back to the mainstream audiences in

France, who might have found her New Wave films obscure. The cinema of the New Wave was the product of a society enjoying considerable material prosperity, but not everybody was living easily with it. As they examined the problems and realities of life in both Paris and the provinces in a new way, some of the more controversial films took time to settle.

After this venture back into the popular consciousness, the time was right for Moreau to go back to Louis Malle. The role was a cameo in his brilliant study of suicide, *Le Feu Follet* (*A Time to Live and a Time to Die*, aka *Will o' the Wisp*). This was their first film together since *The Lovers* five years before and Malle was now romantically involved with Canadian actress Alexandra Stewart.

'I didn't want to cast her,' Malle told me recently. 'She was a huge star and the part was so small, just six minutes. But it had to be done with great bravura and self-irony. I phoned her a week before shooting began, and told her I was desperate. I knew I wouldn't have found anybody else right to grasp the feeling of the character. She said yes and was wonderful. I was thrilled because it turned out to be one of my best films. Perhaps not a very commercial one, but I love it. In the provinces, to commercialise it, they put "Jeanne Moreau in *Feu Follet*".'

In Malle's intensely personal adaptation of a novel by Pierre Drieu la Rochelle, who committed suicide in 1945, an erstwhile alcoholic aristocrat with suicidal tendencies (Maurice Ronet) spends forty-eight hours forlornly visiting his friends in the hope of finding a reason to stay alive. He leaves a clinic in Versailles where they have put him on a cure which has sterilised his body and soul, knowing in his heart that his hopeless search will only confirm the isolation that must lead him inevitably to death. Part of his pilgrimage takes Ronet (the man in the lift in *Lift to the Scaffold*), back to Moreau, a bohemian friend who lives on the artist-and-poet circuit of an evidently emotionally confused Paris.

The film is dark but never bleak. Full of long shadows, made more eerie by Erik Satie's music, the subject matter is intractable, and as suicide is not an accepted option, particularly in a predominently Catholic country, all the more shocking. When asked by *Paris Match* what drew him to the subject, Malle replied: 'It wasn't the subject of suicide that drew me . . . it was the sense of the night in the film'. *A Time to Live and a Time to Die* won the Special Jury prize at the 1963 Venice Film Festival.

From her retreat in Provence Moreau was now lured out to meet one of the great challenges of her career. The French producer Serge Silberman, who financed all five of the films the Spanish director Luís Buñuel made in France between 1964 and 1977, wanted to initiate their extraordinary collaboration with Moreau in the principal role of their adaptation of Octave Mirbeau's ironic *Le Journal d'une Femme de Chambre* (*The Diary of a Chambermaid*).

Silberman recounted to *Le Monde*'s Danièle Heymann how the first encounter went. 'I suggested Jeanne Moreau for the part of Célestine. Buñuel [who had gone into exile for twenty-four years in Mexico after the Spanish Civil War] wanted a Mexican actress. It was at the time of the Cannes Film Festival. Jeanne was in the area and I suggested to Luís that we go and see her.

'He liked Cannes despite one unpleasant memory: in 1954 he had been a member of the jury when the president was Jean Cocteau. One of the films in competition was René Clément's *Monsieur Ripois*, which Buñuel hated. Cocteau begged him to let it get a prize. Buñuel refused. At the closing ceremony *Monsieur Ripois* was awarded the Jury Prize. Buñuel was enraged and walked out of the cinema, went straight to the beach and chucked his dinner jacket into the sea.

'So there we were on the Côte d'Azur. As it was hot, we had a drink on the way to Jeanne's place, Amer-Picon and beer – an explosive mixture. "She's going to talk to me about the film," Buñuel said, "and I'm going to talk to her about birds." Ten kilometres further on we stopped at an *auberge* and had another Amer-Picon with beer.

'Everything went very well with Jeanne, she signed blind, even though she had no screenplay to read, just as if she was an extra.'

Buñuel was nervous to talk to Moreau about her role, but wanted her to agree not just because he thought she was a marvellous actress but also because he loved her walk. 'I have always liked to watch women walk,' he wrote in his book *My Last Breath*. 'Watching Jeanne was a great pleasure. When she walks, her foot trembles just a bit on its high heel, suggesting a certain tension and instability.'

Moreau in turn was fascinated by Buñuel, a director known for his courtesy towards actors. When she first met him, he was already sixty-three, tormented by sciatica, and had been going deaf for seven years. She used to call him Don Luís, her 'Spanish father', saying he was the father she wished she had had. 'He says he wants to be quite deaf in five years so he won't be able to hear anything at all. He will live through his eyes,' she once recorded. She also tells a sweet story about how Buñuel, who died in 1983, used to become so fascinated when the actors were working that he did not notice his hearing-aid buzzing and they would have to stop shooting because of the noise.

The strikingly handsome Buñuel had grown up from prosperous rural Spanish stock into one of the angry young men of the Dadaists and Surrealists. His friendship with Salvador Dali produced the celebrated short *Andalusian Dog*, still a staple of film studies courses everywhere. His 1930 masterpiece, *The Golden Age*, was so bitingly anti-Church and anti-establishment that it was banned in Spain for fifty years for besmirching fatherland, family and religion.

Now came *The Diary of a Chambermaid*, based on a book Buñuel had read many times. Jean Renoir had made a version of it in the States in 1946, with Paulette Goddard as the nineteenth-century serving-girl who causes sexual tension and other troubles in a confined household, but his version had been written off as unpersuasive and artificial. Buñuel wanted to move the story into the 1920s, a change that also allowed the right-wing demonstrators to shout '*Vive Chiappe!*' at the end, in memory of *The Golden Age*.

The chambermaid in question is a poor but ambitious young woman who has come from Paris to work in the petty provincial household of the Monteils, paragons of the rural bourgeoisie, well contrasted here with the hard-working peasantry that they employ. Soon after her arrival, as she minces around in high-laced boots and looks through keyholes, she discovers the hidden vices of her employers – the idle, lecherous Monsieur Monteil (Michel Piccoli), his bitter, frigid wife (Françoise Lugagne) and her father (Jean Ozenne), a shoe fetishist who likes to caress the legs of chambermaids.

Gradually Célestine commences her calm manipulation of all of them: her right-wing boss, the leftish neighbour, the sullen fascist gamekeeper, the old shoe-worshipper. All strong characters, they are delicately but firmly drawn. As her net closes in, she uses the power of her chilling disdain and sexuality to deflate their bourgeois decadence and confused morality.

Remarked Moreau: 'One critic said of my performance that I made Célestine look like a princess. But what a rude thing to say about maids! Why should they look any different from princesses? Servants are forced to live the life of their bosses; they can only lead their private lives at night. They just watch; if they made judgements they couldn't be servants. Célestine is Buñuel himself – the way she watches: critical, humorous. Buñuel has a lot of humour, though it is black humour.'

They started shooting the film during the autumn of 1963. She had signed for a week's work on *The Train* (for FFR 300,000) and Buñuel delayed filming so that she would not lose the money. (For the record she received FFR 250,000 for six weeks on *Chambermaid*.) Buñuel told Moreau that in return she was not to come to the studio in the Rolls with the chauffeur (Anna's husband) – she was no longer working on a Hollywood picture.

Right from the start, however, she was on Buñuel's wavelength. 'When we worked together, we didn't need to talk. Just to look was sufficient,' she remembers. It seems theirs was a delicate two-way understanding. One day she turned up with visible bags under her eyes that showed up horribly on screen at the day's rushes. Buñuel merely apologised to her the following day, saying that they were going to have to shoot the scene again. He tactfully claimed that the fault was his due to a technical problem.

She, in turn, revealed in one interview that she had a fantasy of being castigated by Buñuel, of getting out of bed, having a cold shower and being scolded by him. 'It's not true!' she apparently added. 'It's only a fantasy!'

The result of their complicity is a funny and revealing film that is engrossingly nasty. On contemporary viewing it still holds its own brilliantly. Clearly too sharp for the inflated bourgeoisie of its time, when it first came out the film received a lukewarm reception. Although she does not often see her completed films – she watched *Chambermaid* on TV only many years later and was totally agog – she was full of admiring remarks about Buñuel's direction and predicted in the press that the film was going to prove to be his most scandalous masterpiece yet. The critics nevertheless turned up their noses at it. While expressing their great admiration for the director's glorious past and also for the performances, particularly Moreau's, which was felinely brilliant, they remained generally condescending.

Up till then – and until relatively recently – French cinema as a whole often lacked audacity on trenchant political and social subjects. Buñuel's film had probably trodden too heavily on the *classes moyennes*, that conventional middle class that was still so close to its nineteenth-century ancestors. Nevertheless, for Moreau, her work with Buñuel was distinguished and has endured.

Buñuel and Moreau were to have made another film together, based on the great Gothic novel *The Monk* by 'Monk' Lewis. The project fell through due to financial difficulties, despite the fact that Peter O'Toole was ready to do it for nothing and Omar Sharif was interested too. After years of correspondence between Moreau and Buñuel, and after she took a lot of flak from friends who felt she was ruining her career 'making films like that', *Le Moine* (*The Monk*) eventually emerged in 1972, starring Nathalie Delon and directed by Buñuel's friend, Ado Kyrou. Critics described it as a 'near disaster', and regretted that Buñuel had not directed as well as writing the script. Perhaps Moreau was better out of that one.

8

'Sleeping with people must be one of the best ways of getting to know them.'

There were several films Jeanne Moreau might have been better off out of. One of them was *The Yellow Rolls-Royce*.

Although she was a proud owner of a Rolls herself, she did not look at home behind the wheel of this one. *The Yellow Rolls-Royce* was one of those all-star vehicles with everybody in it, in the worst kind of discreetly daring good taste. The film consisted of three stories written by Terence Rattigan about the owners of one particular yellow model. I would like to think she took her role out of solidarity with her own Rolls, for there can be little other reason to account for her presence or performance.

Designed as a successor to Rattigan's *The VIPs*, a star-filled multistory picture that did well enough by exploiting the real-life Burton-Taylor romance of the day, this film was also directed by Anthony Asquith as a follow-up. Moreau plays the Marchioness of Frinton, no less. She is the wife of an aristocratic diplomat (Rex Harrison) who, on their tenth wedding anniversary, gives her the car. Between dinners and dialogues about postings to Caracas and appointments with Albanian ambassadors, we learn, although the husband apparently has not yet gleaned this minor detail, that all is not well with their marriage. While at the races at Ascot, in a pretty white broderie anglaise frock (by Cardin) and a feather hat, she cuckolds him, steaming up the windows making molten love to one of his underlings (Edmund Purdom) in the aforementioned Rolls. Too bad the Marquess had not sent the bounder off to Caracas sooner.

And too bad, thought her fans, that she undermined her career by making such wrong films. The jump from *Chambermaid* to *The Yellow Rolls-Royce* horrified them. They probably would have been even more vexed had she taken the part she was offered in *The Battle of the Bulge*, the Second World War Ardennes epic, a three-page role finally done by Pier Angeli. Moreau appears to have rejected this one for a never-made Peter O'Toole film, *The Will Adams Story*. Whatever the facts, after making *The Yellow Rolls-Royce* in Britain she was on doctor's orders to take a month's rest to get over her fatigue.

While working in Britain, however, Moreau had met director Tony Richardson and producer Anthony Page, who had just mounted John Osborne's *Inadmissible Evidence* at the Royal Court Theatre. Established in 1956 by Richardson and George Devine, the Royal Court was a powerhouse of contemporary agitprop at a time when British showbiz was generally febrile and lacklustre. Richardson wanted her to act at the Court in their revival of Wedekind's *Lulu*, the piece about a woman who spreads despair, ruin and death among the men who get involved with her. Although she was very keen on the proposition, in the end it fell through (and she was not to play Lulu on stage until years later in Paris). Yet her meeting with Richardson marked the start of a rather spectacular director-actress relationship which was to put her once again in the headlines.

While in London then she did the usual round of interviews and the published results seemed to concentrate with the now traditional zest on her uninhibited ability to talk about love, men, women and life in general. 'Why do people always ask me about love?' she asked a *Sunday Express* journalist with a small bleak smile. The interviewer, Roderick Mann, was stoically unable to answer her, but he wrote in his introduction to the interview: 'Dammit, you think, looking at the clenched agonised face – what can she know about love? Yet the curious fact remains; whenever definitive views on love are sought, it is to Jeanne Moreau that people seem to go.'

I will pick up on the 'clenched agonised face' aspect of Moreau later. Far more absorbing at this stage was the acceptance that she was a philosopher on love and on relations between the sexes. Admittedly, it is a subject on which she has always given as good as she has got. As the actress who symbolised the lover to French adults, just as Bardot had for the less mature, she would go on record and wreak havoc with statements that were all too ripe for quoting out of context. There were the innocent ones, like 'Love is given by God as an extra and you have to work for it all the time.' There were the more provocative ones: 'Sleeping with people is one of the best ways of getting to know them,' 'All my life I've had enough self-confidence to attract any man I cared for,' and 'I'm a sensualist who believes what makes me feel good cannot possibly be bad.'

Of Englishmen she said in an interview at this time that they had a sort of modesty that was very 'endearing' but which seemed to make them hide themselves away. (She has also said she has never really known an Englishman in her life apart from her grandfather.) Frenchmen, on the other hand, she roundly declared on French television, lacked virility. The last remark caused an outcry from all quarters. The list of male company she had kept came under scrutiny as a result and, as the *Evening Standard* pointed out, it was a fairly long one, including such names as Sacha Distel, Philippe Lemaire, Raoul Lévy, Jean-Louis Malle, Trintignant, Cardin and others.

One publication was sharp enough to quote Bardot's ex-husband, Jacques Charrier, as saying that perhaps Moreau should try to enlarge her circle of acquaintances. He added, 'she can have my phone number for a start', thereby adding fuel to the fiery debate that pitted B.B. against Moreau, as France's two top-paid female stars, in the competition for the nation's top sex symbol. In England some called Moreau a Third Programme Bardot!

But the most spirited response to her statement came, quite astonishingly, from Edith Piaf, somebody considered quite an authority on the matter. Commented Piaf: 'Come, come, it is simply not true. For a man to be virile it is sufficient for a woman to persuade him of his virility. I have always been surrounded by virile men. When I love a man I prove it and the problem ends there. Obviously in certain circles men are a little too refined, but then one must know how to choose.'

Moreau further upset her countrymen by saying that Frenchmen were generally afraid of her, basically because a happy marriage for a Frenchman had always to be with a stupid wife. 'I – as a character – am not stupid and sitting at home waiting. I have the strength to abandon a situation. Men want to believe abandoned women have tears in their eyes. It frightens them to discover that a woman can pack up and go as easily as a man can.'

All this was reportedly said by Moreau in the early sixties. Looking back on the period now, it is still great copy. Surely these utterances must have been part of some spontaneous master-plan of Moreau's to get people to open up and live a bit more with their feelings. She had nothing further to lose by being outspoken: according to her, she was already considered the 'scarlet woman of Babylon'.

She told journalist Richard Grenier as a matter of fact at the time: 'In Paris they think I'm some kind of monster, the scarlet woman of Babylon, because I still associate with men I've had affairs with. There's a marvellous line in Apollinaire's letter to his daughter: "The people I have loved, I shall always love." But why not? What's the alternative? Cut them out of my life? From the age of twenty-five on, any man who comes into your life stays there for good. Otherwise it's a terrible defeat, and shows you've chosen badly.' She added that the list of men she had loved was 'not like the telephone directory'.

'You can truly love somebody and know that you hurt him, but you can't help being deeply in love with somebody else. It may sound very scandalous, feeling all women should keep their lovers, but I believe they should, if they can. If I married all the men I'd been in love with, I could make a bracelet from the wedding rings.'

You have to admire her sass and guts to have said this sort of thing on sex, especially as in a considerable number of her films Moreau the bitch-goddess on screen has allowed her leading men indescribable bliss before they spiral, spent but smiling, straight to hell. When the off-screen Moreau came out with such heady equivalents in real life, it is hardly surprising that her audiences began to dub her *la mante religieuse* – the praying mantis, the insect that devours raw meat.

'Anyway, if we didn't have the sensation of love, we'd have nothing and live like bugs,' she said most poignantly. 'When I am in love it influences my acting. It sometimes puts me in a state of grace. It gives me a feeling of resurrection and makes me conscious of my power.'

Time has not changed La Moreau, nor her attitudes. Thirty years later she still has her immense and shocking talent for mesmerising you, she still lives her life without worrying about what other people think of her.

Despite her straightforwardness, which can throw the cat among the pigeons when she expresses herself in a direct manner, Moreau can also display great tact and a demeanour of controlled coolness.

According to Alexander Walker's book *Vivien: The Life of Vivien Leigh*, while staying with Laurence Olivier and his wife Vivien during the fifties at Notley Abbey, the Oliviers' country house in Buckinghamshire, there was some talk of her appearing in a play with Olivier. Apparently during lunch, Leigh commented cuttingly: 'Oh, you speak English well enough, do you, to play with Larry? And you think you look young enough to play the part, do you?'

'It was quite awful,' Anthony Quayle, who was present, recalled to Walker. 'Vivien insulted Moreau all through lunch. Fortunately, Moreau realised she had something wrong with her and didn't let herself be baited. She really was an angel.'

Moreau continued to be a model of tact when I questioned her about the incident. '*Oh, j'ai un trou là!* [I have a gap in my memory]' she said. 'I really can't remember which play it was but I know Vivien didn't feel well that day. She wasn't really there. I was surprised and embarrassed but she wasn't awful to me.'

As if to draw attention to her point that men who come into your life stay there, she next made *Mata Hari, Agent H21*. The director was her recently divorced husband Jean-Louis Richard, and the dialogue was written by Richard and François Truffaut. Fourteen exotic jewelled costumes which showed the Moreauian fine form were designed by Pierre Cardin, of course, and Jean-Louis Trintignant was her leading man.

This was Richard's second film – the first was *Bonne Chance, Charlie* (Good Luck, Charlie) – and without her, it would not have happened. 'It was a project written for her,' he told me recently in Paris. 'It was our image of Jeanne. We both knew her very well. Mata Hari was a spy, but she was also a woman like any other woman. We took so many details in the film from Jeanne's life that the script, in a way, could be Jeanne's story.'

The film was made in the heart of her 'film family', with cast and crew filled with friends and colleagues. As it was made during the school holidays, Jérôme had also come on set from his private school in Grenoble. Moreau explains her needs for this kind of on-set 'family': 'I feel the crew, not the camera, is my audience. I cannot forget them. When I have the lead in a film I have the feeling I'm sort of a hostess and these people are waiting for me, and I like to be there on time and properly dressed, even for a rehearsal. I want to be at my best. I need their regard to be different, to transform myself.

'When you work very closely with people, it is natural to become involved. I have to know everything about those surrounding me. I like them to come to me disarmed and I think I react in an animal way. I always need relationships when I work.

'When the work starts suddenly you're in a strange country, a sort of no-man's-land into which you can't let close friends from the outside. Afterwards you tell them about it, but during it you can't allow them into these secret fields.'

Mata Hari was the stage name of the most notorious female spy in history. Under her real name, Margarete Gertrude Zelle, she might not have fared so well, but as dancer Mata Hari she was as alluring an espionage agent as the Germans could have wished for. She achieved notable success before finishing up in front of a French firing squad in 1917.

A silent film version of her life had been made in 1928 (*Mata Hari: The Red Dancer*, starring Magda Sonja), and in 1931 there was an elaborate melodrama starring Greta Garbo, Ramón

Novarro and Lionel Barrymore. Moreau knew that she would be besieged by comparisons with Garbo, especially in the exotic temple dance scene. Furthermore, there was already another script around for a dumped Mata Hari film production and there were even some accusations of plagiarism from the producers of that project. As a result Moreau remembers having to go to the police station, where she was treated as if she were Mata Hari caught out in person.

I asked her how she felt about being seen, as Mata Hari, nude on screen. 'I was naked in *The Lovers* and naked in *Eva*. I don't understand the big fuss about it. I've never been naked in situations that were irrelevant or vulgar or shocking. I mean, when you feel good in your skin and you don't hate your body, I don't see why not. Anyway, expressing a deep and personal feeling is more revealing than showing your body.'

However, when an editor of a nudist magazine once rang her to ask her if she'd like to endorse nudism, she told him pretty sharply: 'If living without clothes eliminates all secret thoughts, I don't see the advantage. To be honest with you, I enjoy those secret thoughts.'

Moreau once did a spread for *Playboy* while she was in Mexico working on *Viva Maria!*. 'Oh, I was nude with a sort of red chiffon thing next to a fire, but I wouldn't make a fuss over that,' she laughs. 'It was not *nude* nude.'

Sympathetic though the idea may seem, the 'film family' approach does not always mean objectivity. Richard's *Mata Hari* did not make huge inroads into cinema history, except, perhaps, in Moreau's death scene, where she is tied loosely to a post usually reserved for target practice. Head back, eyes closed and unblindfolded, she awaits the final volley. People who were on set say that she slumped in 'death' so convincingly that one of the first-aid men rushed forward, thinking there had been a grievous accident. At the time it was thought of as one of the most savage death scenes in post-war cinema. Now, however, it seems tame.

There is one interesting footnote to all this: in 1985 there was yet another remake of the Mata Hari tale, this time starring Sylvia Kristel, the Dutch actress of *Emmanuelle* fame. Jean-Louis Richard was the one who had originally discovered her, hidden at the beginning of a cassette of hopefuls who were screen-testing in 1974 for Alain Siritzky's *Emmanuelle*, for which Richard wrote the screenplay.

Moreau says that on her next project with Orson Welles he paid her in silver plate. This was his *Chimes at Midnight*. He never had any money and she accepted the silver gracefully, not anticipating that she would have to drag the pieces back through customs on her return to France from the location in Spain.

Welles had promised her that *Chimes at Midnight* (aka *Falstaff*), Shakespeare's tale of Prince Hal becoming King Henry V, would be a dark comedy. What actor would not be tempted by the maestro's promise? She leaped at the offer to play Doll Tearsheet, alongside Margaret Rutherford as Mistress Quickly, John Gielgud as Henry IV and Welles as Falstaff, with Ralph Richardson narrating.

Welles' modest resolve was that it would be a film of close-ups, a sort of comedic telescoped version of the play. Instead, during the shooting, the sleeping cineaste in Welles woke up to the advantage of countless locations that had remained more or less unchanged since the Middle Ages. Thereafter *Chimes at Midnight* became a massive production with teeming gypsy extras and semi-exotic locations on hilltops and plains all over Spain. It had its share of typical Wellesian difficulties. After announcing a ten-month shooting and post-production schedule, Welles faltered in his timing and had to postpone the release. As a result the distributor backed out of the film, making its financial position untenable. Another backer had to be found before shooting could resume. Then Welles fell ill with a serious gall bladder infection, and the problems continued. At the same time, it should be noted, he had also begun work on a version of *Treasure Island* in which he was to play Long John Silver.

Eventually, when *Chimes* made it to the screen, nearly two years after shooting commenced, it was hailed as brilliant and the visual effects stunning. But it was also a film on the edge of a nervous breakdown. This was Welles' greatest performance, but elsewhere there was a desperate clash of acting styles, much unsynchronised dubbing and a lamentable, almost incoherent, soundtrack. Yet *Chimes* is still one of the most stirring of the screen Shakespeares. Welles said of it that, if he wanted to get into heaven on the basis of only one movie, *Chimes* was the one he would offer up. The film won the 1966 Cannes Film Festival's twentieth anniversary award.

The first time I saw it, in the early seventies, was at an outdoor summer cinema in Athens one hot, balmy evening full of moonlight, jasmine, cigarettes and *ouzo*. Apparently, they played the reels out of order, so that the dead lived again and the friendship between Falstaff and Hal became a rather on-off affair. Throughout this jumble Moreau looked as if she was having a ball, even though I considered her unbelievable as an Elizabethan wench with wild long hair and pretty feet, revelling bawdily through the night, in bed with the hippopotamic Orson at Mistress Quickly's tavern in Eastcheap-in-Madrid.

Ultimately, during her four-day shoot, Moreau had little to do, but as Alexander Walker of the *Evening Standard* put it, she did it 'fetchingly'. Somebody else opined that she was sometimes acting as though she had 'just wandered on to the set of *Chimes at Midnight* in the middle of making a French New Wave film by Jean-Luc Godard'. All fair comment, but the bottom line for Moreau has always been the experience of making the film. She loved working on it and she loved working again with her beloved Orson.

In a BBC documentary on Welles she tells a sweet story of how he was always plagued by stage-fright and would go to all extremes to avoid acting. 'I'd waited two or three days to do a certain scene with Orson,' she says, a smile playing on her face, the brown squirrel eyes gleaming naughtily. 'He'd take me out to dinner and talk about different things until eventually I asked why we were waiting. "Oh no," he said, "we can't do our scenes yet, I haven't got my make-up. My little make-up suitcase is lost. I can't do any scenes till it's found. We'll start with the reverse shots of you, the close-ups."

'"But Orson," I said, "close-ups are so difficult to start with, but OK, I'll manage if I have to." So I arrived at the studio and went into the shabby little room which was the make-up room and sat on the floor – there was no chair – to wait my turn. And what did I see under an old settee but Orson's make-up kit hidden underneath. "Oh look!" I shrieked. "Shhh, don't say it," whispered the make-up woman. "He has stage-fright and hid it himself."

'Anyway, after two hours of shooting I told him that I'd discovered his make-up and let's go. We finally got to do the famous scene when Doll Tearsheet jumps up and down on Falstaff in the bed. I rehearsed with another actor and then when it was time for me to jump on Orson, he yelled, "Cut, cut! You've destroyed my nose – we can't shoot this scene today." That was Orson. He was a shattering, marvellous man. There was a sort of madness on the set when he directed, but he has done more than anyone to extend the cinematic language.

'Each time we made a film together there was a different mood. He improvised and drew things out of you. Sometimes he would speak lines to you and you would have to give them back, like birds do when they eat a worm and then give it to their baby.'

In the documentary she screws her face up and giggles. Once again I am surprised at how easily she slips in and out of character, chameleon-like, in the flick of an eyelash, from a sultry girl drifting dreamily to a *soignée* woman, eyes full of experience and almost insolent directness – a mixture of the old-fashioned romantic and the modern liberated women, says Marguerite Duras. On camera Jeanne Moreau somehow *always* looks sensual, eager for life, poised, her golden skin, tiny hands and face both childlike and world-weary.

Yet off camera she can be shockingly plain. I personally have never seen her present herself as anything other than a screen legend, but others have caught her out and put the results down in brutal black and white. In 1965 C. Robert Jennings of *Los Angeles Magazine* found her with 'dark circles under large bulging frog eyes, uneven teeth in a styptic hungry mouth, both flaccid and puffed up, something like a prune'. Of course, he was, in due course, to be totally swept up in her charm and after their interview at Le Préverger left reluctantly.

Sue Summers in *Harpers* in 1992 found her 'tiny and plump while the hair, once so chicly dark, was pulled back severely behind rather prominent ears'. The *Daily Mirror*'s Donald Zec, when invited to dine with her during the filming of *Viva Maria!* found her, on first impression, 'a thin, pale, unbeautiful Miss Average Woman who needs to catch up on her sleep'. Oriana Fallaci, in her book *Limelighters*, writes that as faces go, she actually found Moreau's 'a little on the ugly side, with that bitter mouth, those sunken cheeks, those dark ringed eyes'. The *Observer*'s John Gale wrote that at first there was 'something almost plain, almost schoolmistressy about her'. Moreau herself claims she does not like her face, but has 'grown accustomed to it'. 'Now I'm more like the title of the book, *My Face for the World to See*. That's what I am, and as time goes by my face reflects more and more of what's going on inside.'

In the mid-sixties, that face became indelibly imprinted on the minds of cinema audiences everywhere, whether it was before a firing squad or romping with Welles.

9

ℳ

'We were like two pals in the Army: there were good and bad moments.'

Viva Maria! has gone down in film history as the first female 'buddy' movie. Starring Jeanne Moreau and Brigitte Bardot as sisters, it was directed by Louis Malle on location in Mexico. He had to have Moreau in the production in order to raise the finance for it. Although it is said that Moreau had not wanted to appear in any further Malle films, she had agreed to do it out of loyalty to him. He was, after all, the man who'd 'discovered' her.

For his part, according to Moreau, Malle had to get rid of his hang-up about the Malle family's wealth, which was a burden to him. He chose to prove himself on a big-budget ($2 million) epic, with a crew of 150, starring the two top French actresses of the time. The absurdly handsome George Hamilton, then only twenty-five, was the love interest as a virile revolutionary with whom one of the Marias (Moreau) falls in love while he is helplessly chained and pinioned, half naked, to a rack in prison. Of the sequence Moreau said: 'It's a slight reversal of the roles, but novel, don't you think?' Rumour had it that he and Moreau had an off-set flurry. ('I think of actors as men and treat them as men,' she said), but this seems unlikely – she had by now become engaged to Pierre Cardin, and although their engagement was soon to be called off, Pierre was in evidence on set.

Viva Maria! was a huge undertaking, designed to be very commercial, and its spin-off potential was maximised. The money made from the merchandising side of the James Bond films had increased awareness of the markets to be exploited. By the time of the film's launch no fewer than eighty licences had been granted to exploit the 1910 *Viva Maria!* frilly pastel look in blouses, bras, knitwear, skirts, belts, swimsuits and even handbags.

'At the end of *Feu Follet* everybody was depressed and about to commit suicide,' Malle says, only half joking. 'One Sunday I came across the premise of *Viva Maria!* and it seemed just what we needed – a musical comedy, fun with adventure, with women, with colour. It was a brilliant idea at the time: a parody of a buddy-buddy movie.

'Jean-Claude Carrière, who wrote the script, was pretty much a beginner at the time. He had to be very careful to balance the script equally between the leading roles. We sent the script to their [Moreau's and Bardot's] agents and within twenty-four hours had phone calls from them saying that the other actress's role was much better than their client's. It was a bad start, but we knew there was going to be an ego problem created by the entourage and the press. It was going to be Muhammad Ali versus Sonny Liston.'

Neither actress had ever performed outside Europe, or with each other. Bardot, whose role had originally been pencilled in for Shirley MacLaine, was to have top billing.

'At the time I was the only one who'd worked with both Jeanne and Brigitte. Brigitte and I had worked well together in *Une Vie Privée* (A *Very Private Affair*) (1961), but I knew from the start that directing them both in the same picture would require diametrically opposite techniques. Bardot is impatient and has to be kept amused; you play a game with her. Moreau has to be kept at the end of her nerves. I know Jeanne doesn't remember the film very fondly!'

He says he alternated between tact and firmness to hold the women's temperaments in check while encouraging a slight undercurrent of competition between them. Each actress definitely responded with a determination to out-troupe the other. Their on-screen relationship is funny and spirited and very special to watch –

one would be hard pushed to find two huge names playing in such a daft and exuberant colour supplement of a movie nowadays.

However, shooting the film during four months of hot, hard weather was not Malle's favourite experience. While it seems that his stars got along fine, the press – a barrage of 140 and three TV teams – drove him crazy. This was the film Hollywood had been waiting for – the cat fight between two sex symbols while the baking Mexican sun beat down by day and the tequila took its toll by night.

'The horror was reading daily about the "terrible fights" they were *not* having. Of course, they ended up having them,' says Malle.

Luís Buñuel, who lived in Mexico, recalled it being so fraught on set that when for a joke he visited the set, put on a wig and walked across the location right past Malle, the director did not even recognise him. 'No one did – neither my technician friends nor Jeanne Moreau, who'd recently made a movie with me,' he remarked.

This film must have been sheer hell to make. The sun was indeed swelteringly fierce, but they did not have the budget to wait for better conditions. Reportedly, there were additional harassments, such as Bardot claiming that Moreau's rented *hacienda* in the foothills above Cuernavaca was more commodious than hers. Moreau also got the only air-conditioned trailer dressing-room. (The French public was less categorical about the cat-fight aspect, but smirked behind their well-manicured hands as they knew that B.B. had been thoroughly rattled when Moreau replaced her as the person who wished French television viewers a Happy New Year. The producer, François Chatel, had said he would not tolerate Bardot's eccentricities any longer.)

Bardot arrived first in Mexico City. Riot police with tear-gas pistols had to hold back the crowds. When Moreau, the 'other girl' in the film, flew in five days later, the producer had to identify the slim, small woman stepping off the Air France flight from Paris for the waiting photographers. She arrived still tired from a bout of pneumonia and with luggage 260 lbs overweight, filled with Cardin clothes. Her *maquilleuse*, Simone Knapp, and Anna Pradella were in attendance. Bardot had arrived with only her small boyfriend, Bob Zaguri, in tow.

Viva Maria! is a tale of two turn-of-the-century dance-hall *soubrettes*, hoofers who get bogged down in a Latin American revolution. Maria II (Bardot), the daughter of an Irish anarchist and skilled in the use of firearms, is fleeing her late father's final act of terrorism and encounters a travelling variety show somewhere in a South American banana republic. Maria I (Moreau) is the singing act. They link up, going on to travel across the country, first as performers – The Marias from Paris – and then as revolutionaries who take over the rebellion when the leader is killed.

Basically it is about two women, a stripteasing sexpot and a cool seductress. It's a wonderfully silly story, one man's fantasy filled with two mouthwateringly beautiful women, remarkable scenery and colourful madness (like a church spire that does semaphore). Malle's complaint that 'the trouble with movies today is that they are too intellectual' was utterly rectified with *Viva Maria!*

At first the film was called *Que Viva Maria!*, a parody on the Russian director Eisenstein's massive but unfinished Mexican documentary *Que Viva Mexico!*. Malle and Carrière (who co-wrote *The Diary of a Chambermaid*) penned it as a sort of burlesque match between the sexpot and the seductress, or, if you prefer, the real sex symbol and the intellectual one. On set, most people hung around, sweating in the midday heat, batting away at the flies with their sombreros, waiting for the fists to fly in a real-life epic duel under the Mexican sun. *Les Girls* in Mexico, or 'How to Play a Pair of Queens', as *Life* magazine put it.

Reams of loaded anecdotes came off the set of the film and flew around the world, yet both actresses have always insisted there was professional harmony on set. Whatever they may have done after work was private. Their collected views on each other in fact boiled down more or less to the following. Bardot on Moreau: 'Jeanne is an actress. I am a phenomenon'; Moreau on Bardot: 'Brigitte is a champion. I am a challenger.'

'To me there are two kinds of women,' Bardot has also said, 'those who have a wholly feminine character, with all the faults that implies, and those who have the character of a man, completely open and spontaneous. I am of the latter kind, and so is Jeanne.'

Agreed Moreau, B.B.'s senior by seven years: 'Like me, Brigitte is an animal, but of a very different species. I guess we are both free women – we have that in common. We were like two pals in the

Army: there were good and bad moments.' Sex appeal, after all, is flesh, while the rest remains more mysterious, indefinable. Moreau feels she does not have the first, so she exploits the mystery. 'I suppose I don't think of myself as a glamorous piece of meat, so the roles are there,' she said years later. 'I've continued because I have always taken risks and am driven.'

Viva Maria! was Jeanne Moreau's forty-first picture. On set she told *Look* magazine's Chandler Brossard that she was searching for a new Moreau. 'I feel I have used up a particular image of myself. You know, the way a strategist exhausts a particular strategy. I have a great fear that I may start imitating myself if I don't do something entirely different. I feel that an absolutely new Moreau is waiting to be brought to life. It is amazing how people refuse to think of themselves as endlessly rejuvenatable as personalities. One's soul is like a vast, unexplored country, don't you think?'

When the film opened in New York, the two Marias rode in an open car down Broadway, followed by a caravan of no fewer than eleven orchestras. It opened the new Curzon Cinema in London, and in Paris Alain Delon escorted both ladies, one on each arm, to the première. The film featured in cover stories in magazines worldwide and both actresses became thoroughly international. The exposure prompted a fawning *Time* magazine cover story on Moreau, she was listed in *Esquire* as one of the hundred outstanding personalities of the world (Charles de Gaulle was the other French person who made the list) and she earned inclusion in the *International Who's Who*. From Los Angeles she was soon to receive the Oscar of Elegance, chosen by a jury of dignitaries, and from London the Best Foreign Actress award from BAFTA. She chalked up the Francis Carco Prize for best singer of the year in 1966 as well.

La Moreau was now thoroughly international.

Still exhausted from the Mexican circus, Moreau arrived in the abandoned village of Le Rat in Limousin to make the film that was to really shock the world. It was called *Mademoiselle (Summer Fires)*. In theory this was her best try yet at international stardom, for it was directed by Tony Richardson, then the husband of Vanessa Redgrave, from a story by Jean Genet.

In *Mademoiselle* she plays a demure but neurotic and sadistic country teacher. When not instructing her pupils she burns farms and poisons wells. In an undemure moment she surrenders to an Italian migrant worker (Ettore Manni) for what must be the longest celluloid cross-country love scene ever filmed. The movie leaves her driving off into the countryside, much satisfied, after her lover is battered to death by shovel-wielding villagers.

The poster for the film, which played at the London Pavilion in Piccadilly Circus, announced: 'Genet's story shows what can happen to a woman who is loveless. As the film plunges into the roots of her evil, it is unflinching and unsparing, with a realism no other picture has ever attempted.' Even now it comes over as pretty nasty.

Moreau has said that she detested the part, but liked doing the film. In the original screenplay Genet had let the character convert the repression of her sexuality into pathological release, with the logical conclusion of self-destruction. Richardson changed all this into an orgy of love, after which she announces to the village that her lover has raped her.

Moreau said: 'It is not a pretty film. Genet's eroticism is ferocious and there is a lot of morbid violence in it. I had no pleasure making it. It was painful, because it was a difficult and unhealthy role. She was so unhappy, that woman – someone I wouldn't like to be. She's an inhibited virgin, a dry fruit. You can't tell what the part will be like before a film starts, not completely. That's where the director is so important. I put great faith in Tony – absolute faith. He had a mysterious quality which is hard to define and when he said I should do the film, why, I just did it. I feel the same with Truffaut, with Buñuel, with Orson.'

Richardson was then the king of the British Free Cinema Wave and still hot from *The Loneliness of the Long-Distance Runner* (1962) and *Tom Jones* (1963). He wanted desperately to work with Moreau, having seen her many times on stage and loving what he called her 'precision, elegance, her understanding of film and how it works'.

'What no one knows until they have worked with Jeanne is the completeness and accuracy of her professionalism,' he writes in his memoirs, *Long-Distance Runner*. Clearly Richardson had never met a woman like Jeanne Moreau before. He described her as 'sophisticated, skilled, mature, lighting up and taking over everywhere she went'. 'It was as if I'd never grown up before,' he wrote.

They had met in Paris, and he had told her she could choose her own script. She immediately thought of the story Genet had written seven years earlier, a text of a hundred pages, which she had found very striking. Genet lived close to her in Paris and they had already talked lyrically about the story. Joseph Losey had wanted to make it, starring Romy Schneider as Mademoiselle, the teacher, but he had let the cat out of the bag and lost it to Richardson.

'Once again, I talked too much and told somebody over dinner one night that I was going to do it,' admitted Losey in his book. 'Genet wanted $50,000 for his old script. Producer Sam Spiegel said it was too much. Schneider offered to lend him the money "from the receipts". "No hurry," said Spiegel, "the script has been lying around for centuries." Over the same weekend, Richardson paid the $50,000.'

When the film was entered at Cannes 1966, it caused an outright scandal. Some termed it pure pornography, and worse, it was tittered at in screenings. The reviews were disastrous, audiences were bored. It lost its distributor, United Artists, a lot of money and critics found it in such bad taste as to be irritating. Moreau was even accused of being a female Gilles de Rais, Joan of Arc's monster warrior who organised bloodthirsty orgies, sacrificing hundreds of children at his château. People also began to question Moreau's talent, and her talent for selecting work.

Undaunted, Richardson and Moreau went on to make a second film together. This was *The Sailor From Gibraltar*, based on her friend Duras' novel of the same title. It was Moreau's favourite book of the moment and she was dying to play the role of Anna, the wandering American divorcée.

Once again this was a project that had slipped through Losey's fingers. Losey was passionate about Duras and had wanted to produce *Sailor* with Moreau, to whom he had spoken about the project. According to Losey, she gave the idea to Richardson, who set things up, doing the film with a screenplay by Christopher Isherwood and theme song sung by Moreau. As both directors are now dead, the finer details of the story have gone with them to the grave.

The story of Anna, 'a female Flying Dutchman', as the *New York*

Times called her in its review, is about a wealthy predator who cruises the harbours of the world in search of her lost love. In one port she meets an Englishman (played by Ian Bannen, until then known mainly for his distinguished Royal Shakespeare Company career). He joins her on the mysterious search. They fall in love and, in the end, he becomes more obsessed with the phantom sailor than she is.

To shoot the film Richardson whisked his cast and crew, like a gypsy caravan, off to locations in Italy and Greece, Egypt, Ethiopia and even a jungle near the Sudan. He cast Vanessa Redgrave as the 'other' woman, Bannen's screen fiancée Sheila, who loses him to Moreau. Orson Welles had a small role as Louis of Mozambique and the rest of the cast included John Hurt, Hugh Griffith and Eleanor Bron.

It was the first time Richardson and Redgrave had worked together on a film and, considering the nature of the story, it was a difficult one on which to prevent personal life spilling over into professional life. They were experiencing difficulties in their marriage, problems caused partly by their separate desires to pursue their own careers and neither countenancing the suggestion that they should do anything less.

In her autobiography *Vanessa Redgrave*, the actress writes that she had felt miserable and left out while on location with Richardson in France for *Mademoiselle*, trundling their baby daughters, Natasha and Joely, around in a pushchair and feeling 'terribly in the way'.

'Neither of us knew any longer what to do for each other and I didn't know what to do with myself,' she writes. It seems it was not being part of the action which hurt her more than her husband's obsession with Moreau, which she says she found 'completely understandable'.

'She was enchanting. The crew, the cast, the whole village were in love with her. But I felt miserable and excluded.'

Consequently, being cast in *Sailor* was a double-edged sword for Redgrave. She was part of it all, but playing the woman who loses her man to Moreau.

Relations between the director and the rest of his cast appear to have been fairly tense on several fronts during shooting. Ian Bannen, when asked for his comments on the film, faxed me: 'Although the film turned into a nightmare for most of us from day one, Jeanne was a joy to work with. After the first two weeks she said: "Do you know, Ian, what we should all do with this film?"

"No, what?" I asked.

"Stop working on it and go away and work on something else and perhaps come back at a later date."

'How right she was! She had a magnetism all of her own which she could particularly turn on when the camera whirred, and whirr it did, as the entire film was shot with an unblimped Arriflex. At times it was almost impossible to hear oneself speaking, never mind one's fellow artists. But the whole idiotic idea was one of many eccentric whims of the director, a fellow called Tony Richardson. Orson Welles summed it up beautifully when, after a couple of days, he asked me: "Is this director from outer space?"'

Moreau counters the 'outer space' quip by saying that from Welles it was quite a compliment. 'Orson knew what it meant to be from outer space,' she chuckled, while admitting there were difficult moments during shooting. 'These moments always had to do with creation. Even if there is tension between people, a film can't be all bad. But there was no real script and Tony did it far too quickly. We had just finished doing *Mademoiselle*. We had terrible weather, so lots of the days were spent idle, postponing the shooting. But he wanted to do the film immediately. Was it in relation to his infatuation with me? I don't know. But we were not ready to shoot.

'Part of the problem was that I had the idea to bring in the cameraman whom Godard and Truffaut used, Raoul Coutard. But I forget things. He had made François very unhappy in *The Bride Wore Black* because he was aggressive and François was gentle. But I spoke to Tony about him because he is a genius with the camera and knows how to work a hand camera. At that time it was not easy to find people who knew how to do that. As we were supposed to be shooting in the desert and shooting on the boat, using very light equipment and no lights, much of the camera was hand-held. I thought Coutard would be perfect.

'But it was terrible, Coutard with Tony. And *en plus* there was the barrier of language and I understood everything. Ian was so infatuated with himself and his part that he didn't notice that part of the problem during the filming came from that aggressive relationship. Tony was a very gentle man.'

Meanwhile, there was another personal drama unfolding behind the scenes of *The Sailor From Gibraltar*. Richardson had cast a young Greek sailor from the naval academy of Hydra, Theodore Roubanis. Young, dark and Macedonian, Theo had escorted the director and his team around Greece and the islands, doing recces for locations. He had aspirations towards acting and had studied acting in New York, but was back in Greece for his military service. His part in the film was as a member of the yacht's crew.

Not long after shooting started, rumours began to drift about that Moreau had fallen in love with Roubanis, at twenty-four, thirteen years her junior. Their own rapport upset the balance of the actress's relationship with her director. While he tried to ignore the romance he became 'insanely jealous' (Richardson's own words). He fired the Greek.

The photographers went wild, snapping the couple coming out of nightclubs or going into airports. French television filmed an empty rumpled bed to illustrate Moreau's adventure in Greece. Greek newspapers reported that they were to wed, at a huge public ceremony in which the couple would be drawn by white horses in a carriage around Constitution Square. Moreau denied these reports as 'pure imagination' but naturally the news travelled worldwide, augmented by the gossip columnists noting that Richardson had cast Moreau as the lead in his film while his own wife was in a secondary role.

On *Mademoiselle*, Richardson had made much of how he enjoyed working with Moreau. After *Sailor* he was quoted in *Cosmopolitan*, still saying that she was 'the most marvellous actress I have ever worked with, and the most marvellous person'. As nobody believes what they read in the press, nobody really cared, but further mutterings along these lines were to bubble up a year later when the Richardson-Redgrave marriage finally collapsed.

Sailor did not do much at the box office, but it remains a wonderfully scenic piece enhanced by the romantic rifts and valleys that weave their way through it. When it finished Moreau took time off, for the first time in years, at home in Provence to recharge her batteries. Richardson spent Christmas with his wife and children, but then had a fortnight 'being spoiled' by Moreau in La Garde-Freinet. Apparently the Roubanis-Moreau link had been amicably severed, for the person the young Greek later married was no less than Lady Sarah Churchill. Richardson flew off as far away as he could get – to Tahiti and Bora-Bora – and Moreau, never very good at doing nothing for more than a week at a time, recorded a second album of a dozen new songs by her friend Bassiak/Rezvani. The record went on to win the Grand Prix de l'Académie Nationale du Disque Français.

When summer finished at Le Préverger and the evenings started to close in, Moreau returned to Paris for a little job *parmi les copains* back home at the Bois de Boulogne studios, playing a French Revolution whore called Mademoiselle Mimi in a compendium piece on prostitution called *Le Plus Vieux Métier du Monde* (The Oldest Profession in the World). It did nothing much for her career, but perhaps it paid a few bills, and it put her in touch again with old friends like Jean-Claude Brialy, Jean-Luc Godard, who was directing his wife Anna Karina in an episode, and director Philippe de Broca, known for his comedies with Belmondo.

De Broca and Moreau had first met when he was assistant director on *Les Quatre Cents Coups*. They were to go on and make the excellent *Chère Louise* together. But before that she had another date to keep with Welles and other *copains* – or *copines*, as it turned out.

The Immortal Story was made for French TV and dubbed appallingly for cinemas abroad. Welles' first film in colour, it was co-produced by Moreau's agent, Micheline Rozan, and adapted by Louise de Vilmorin. The screenplay is based on a tale by Karen Blixen/Isak Dinesen set in nineteenth-century Macau. For the third time Welles cast Moreau as a courtesan.

A rich merchant (Welles) tries to make an old seaman's tale come true by hiring a young sailor (Norman Eshley) to sleep with a beautiful girl. Naturally, as with all moral tales, the plot recoils upon the old schemer. Welles is his usual megalomaniacal self, but the film fails to work, even with its Erik Satie 'Gymnopedies' music, Cardin costumes and a wonderful location. It took two years for it to be screened on television, and another four before it reached cinemas.

Moreau remembers Welles having big money problems at the time. He was depressed, sometimes so violently he would walk around all day with tears in his eyes. He knew his career had slipped away from him – he was to make only three more films, two of which were never finished. But he was still a person of inspiration and influence for those in his pool.

Very late one night, after a few drinks too many, Welles and Moreau were sitting together in his hotel, Le Meurice, in Paris, talking about their hopes, fears and frustrations. Stirring her champagne to get rid of the bubbles, she said to him that what she really wanted to do was direct. He said simply: 'Do it.'

'Sometimes the strongest and biggest obstacles are inside,' he rumbled. 'Once you have cleared your mind, your energy is so strong, your conviction is so strong that you get the money.' What he also drummed in to her was that realism was uninteresting and 'artistically non-existent'. These things she took away with her to reflect on during her long walks across the hills at Le Préverger, or in the Rolls returning through the long haul of central France back to Paris from the south.

Eight years later her ambition was realised when she wrote and directed her own film – *Lumière* – and three years after that, a second, *L'Adolescente*. Her third is being planned as I write.

'I never thought I would make a career as a film director but as long as there is something I want to say, I can plan to make another one. My life is not finished, so my work is not finished. To me, life is given for me to do something with and to make use of everything I have been given. So right up to my last breath I have something to do.'

The route towards achieving her goal was, however, to be an arduous and fraught one in the difficult business in which she had chosen to live her life.

10

'Poor Don Luís with my French corpse in his arms!'

By now Jeanne Moreau was considered by the Americans as one of
the most exciting women in the world. French actors, unlike French
wine, seldom export well to America, for reasons perhaps best
encapsulated by Yves Montand in his warning to his fellow countrymen to beware of American puritanism as they are 'touchy about
things that seem a joke to us'. Nevertheless, Moreau was one
Frenchwoman they welcomed.

Perhaps it was her English, now spoken with a marked American
accent, that smoothed the way. Perhaps it was the frisson of lust
they felt when – unlike Bardot and using fewer tricks and more
clothes – she conferred an aura of greater reality to the noble art of
sweet seduction. Whatever it was, director Mike Nichols had set
his heart on her for Mrs Robinson in *The Graduate*. He insisted on
her, but she said no, she was busy, and his insistence was in the face
of great adversity from his peers, because *The Graduate* was thought
of as a fiercely American story, set as it was in California in the sixties. No, Mrs Robinson had to be American. Yet, in fact, the
scenario of the son falling for the wife of his father's friend, then
falling in love with her daughter, is an old and much-used theme

which apparently originated in France centuries before, *mais tant pis!*

Anne Bancroft was duly chosen instead and Moreau went off to Britain to plunge into costume for the eighteenth-century Russian drama *Great Catherine*. There she looked utterly magnificent, in a plain black velvet gown, as the capricious czarina, with a hint that she might just turn into a Jean-Luc Godard heroine, given the chance. It was not the right film for her but she got to wear the genuine Romanov crown jewels, which is more than could be said for her predecessors in the role: Dietrich in Josef von Sternberg's *The Scarlet Empress*, Tallulah Bankhead in Ernst Lubitsch's *A Royal Scandal* and Elisabeth Bergner in the Alexander Korda version, *Catherine the Great*.

Shot at Shepperton Studios and based on George Bernard Shaw's early comedy, *Whom Glory Still Adores*, it co-starred Peter O'Toole (who also co-produced it) as Captain Edstaston. The two leads seemed to get on famously. Michelle Moreau remembers an evening with them, when O'Toole had come over to Jeanne's rented flat near Park Lane to work on the script, as one of hilarity with flowing wine and 'his shoes being kicked to the ceiling'. The film was made in the true old British film manner – grandly, honourably and traditionally, with Gordon Flemyng directing and Zero Mostel and Jack Hawkins co-starring.

Producer Jules Buck's daughter, Joan Juliet Buck, who was in a £10-a-week job as Moreau's public relations person, describes the actress's singular style years later: 'She was not yet forty; her wardrobe stretched into an infinity of Cardin creations with cut-outs and colour slashes; she boarded aeroplanes carrying only a tiny handbag, followed by Anna, her housekeeper, and sometimes Anna's husband Louis. A Rolls-Royce took her from her flat to the studio every day and she was generous about sharing rides in it, though steely about keeping her seat, the one diagonally behind the driver. She smoked Benson and Hedges and gave me presents – rafts of the Cardin stuff, Chanel jewellery in gold and diamonds, shoes. My father always used to say I must give the stuff back! I was the only girl at college with a complete Cardin wardrobe. Jeanne was deeply generous.'

At the time Moreau's boyfriend was a *Paris Match* photographer called Cyril Morange, a handsome, pleasant young man. Her PR assistant wondered why a woman of Moreau's depth, impact, stature and dramatic weight did not have a man as deep and dangerous as she was. 'I didn't know a thing,' acknowledges Buck.

The only irritation the actress appeared to show was when journalists came on set. Cited as an example of an interview that allegedly went badly is one with John Gale for the *Observer*. I tracked it down and found it a small gem of insight into Moreau's English roots. One paragraph practically says it all: it describes the time when her mother and uncle came to see her in her dressing-room in the studio. 'Miss Moreau kissed her mother, who was small and kind and wore tinted glasses. She offered brandy to her uncle, who said, "I won't refuse." He said he'd lived in the Isle of Man for forty-seven years: "I wouldn't leave it for anything".

"All the ashtrays here are from the Isle of Man," Miss Moreau said.'

The press made much of the wayward 'French' daughter, with her foreign ways and wanton attitudes, being back on her own 'home ground'. Her lovely anecdote about desiring a house big enough for all the men with whom she had had deep and strong relationships went down brilliantly, especially when she added, with typical French candour, 'It's just a dream, I couldn't afford it and it would probably be hell.' Then there was, 'I am always in love unless I am recuperating from love,' and 'I'm a pantheist. I see God everywhere in nature – and in men.' Better still was the one about the meaning of freedom, which for her was to be able to 'choose whose slave I want to be'. This she compounded by adding that it was so conventional (then) to live with a person without being married that to marry had become quite unconventional.

It was not, remarked some, quite like that in Britain in 1967, even though it was England's 'summer of love' and love-ins were all the rage in the metropolis.

Moreau made much of practising her English and seeing her family. Her mother and stepfather were now living in Brighton. Michelle was by then the mother of two children, married to but breaking up from Desmond Cavanaugh, who ran the Black Angus Grill and the Pickwick Club. The Pickwick was a favourite den for the London showbiz crowd, people like Michael Caine and Terence Stamp, for whom Michelle later went to work, managing his Trencherman restaurant in Chelsea.

The press now loved anything Moreau did. They even covered the trivia, as when she, Mick Jagger and Ava Gardner were reportedly locked in combat for a sixty-guinea box for four (now it would set you back more than £500 for a Wagner opera) at the gala première of Roland Pettit's ballet *Paradise Lost* at the Royal Opera House, Covent Garden. (Jagger pipped Moreau and Gardner at the post.) If she went shopping down the Portobello Road, somebody with a camera and notebook was there to immortalise the event. Moreau was burdened with fame then, the way Hollywood topliners are now. But midway through shooting *Great Catherine* something happened that was to turn her world upside down.

In the middle of February 1967 she was named in a divorce petition brought by Vanessa Redgrave against Tony Richardson. They had been married for five years, Redgrave had just been nominated by the Variety Club of Great Britain as the stage actress of 1966 and was in Hollywood playing Queen Guinevere in *Camelot* opposite Franco Nero, the man who was to become her partner for several years.

Moreau was hugely surprised to find her name in this petition and flew instantly to Paris to see her solicitors. She told me in 1993 that she found the entire case extraordinary. 'To me Tony Richardson wasn't a lover. In his book [*Long-Distance Runner*] he says he left Vanessa for me. I have no idea about that. I know what it is to be the lover of somebody, to live with somebody, to sleep with somebody. But that's not the relationship I had with Tony. We made films. The only time we were together, Tony and I, was when we were making films. My relationship with Tony was like my relationship with François Truffaut – a profound friendship. The director with whom I had a very important love relationship is Louis Malle. I never shared a flat or a night with Tony.

'So when I learned that I was cited, I didn't react because I thought to myself, "It's me, but it's not me." It's what they made of me. I'm sure Tony was infatuated with me. They had their problems to solve as a couple. Maybe I was cited, but I didn't know about their relationship. One lives one side of the fence and I was living in France.

'I can think of no reason why I was cited as "the other woman" unless Vanessa Redgrave was advised to name me because Mr Richardson and I had made two films together.'

I read somewhere that she had said it was 'Vanessa's gift to me', and I asked her about that.

'It's a lovely quote but I never said it,' she replied with a husky chuckle. 'Maybe it was a gift to Tony that she cited me!'

Redgrave got her decree nisi on grounds of adultery committed by Richardson with Moreau. Both women had separately been called the New Garbo and both women were also the epitome of the independent woman of mystery. Years later, in June 1993, when Redgrave opened with a touring one-woman show, which she dedicated to Richardson after his death, she asked Moreau at the Comédie des Champs Elysées to introduce it.

'I said yes, I was very moved,' says Moreau. 'For years I knew that she didn't want to see me, but time passes. I went on stage and said some words and sang the song I'd sung in *Sailor From Gibraltar*.

As soon as filming *Great Catherine* wrapped, Moreau headed back to Paris, undoubtedly with a huge sigh of relief, to the familiarity of her 'film family'. She was to make *La Mariée était en Noir* (*The Bride Wore Black*) for Truffaut. With her she brought back all the English things she loved – crumpets, tea, linen tea-towels, shoe trees, the washing-up brushes she swears by. There was also a sweater for François, a first-day-of-shooting gift, a ritual that had grown up between them. This was their third venture together.

Jean-Louis Richard had again collaborated with Truffaut on the screenplay, taken from William Irish's novel of the same name. (Irish is a pseudonym for Cornell Woolrich, best known for *The Window of Ted Teztlaff* which Hitchcock filmed as *Rear Window*.) Truffaut later made the film of another Irish book, *The Siren of Mississippi*, starring Catherine Deneuve. He had first read the book against his mother's wishes, when he was thirteen. Years later, he tried to remember the title, and with Moreau's help eventually tracked it down.

Having decided that he wanted to make *The Bride Wore Black* with his friend Jeanne, Truffaut set about acquiring the film rights. He saw it as an opportunity to make a *film noir*, intended as a homage to Hitchcock: how to make the images of a film carry the story, how to free film from the dependence of dialogue (the murders take place on the screen, but the soundtrack ignores them).

The story deals with a widow whose relentless quest for

vengeance leads her to murder all five of the men who killed her groom on their wedding day. In her attempt to find out why her husband was gunned down, she also discovers from her informers various sides to his character. (The actor with just about the shortest role on record in a Truffaut film was Serge Rousseau.)

Moreau, as Julie Kohler – dressed throughout the film only in symbolic black and white (by Pierre Cardin, *bien sûr*) – is a woman ravaged by an almost religious approach to her mission, picking off the men played by Claude Rich, Michel Bouquet, Michael Lonsdale, Charles Denner and Daniel Boulanger. Truffaut told her not to be 'tragic; play it like a skilled worker with a job to do, conscientious and obstinate'. Methodically she pinpoints her victims, chats them up and then chops them down.

When questioned on the gruesomeness of his subject, Truffaut said at the Unifrance conference for the film, producing a clutch of press cuttings to prove his point, that shootings occurred daily at weddings. Far more exceptional, in his opinion, was that it was his first film with the line *'je t'aime'* in it.

'This used to be unthinkable to me because my main character must never put into words exactly what he is thinking,' he explained. (Another first was Truffaut's commission of a series of paintings of Moreau by the artist Charles Matton, which appeared in a section of the film concerned with one of the men, an artist. These were later shown in Paris and led to Matton himself becoming a director.)

In a way this was a feminine version of Truffaut's *Shoot the Pianist*, with Moreau taking over the role of Charles Aznavour. The subject matter, the Clint Eastwood-type killer role being female, was decades ahead of its time.

There might have been some things unsaid as regards her next film, *The Deep*, once again with Orson Welles, and if there are, Moreau is leaving them unsaid.

The Deep (aka *Dead Reckoning* and also *Direction Towards Death*) is a film she, Laurence Harvey and Michael Bryant made with Welles in 1967 off the Dalmatian coast of Yugoslavia. It was based on the novel by Charles Williams, which was to become the wonderful Philip Noyce thriller *Dead Calm*, setting up Nicole Kidman and

Billy Zane as Hollywood new faces in the late eighties. Welles' version, however, had a less rewarding life.

Michael Bryant remembers little of the actual filming. 'There was very little live sound as Orson had sacked the sound crew. I tried to do the post-synch, but we had no record of what I had said as he had sacked the continuity girl, so I had to give up. I certainly did not complete the film in the sound sense.'

Allegedly the film was never completed. However, Moreau feels that whatever Welles said along those lines was simply not true. She had tried to speak to him about the project, but due to his fear of exposing himself to the criticism of others, he refused to discuss it.

Paris audiences were now beginning to see retrospectives of Moreau's films, yet, after the fiasco of *The Deep*, she did not work for a year. Often she has said that when she is making a picture she becomes progressively more exhausted, and by the end of the film thoroughly depressed. It is for her that feeling of having to do the bits and pieces, and rebuild them into a whole. One of those times was now. For her to stay away from the camera for such a long time meant something was definitely not right. It would be feasible to speculate that she had become a prisoner of her own cinematic past. *The Deep* had not helped boost her own morale, dampened by recent films which were forming a downward curve in contrast to the early films, whose graph had endlessly soared upward. How to break the slide, avoid the fall? How to rekindle the embers?

During those months of retreat at Le Préverger in 1967-68, she needed to sit and think and soak in the feeling of place, the sense of self. She settled for homely routines: making jam, tending the vineyards, looking after her father, who a few years previously had become seriously ill. She recalls reading a lot of books and making another record of traditional *chansons*, *Les Chansons de Clarisse*. But the playful, extended family was now quieter. Life lay, for a whole, in a chrysalis state.

She had had therapy on and off for a while, from 1963 for about six years, and took it very seriously. Joan Buck remembers: 'One summer when I was staying at Le Préverger she had discovered Groddeck [Dr George Groddeck (1866-1934), an early German practitioner of psychiatry and the first proponent of psychosomatic diagnoses]. She gave me his *Book of the Id* to read. Afterwards I woke up at four o'clock in the morning screaming, a reaction she handled with great empathy as she'd been through psychotherapy, and was at that point considering medical school.'

'I had therapy three times a week,' Moreau told me, 'the kind you're not allowed to miss. I had a wonderful male therapist and we had a very free relationship. He always said: "One day I will tell you everything is over and I will invite you to lunch." But once we had a discussion about incest and I said, "You bloody men, you only think in terms of incest between the father and the daughter; you never think of the real incest, between the mother and the son, Jocasta and Oedipus."

'I remember he was very shocked and said that he was not eager to dwell on the subject. I said: "OK, you're not? Then I invite you to lunch," and that was that. Interesting reaction, don't you think?

'I went on calling him. He was a much older man. He'd say to me: "I'm dreadful, I'm old," and I'd be very shocked to hear such an intelligent man who had done so much work, particularly on Freud, saying things like that, about being old and not being able to cope with it. Years later, before he died, he told me that he was in love with me.'

Jeanne was now forty and had made fifty films – counting the episodes in collaborated movies and not counting the brief cameos. It was a difficult period which, she has said, made her afraid that she would die. 'I telephoned Buñuel in Mexico because I wanted to die next to him. Poor Don Luís with my French corpse on his arms!'

Moreau's up-and-down health seems to be almost part of her lifestyle. 'She is very *cyclothémique*, like so many actors,' says Florence Malraux. 'She is either up or she is down. It is the way they live, working and then being between jobs. She is enormously energetic on a film and then has to go home and collapse. If something doesn't work, she will have a physical reaction and sometimes become quite ill. Her body is where she hides her fears.'

By the end of 1968 Moreau at last felt ready to go out again, but only with her 'family'. Virtually the only 'public' appearance she had made was in February of that year when the French government dismissed Henri Langlois from his position as head of the Cinémathèque, the world's largest film collection. In protest a crowd of actors, film-makers and enthusiasts converged on the Place du

Trocadéro outside the Cinémathèque Chaillot. Among the protesters were Yves Montand, Simone Signoret, Alain Resnais, François Truffaut and Jeanne Moreau, all deeply involved with the defence of the Cinémathèque. For the first time in their lives, she and Truffaut were actively involved in politics.

They were all demanding the resignation of Langlois' 'replacement', Pierre Barbin. The TV crews gathered to watch the protest. When one celebrity suggested marching on the building, demanding that Langlois be reinstated, another countered that they would be bludgeoned by the police.

'Really?' Moreau asked coolly. Inviting the others to join her on the front line, she moved forward. 'We'll see if, with all the cameras here, they dare attack us.'

The police did lunge, but were beaten back by other policemen only too aware of what the bad publicity could do. Langlois was eventually reinstated and Moreau returned to Le Préverger. 'Politics are no immediate concern to me,' she says. 'To me, politicians are all rotten. Politics is like income tax: a complete blankness. I don't understand a thing. It's too related to egotism and ambition for me. Cinema can bring pleasure, knowledge, emotion, warmth, music; to make people feel good, not be political.'

She was still out of Paris when the student riots at the Sorbonne broke out in May 1968. The barricades and bombs might have gone unnoticed by her, except for the fact that her son Jérôme now left his studies for the movement. 'For the moment he's more interested in revolution, in fighting against society, than anything else. Young people are fighting for their lives,' she commented.

Another unplanned political step was taken at the end of that year as she came out of her retreat, when she joined forces once again with her ex-husband to make another film, *Le Corps de Diane* (*Diana*).

'This was a film about the jealousy of a couple and how jealousy can push people to madness,' Richard explained. 'Originally I wanted Anna Karina for the role, but I gave Jeanne the scenario and when she said she'd like to play it, I changed my mind. Because of finances, we decided to make it a co-production with another country. When Denmark fell through – Copenhagen would have been a perfect location – we approached the Czechs and made it partly at the Barrandov Studios and on location in Prague.'

Both sides were pleased by the move. Barrandov, with its advanced Technicolor facilities, was the nurturing ground for the Czech New Wave of the 1960s. Built in 1931 by entrepreneur Vaclav M. Havel (father of the playwright and first president of post-Communist Czechoslovakia), it was the most advanced production studio in central Europe.

When Richard and his cast and crew arrived, it was the year of the Prague Spring. Czech Communism was liberalised and Dubcek was in power. When Moreau landed at the new Prague Airport, which had just been completed, she was mobbed by the press. There are lovely pictures of her with a bouquet and her miniature dachshund, Quick, in her arms being swept into an airport press conference. They remembered her from when she took the Best Actress prize at the festival in the mountain spa resort of Karlovy Vary (formerly Karlsbad) a few years before for *Chambermaid*. She told them she thought Czech cinema was the most original in Europe. They were overjoyed when they found out she was friends with Milos Forman and his co-scriptwriter Ivan Passer (now both successful Hollywood directors), was well acquainted with the Prague Film Faculty and would like her son to study there. (Jérôme, who was a nineteen-year-old version of his father, but with his mother's mouth, was working with them on the film as Richard's assistant.)

'Then the Russians arrived,' Richard sighs. 'They invaded in August and everything changed. There were lots of problems for both locals and foreigners. It was not an easy film to finish in a country suddenly caught in trouble.'

In *Diana*, Moreau plays a costume designer and choreographer putting on a theatrical production. In a way this is her first delve into her own classical dance training. She has said that it was a completely different role from her previous parts, although once again she is a thoroughly feminine figure who meets the ultimate masculine man, resulting in tragic love. As Diana she links up with an architect she has not seen for some years (her old friend from TNP and, more recently, from *The Bride Wore Black*, Charles Denner.) He falls in love with her but also kills her.

Diana is a wonderfully stylish film, with colours to dream about and Prague backgrounds on which to feast the eyes. Yet it did little at the box office and did not halt her slide down the scale. In fact, it was the first of her films in ten years to find no takers in the Anglo-American market. While it must have been fun working *en famille*, it was not the right place for her then. She needed something new, something different, fresh horizons.

There was talk of her doing a film in England with Richard Lester, still hot from *The Knack*, but instead she bumped into Jean Renoir and took a three-minute role in his last-ever film, *Le Petit Théâtre de Jean Renoir*, which was designed for television and later went cinematic.

Jean Renoir, son of the painter Auguste Renoir, was perhaps the greatest of French directors, at his incomparable best in the thirties with classics like *La Règle du Jeu*, (*The Rules of the Game*) *La Grande Illusion* and *La Bête Humaine* (*The Human Beast*, aka *Judas Was a Woman*). He and Moreau had first met in the mid-fifties in a café when she was taking coffee with Jean Marais, who was working with Renoir at the time.

At their second meeting Renoir asked her to sing the *Belle Epoque* ditty, '*Quand l'Amour Meurt*' (When Love Dies) by Octave Crémieux. She did it, alone on a bare stage, in an infinitely sad voice, even sadder than Dietrich's in Sternberg's *Morocco*. Dressed in a stylised yellow and black evening gown, with swirling Fortuny skirt and long black gloves, Moreau compressed her entire acting ability into those three short minutes. The sequence is a glorious example of the pure fantasy of the Seventh Art and how it can work. In terms of a curiosity, it is golden, watching Jean Renoir and Jeanne Moreau poke fun at the period which inspired so many of his films.

The two of them talked about doing more films together. He wanted to make her into a female *clochard*, a tramp like the one in his hit black satire *Boudu Sauvé des Eaux* (*Boudu Saved From Drowning*), which was remade as Hollywood's *Down and Out in Beverly Hills*, starring Nick Nolte. But Renoir was not to make any more movies.

Moreau, on the other hand, was destined to end the long dip in her career by moving to Beverly Hills, but as a celebrity, not a *clochard*.

11

**'I believe in nature's cycles, a process of ripening.
Some days it's fine but you can't personally see the sun.'**

The close of the 1960s very much marked the end of an era, on both a general and a personal level for Jeanne Moreau. From here her life diversified.

Far-reaching changes were occurring in France. The *événements* of May 1968 – the student uprisings which showed their hostility to the establishment – left a lingering impact throughout the nation. In 1969 Georges Pompidou took over as Charles de Gaulle's successor, putting into action his policy of breaking with the traditional and encouraging the abstract. Modernisation promoted the growth of television, as a result of which French cinema entered a recession. Audience attendance, more than 400 million in 1957, had dropped to 180 million by 1969. Generally it is accepted that the *Nouvelle Vague* ended around the close of the sixties, and post-1968 French cinema became known as the post-New Wave movement.

The bright new promise of the sixties had come and gone. Jeanne Moreau had starred in more than fifty films, was in her early forties and, as the queen of the *Nouvelle Vague*, did not have to prove anything. She did, however, have to avoid becoming trapped as a victim of her own fame. Even as a symbol of ageless seduction she had reached a time of transition. The tunnel she had been in opened on a wide empty space and she needed somehow to fill that expanse.

Forty has always been a difficult age for film actresses, an age when parts come less frequently. That old Hollywood truism about pretending you are not forty in order to survive is perhaps less true in the nineties, when the forty-something woman is still an attractive option. But in the seventies women of forty were generally considered too old for romantic leads.

The roles she was being offered did not appeal to her. Sometimes, she told me, she actually went as far as to contact the producer or director and advise them who might suit the role better. The next couple of years were to be a period of deceleration and of introspection for her. Thanks to the absence of decent film projects, she retired to her beloved Le Préverger with her dachshund Quick. There she spent languid afternoons under the trees in her hammock, surrounded by poppies, sorting out the uncomfortable person inside her. Alone with herself, in the insecurity of uneasy solitude, she needed time to regain her inner composure. With her father living there, as well as Anna and husband, and the usual round of friends, she might not have been physically alone in this fallow period, but she remembers being emotionally lonely.

'There's never been a conscious thought in the organisation of my life,' she says. 'I've always been ready to accept things as they come. I'm not a workaholic. I can stay idle, I can enjoy holidays. I'm told that whenever I'm away from the telephone and the pressure of the city, I am bored within a week. But I'm not, not at all. I accept whatever comes my way. I can deal with any rhythm and I know when the rhythm is too much. Then I cut down.'

Cutting down at this point meant reshaping her activities. Although she patently loves the frenzy of a lifestyle in which she is Queen Bee in a smouldering outfit, buzzing around with the gleam of being in control in her eyes, Cardin's 'country girl' does indeed emerge when she's 'off stage'. Friends tend to remember her better as the barefooted Jeanne in a kaftan or jeans, her hair pulled back in a ponytail, rather than one of the best-dressed women in Paris. Michelle Moreau has a permanent image of her sister, still in her nightdress with a large apron over the top, chopping vegetables in the kitchen, preparing the *soupe du jour* de Chez Jeanne.

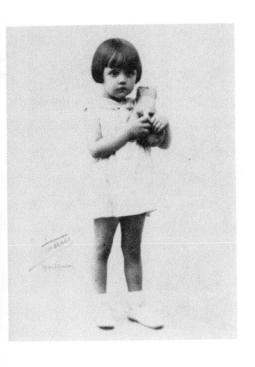

Jeanne Moreau, aged three, with her toy cat.
(*Michelle Moreau*)

As the youngest *pensionnaire* under contract to the Comédie Française in 1948, aged twenty.
(*Michelle Moreau*)
(right)

Portrait of Moreau in the mid-fifties.
(*J.C. Moireau*)

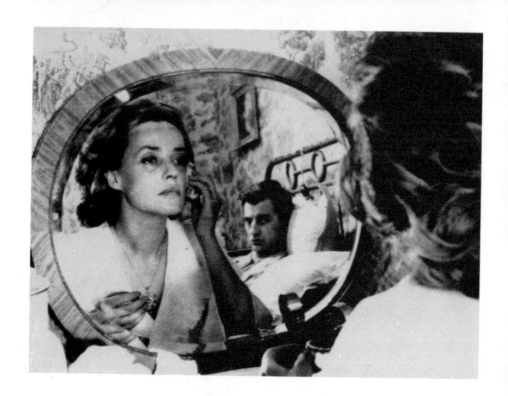

Cresting the start of the New Wave with Henri Serre in François Truffaut's *Jules et Jim* (1962). (*Tony Crawley*) (above)

As 'the Devil's Woman' Eva in Joseph Losey's 1962 shocker *Eva*. (*J.C. Moireau*) (right)

*W*ith on-screen, off-screen heart-throb Philippe Lemaire in *M'sieur la Caille* (1955), directed by André Pergament.
(*J.C. Moireau*)

*W*ithout her boots in Luís Buñuel's most scandalous masterpiece *Le Journal d'une Femme de Chambre* (*The Diary of a Chambermaid*) (1964).
(*Tony Crawley*)

Viva Maria!, Louis Malle's 1966 female 'buddy' film, starring Brigitte Bardot and Moreau as turn-of-the-century revolutionaries. (*Tony Crawley*)

A calm moment with Ian Bannen on board *The Sailor from Gibraltar* for Tony Richardson in 1966. (*Tony Crawley*)

$\mathcal{D}$uring the filming of *Great Catherine* for Gordon Flemyng at
Shepperton Studios, co-starring Peter O'Toole in 1967.
(*Tony Crawley*)

Covergirl of 1970
Christmas issue of
French *Vogue*, edited
by Moreau.
(*Tony Crawley*)

Chère Louise
(*Dear Louise*) (1972),
another film written for
Moreau, directed by
Philippe de Broca, about
an older woman and a
younger man.
(*Tony Crawley*)

With Patrick Dewaere and Gérard Depardieu in
Bertrand Blier's film that set a new trend in modern
French film-making – *Les Valseuses* (*Going Places*) (1974).
(*Tony Crawley*)
(above)

$\mathcal{T}$wo icons of the French screen, Alain Delon and
Moreau, in Joseph Losey's classic *Monsieur Klein* (1976).
(*J.C. Moireau*)

$\mathcal{I}$n Rainer Werner Fassbinder's last film *Querelle*
(1982), a dockside drama of homosexual lust and death,
Moreau plays an ageing brothel proprietress Madame Lysiane.
(*Tony Crawley*)

Moreau's triumphant stage comeback in 1986 in Klaus-Michael Grüber's tale of *Zerline*, which in 1988, when she was sixty, won her the Molière Award for Best Actress.

(*Tony Crawley*)

(left)

The role that won her a César, as the arthritic con-artist Lady M. in Laurent Heynemann's cutting comedy *La Vieille qui Marchait dans la Mer* (*The Old Lady who Walked in the Sea*) (1991), with Michel Serrault.

(*Tony Crawley*)

*W*ith her sister
Michelle in Versailles,
winter 1991.
(*Michelle Moreau*)
(left)

*A*s the Anglo-
Egyptian Lili in the 1992
BBC TV film *The
Clothes in the
Wardrobe* which became
successful on the
theatrical circuit in the
United States as *The
Summer House* in 1994,
directed by
Waris Hussein.
(*Tony Crawley*)

I do not believe that Jeanne Moreau needs constantly to be lauded for her talent, with her name in headlines and her face on covers, just to keep her ego going. I do think that she needs to be constantly stimulated, busy doing things which challenge her and fill that wide open space before her. It seems that it is not ambition that drives her, but the desire to get the best out of herself, even if it means paring her emotions back to the core.

'I believe in nature's cycles, a process of ripening. The right moment will come. Some days it's fine but you can't personally see the sun.'

Life was ambling along aimlessly. The complexity and conviction she usually saved for the screen she now used to sort out the state of play of life then and life now. There were some welcome intrusions, such as the magazine *Marie-Claire* featuring her in a huge cookery spread, complete with her favourite recipes, illustrated with photographs by her former boyfriend Cyril Morange, but mainly time was spent doing things she had been meaning to do for ages. It was around then, she says, that her 'Rolls-Royce period' with the furs and the champagne ended.

'I don't remember exactly when it ended but somewhere around 1967 to 1969,' remarks Moreau. 'I gave my lovely Rolls, with its grey leather interior, to my friend Emilio because he had money problems.'

Just when the sap was rising again, an offer came from America. At an age when most European actresses would shrink from carving out a new career on the other side of the Atlantic, she headed for Hollywood.

Moreau was not familiar with Hollywood. She was a great admirer of the American cinema of the thirties and forties, 'when actors and actresses were under contract, and not manoeuvring on slippery ground from one film to the next'. She had also started to notice and become interested in the American New Wave. Low-budget independent films, like *Easy Rider* (1968) and *M*A*S*H* (1970), were beginning to break through into the mainstream and people like John Cassavetes and Martin Scorsese were developing a new sort of film-making.

It was not, however, the prospect of a New Wave film that took her there but, almost unbelievably, a mainstream Western starring establishment backbones Lee Marvin and Jack Palance, no less. William A. Fraker, who had been cameraman on *Rosemary's Baby*, was making his first feature, a Western to be set in Arizona in the 1880s about two ageing cowboys. He came to Paris to ask Moreau to play Marvin's 'love', a Frenchwoman who works in a saloon.

When she first arrived in Hollywood she knew hardly anybody and remembers being terrified as she moved into the lavish villa rented for her in Bel Air. 'I wanted to go and see how it was,' she said, 'and it was, for me, good. I was lucky enough to have my friend Anaïs Nin living nearby. We had met in Canada, and later in France and in LA. When I was making *Monte Walsh* she and her friend Henry [the novelist Henry Miller] would come to my house for early dinner, early because I had to get up so early during shooting. Miller would take care of the wine and Anna [Moreau's housekeeper accompanied her to America] would prepare the food and set the table. Miller would arrive early and check the wine and prepare everything for our evening together. It was a marvellous friendship. Regrettably I never met his friend Lawrence Durrell. I was a great admirer of his books. In fact, so much so that I nick-named my Rolls 'Justine', after one of the women in his *Alexandrian Quartet*.

'Coming to Hollywood is quite exciting for us foreigners. It is the centre of cinema. There's a sort of aura about it,' she said at the time. 'Anyway, I liked the story of *Monte Walsh*. It's a modest entry into American films. It's a melancholy film. I'm not a fan of Westerns but this one is unusual. All my scenes are with Lee Marvin and we have a tender love story.' These scenes inevitably led to reports that she and Marvin were romantically involved off screen after the seemingly unmovable Marvin praised her as 'an excellent lover'. Moreau refuted the rumours.

'It was good for me to see how they make films over there. We had a huge crew, unlike on French films. At my wrap party I invited all the crew and discovered myself surrounded by a hundred and twenty people of whom I knew only a quarter. In France I know everybody by name.'

Such a claim, according to friends who have worked with Moreau, is true – certainly not the usual star 'bullshit'. With her frighteningly accurate memory, she knows every technician on set and remembers their contributions. Tony Richardson called it her 'gift of instant, non-patronising intimacy', something she somehow also manages to establish with individuals in the audience. This is quite a disarming feeling for, of course, when one leaves the cinema, one knows the private woman no more than when one went in. I have that feeling myself about her.

'She treats the technicians all like artists, and naturally they respond like artists,' Richardson commented in his book, discussing the completeness and thoroughness of her professionalism.

While in Hollywood, she read lots more American scripts, but took only one small role, playing herself in Paul Mazursky's *Alex in Wonderland*. Mazursky, who had done well with *Bob and Carol and Ted and Alice*, was a dedicated *Jules et Jim* fan. In 1980 he made his own version of it, a pleasant but forgettable *ménage à trois* film called *Willie and Phil*, starring Michael Ontkean and Ray Sharkey, with Margot Kidder in the 'Kate' role.

The Mazursky script was about a young film-maker, played by Donald Sutherland, then a hot new actor, who encounters Moreau, Fellini and other luminaries in scenes that are tributes to any number of French and Italian films. For example, when he meets Moreau on Hollywood Boulevard he is so enchanted that the Avenue of the Stars becomes a romantic vision with a crossroads called Belle de Jour and Jules et Jim. Some called the film a pale imitation of Fellini's fascinating self-portrait, *Eight and a Half*, others dubbed it 'One and a Half'. Sutherland, a man usually full of volatile recollections, refused me any comment. 'I have vivid memories,' he said jovially, 'and I'm not going to tell you any of them. It was never a pleasant film.'

'Maybe the film never came out,' says Moreau, looking at me, her head slanted, her eyes firmly focused on mine, telling me everything and nothing.

When Moreau left Hollywood to return to France there was talk that she would work again for Jean Renoir in a film with Dirk Bogarde. There was also supposed to be one directed by Jacques Rivette, a film set in the milieu of turn-of-the-century Parisian theatre life. Another project was to work for the first time with a female director, Carol Eastman, who wrote the script for *Five Easy Pieces*. I have also read that Ken Russell initially wanted her to play the older lover in the unconsummated affair with sculptor Gaudier-Brzeska in *Savage Innocent* – the role eventually went to Dorothy Tutin. In 1967 Tony Richardson was asked to direct *Reflections in a Golden Eye*. He had approached Marlon Brando to play the role of the Major but Brando was scared of the homosexual aspect of the character and said no. Richardson wanted Moreau for the Elizabeth Taylor role but the producer said no. In the end John Huston made the film with Brando and Taylor.

'If I made a list of the films I was supposed to do, it would be *this* long!' she says, stretching her arms.

Once again, she gave one of her *je m'en fous*, who cares? shrugs and got on with her fourth album, *Jeanne Chante Jeanne*, this time writing the sad and sweet songs as well as singing them in her gravelly voice. Perhaps her greatest regret to date is never having done a musical, although there was talk of one with Georges Moustaki at this time.

Eventually, after a two-year absence, Moreau returned to Paris, to the good old film studios for a good, old-fashioned *film noir*, a traditional gangster movie called *Comptes à Rebours* which could just as well have been made in the forties, fifties or sixties. Falling again into the easy pattern of working with friends, she took the role of an older gangster's moll, she says, out of friendship for Serge Reggiani, the leading man. It was director Roger Pigaut's first film.

'Sometimes the distributors need the director to engage actors of a certain standing, "names" to promote the business side of things,' she has said. Moreau's name no longer being enough to do the trick on its own, Simone Signoret – another friend of Reggiani's – also agreed to appear in it.

Signoret looks formidably powerful there, but Moreau's role rather harks back to earlier decades when she played the token woman in a man's world. About a gangster who comes out of prison to find the woman he loves married to one of his best friends, the film covers roughly familiar themes: crooks, cash, corruption in casinos, underground car parks, deserted streets and so on. Moreau, all lips with heavily lined eyes and fringe, looks tired. Somehow it is a tired film. However, to work with chums on a film that achieves little and get paid must be better than not to work and have no cashflow.

To Moreau money is ephemeral. When she has it, she spends it –

on family, on friends, on entertaining, perhaps on a painting or piece of furniture. She is spontaneously generous. Anthony Higgins, with whom she made the Granada TV film, *The Last Seance*, in England, remembers an incident after a small champagne party to celebrate the end of filming. They were staying in a Manchester hotel, and he, being the only man there, was presented with the bill.

'Of course I paid it,' recollects Higgins. 'The next morning I noticed something in my pigeon-hole in reception. It was an envelope full of cash and a hand-written note from Jeanne saying that I shouldn't have had to pay the bill by myself.'

When asked in an interview with *Queen* what she wanted for the future, she replied that she would like to become less dependent on money. 'I have commitments, and of course, I love the things that money gives me. But what I would like for the future is to be happy without it,' she said.

Maybe this lack of financial ambition, in somebody who has always paid for herself and her commitments, comes from knowing that money does not buy fulfilment – just the restless trappings of quality of life. I will always be struck by an anecdote I read about Moreau in a piece written for the *New Yorker* by Penelope Gilliatt. Once, after a dinner of her rabbit stew, she made a rose out of a piece of old silver paper for Gilliatt's daughter. Moreau pulled out a box of buttons from a chest full of knick-knacks – used buttons, gloves, old shoes, little cardboard boxes that might come in handy – and with a needle and thread she carefully sewed a red button into the middle of the pleated fold of the rose. A loving, stylish present for a child, worth infinitely more than an expensive gift from a shop.

Having been through first the Chanel, then the Pierre Cardin 'school of fashion', Moreau knows well enough how to use style and make it work. She has never shied away from being stylish, even if this means travelling with a caravan of trunks bearing frequent changes of clothes (as well as a few other essentials, like a teapot complete with tea-cosy and tea, the cup and saucer that used to belong to her mother, pots and pans and a battery of cooking utensils, which she unpacks first, as a sort of a ritual). Friends say she changes her outfit as many as five times a day, each new ensemble having its own accompanying pair of shoes, handbag and hat, if necessary. For a trip to Cannes or Los Angeles she will take a small suitcase filled entirely with evening bags, all wrapped separately in silky paper, tying each with a pretty ribbon as a little girl would.

Her natural style and fashionable connections all came together when, as guest editor-in-chief, she produced the 1970 Christmas issue of that high temple of fashion, *Vogue*. Her name might no longer have been bolstering up films in need of funds, but *Vogue* showed her eye to be as sharp as a laser beam when it came to focusing on fashion.

I do not know how long it took her to create, but from foreword to final page that issue is filled with the people and things that make up her unbelievably styled world of the chic and the celebrated. Naturally Moreau is the 'cover girl', clad in white Russian lynx, peeking (those bronze-ish eyes!), smiling (those lips, those lips!), through a Bentley Mark VI window and snapped by Helmut Newton. Caught by the provocative look on her face, you dive in and turn page after page of chic style, spiked with sabre-toothed humour and heavy with dropped names.

Here are some examples of Mademoiselle Moreau's Utopia of the printed page:

Silvana Mangano posed for Eva Sereny in a 1910-style gown designed by Piero Tosi and styled by Worth for Visconti's *Death in Venice*. Moreau wrote the caption.

Five of the most glamorous chaps in the business pose for Henri Cartier-Bresson, accompanied by five views of a bare woman angled to show the aspect they liked the best – the sweep of the back, the hills of the buttocks, the slope of the stomach and so on.

Jean-Louis Trintignant, Nathalie Delon and Marie-France Pisier in a deliciously tacky ten-page photo-romance comic.

A fashion section entitled 'Film', which features couturiers Yves Saint-Laurent, Pierre Balmain, Marc Bohan, Ungaro and others, designing robes to suit the methods of certain directors. For example, Ingmar Bergman style, as seen by Cardin, is a wistful model clad in a long black skirt and an impeccable short white *smoking* with a train to the ground; Pasolini seen by Crahay chez Lanvin is a zippy city girl with bouffant culottes and nipples.

In the Christmas Gift section Moreau has handwritten poems as captions while buddies like Jean-Claude Brialy fill in as models wearing or holding the item in question. The final flourish is poet Jacques Prévert as a photographed by Robert Doisneau and captioned by Brassai in preview of one of his books.

For the humble reader who probably normally shops at Galeries Lafayette, the entire issue was a priceless daydream in the inner world of the aristocracy of French arts. For Moreau it was a great way to see out 1970.

Jeanne Moreau's New Year, however, started at a low point.

In February 1971 she had a gallstone operation at the American Hospital in Paris. Shortly afterwards, instead of starting on Broadway in Edward Albee's *All Over*, she went to work with Michel Bouquet on *L'Humeur Vagabonde* for director Edouard Luntz. Here she plays a worldly Parisian who becomes the older woman to a young provincial man (Bouquet) who hopes to take Paris by storm. Although it is Bouquet's film – he has nineteen parts, playing everyone he meets and finding people to look much the same – it is a good showcase for the more mature Moreau. Despite the fact that the film represented France at the 1971 Venice Biennale, it later sank without trace. Her record of the film's theme song came out a year later.

In April Moreau joined forces with some of her friends in another untypically political move to campaign against the French abortion laws. At that time in France a woman still risked six months to two years in jail and a fine of up to £600 for undergoing an illegal abortion. On 5 April, 343 Frenchwomen who had had enough of these oppressive regulations joined forces in signing a statement admitting that they had had abortions, called the *Manifeste des 343*.

Moreau was one of the first to sign. Actresses Catherine Deneuve, Delphine Seyrig and Stéphane Audran and writers Simone de Beauvoir, Françoise Sagan and Marguerite Duras also signed the petition, which stated that a million women in France had abortions in dangerous conditions. They called for free access to birth control and free access to abortion.

Explained Moreau: 'Unfortunately I remember only too well all the humiliation associated with this sort of thing. I had three abortions when I was very young, before my son was born. There was no information on how to avoid it. The fear now is AIDS. At that time the fear was of being unmarried and pregnant. It was absolutely forbidden to have an abortion. You were in constant danger if you had one unless you had the money to go to Switzerland for it. It was terrible. We had to make a political stand over it.'

Their efforts changed the law and in 1976 it became legal in France to have an abortion on the state up to ten weeks into pregnancy.

In June she gave a recital of her songs in the abbey of Royaumont and, at Cardin's l'Espace theatre, paid homage to Marcel Proust, reading extracts from his *Temps Retrouvé*. There was also the short film, *Côté Cour, Côté Champs* done for a new young director from Algiers, Guy Gilles, with herself walking with her dachsund Quick, appropriately on Allée Marcel Proust. Gilles always writes a role for Moreau in all his films and she has appeared in two of them, *Absences Répétées* (Repeated Absences) (1971) and *Le Jardin qui Bascule* (*The Tilting Garden*) (1975).

There was also work on another film with Orson Welles, *The Other Side of the Wind* – again one of his unfinished efforts, this time about a Hollywood director. In spite of Welles going hat in hand to the assembled leaders of the movie community when they honoured him at a celebrity-studded dinner in Los Angeles, he never managed to raise the funds to complete it. Like his *Don Quixote* and *The Deep*, it remains uncompleted and, sadly, unseen.

Encouraged by the success of the *Vogue* issue, Moreau now went into publishing by starting an audio-visual magazine. Called *IN* and produced on colour cassette Super 8 film, it was designed as a magazine for posh beauty salons in Paris and key cities. Moreau went into this business venture with her ex-husband Richard and the commercial film-maker Christian Gion. She was the editor of this sort of visual jukebox, showing small films with music, while the men were directors. Programmes featured obliging colleagues like Sagan and Georges Moustaki and covered issues in the arts and current affairs.

The idea was to expand the magazine into airports and stations, even trains and planes. It sounded like enormous fun: items included actor-director Claude Berri (of *Jean de Florette*) showing how a man's way of smoking reveals his character; Moreau with her own smoked-out voice at the Oscars, or interviewing Ingmar Bergman (for whom, she said, she would work as a script girl); Simone de

Beauvoir on abortion, why women were taking up motorcycling and the oddities of interior design. But it did not last.

'We were too creative,' mourns Richard. 'We didn't have enough administration. It ran for eighteen months. We produced eighteen editions but made no money to expand. Neither of us has even one copy of the magazine any more. They all disappeared.'

12

'People get together the way they want. The age gap is in the minds of the people watching.'

Chère Louise (*Dear Louise*) was the film that put Jeanne Moreau back in top billing. The perfect role for her then – a woman of forty in love with a boy half her age – there was so much of her in it that she admitted the film could just as well have been called *Chère Jeanne*.

'The role was written for me,' she said during filming on location in Annecy in the foothills of the Alps. 'I loved making it, particularly as all the roles I'd been offered until then were for women of forty-plus with husband trouble. I loved the idea of a woman of forty loving a boy of twenty. People aren't surprised when they see a man of sixty with a young girl of twenty – why not the other way around? Nobody feels sorry for the old man; if he has a young chicken in his nest, that's fine for him. Why can't a young man have an older chicken?

'People get together the way they want. Some people are old at twenty-five, others never grow up at all. The age gap is in the minds of the people watching. The young, the old – that's racism, like blacks versus whites. Age is of no importance. What we all have in common is life. It is essential to be alive. You can look young, you can be young, but once you have passed the age of youth, what you feel shows on your face. The youthful expression goes from the eyes, to be replaced by the expression of experience, of life.'

The film is a simple story about two lonely people. Louise is a provincial art teacher, divorced and left to start a new life when her mother dies. Luigi is a young Italian forced to look for work in France. Unknown Romanian actor Julian Negulesco took the part at a moment in his life when he was about to look for work in Italy. Louise and Luigi have nothing in common, but they are both alone. While the rest of the town shows its disapproval, Louise carries on unconcerned, until Luigi starts to notice the world beyond their life together.

This is a fairly typical tale of an older woman/younger man affair, with her giving him support until he is strong enough to fly. But there is an interesting twist here when Louise ends up pretending to the fiancée he later acquires that she is his mother – until she is found in a compromising situation with him, that is, and then she regains her former status as his mistress. In 1971, even though the Swinging Sixties had been and gone, such material was still quite strong stuff in the cinema. The film went to Cannes as part of the film festival's official selection, but it was not warmly received in France. In contrast, in Britain, after the English version was shown on BBC television, Moreau says she had more fan-mail than she had ever received for a film.

Moreau next joined forces with the female branch of her French film family to make *Nathalie Granger*. Moreau's women friends are, as is to be expected, rather like her in their outlook – independent-minded, fiercely determined and possessing an intellectual acuity with which one does not meddle.

They frequently use the title Mademoiselle rather than Madame, as is customary in France for females who are clearly no longer girls. 'How could I be Madame Moreau?' Moreau demanded of me. 'I was never married to Monsieur Moreau. Madame Moreau was my mother. I am Mademoiselle Moreau.' I felt crushed and stupid, having always called her, out of respect, 'Madame', but cheered up when Nickolas Grace told me she had been very fierce with him too as he launched into a 'Madame' greeting in French when they met on the BBC film *Vicious Circle*.

Marguerite Duras used to be one of Moreau's closest friends. Like the distinguished writers Louise de Vilmorin, Françoise Sagan and Simone de Beauvoir before her, Duras had been a symbol for young liberated women. A much translated author, she has fascinated feminists (and also psychoanalysts), who have taken her work as emblematic of the category of 'women's writing'. Duras and Moreau (never a feminist) had worked well together on *Moderato Cantabile*, and when Duras decided to make a movie of her book, *Nathalie Granger*, at her home in Neauphle-le-Château, she wanted Moreau for the lead. But Moreau, for some reason, was uncontactable at the time, so Duras gave the role to Lucia Bosè.

Duras later did make contact with Moreau, who then said she would love to be in the film. Duras decided to divide the role into two and drive the film as a piece about the conflict of two women (Bosè and Moreau) and their fear of the outside world. The result is a curious, somewhat intellectual 'art film' about a fatherless family, the Grangers, who live in a country house with a nameless woman (Moreau). The film did nothing at the box office but I rather enjoyed it, particularly for its self-assured pretentiousness. However, in the *New York Times* Vincent Canby called it 'a dead-end film which I would sincerely hope not many of us are ready for'.

In *Nathalie Granger* not much happens, but against a background of domestic life you hear on the radio news of a couple of young killers in the region. At this point a door-to-door salesman arrives. The ominous washing-machine salesman, who tries to sell his wares to Jeanne Moreau, is Gérard Depardieu.

'I wondered where Marguerite had found this unruly, extraordinary-looking giant who talked like a Shakespearean actor but was a total primitive,' said Moreau. He, too, was somewhat bowled over by Moreau, who before he met her had been just 'a mouth, hair and a voice – particularly a voice'.

'Working with her I found that she had everything,' said Depardieu. 'She was a great influence on my early work.' (They were to collaborate again, fifteen months later, in *Les Valseuses*, Depardieu's breakthrough film.)

'I haven't really seen Pierre Cardin since the Brazilian film,' Jeanne Moreau told me in Paris when we were stocktaking her life. It was

1973 when she made 'the Brazilian film', *Joanna Francesca (Jeanne la Française)*.

Shot in the torrid summer in the sugar cane plantations of northeast Brazil, inspired by a true story that took place there in the twenties, it is said to be one of her worst films. Pierre Cardin himself took the part of the French consul, his cinematic debut, and had two scenes with Moreau. As usual, he had designed her costumes, but he had also part-funded the project for a new, young Brazilian director called Carlos Diegues, who had seen all of Moreau's films and written to her. This was to be one of the big films of the emerging Brazilian *Cinema Nuovo*.

The story tells of the struggle for power of a Frenchwoman who had gone to Brazil from France after the 1914-1918 war to live in São Paulo. She is a successful brothel madame and marries a rich sugar baron, systematically becoming the head of his family by terrorising the rest of them.

Set at about the end of the sway of the large landowners of Brazil, the film uses the woman as an allegorical character to underline Brazilian oligarchy – a woman devoured by a country. It was shot in Marechal d'Oro, a remote village full of ancient, pastel-painted buildings.

'They wanted to treat me like a big star. My contract was incredible,' she told the *Los Angeles Times*. 'My private house, my private car, a driver. But you should have seen it! The driver had a huge dirty handkerchief around his head and I could feel the road beneath my bottom when we drove. By the time we got to Marechal d'Oro I was covered with dust – like that scene in Visconti's *The Leopard*.'

She could not sleep in the local convent because it locked its doors at 10 p.m., so she stayed at the hotel, which had no electricity or windows, just grilles, sleeping in 50-degree heat and covered with anti-mosquito lotion. At the end the locals threw a carnival for her. They all arrived on horseback and spent the entire time in the saddle, getting unbelievably drunk. 'It was the only way they could have managed it, by staying on their horses,' she commented.

Although Moreau learned sufficient Portuguese to record her own dialogue, she was dubbed by a well-known Brazilian actress, Fernanda Montenegro; her voice was only heard singing the theme tune, 'Joanna Francesca'.

Apparently Pierre Cardin 'was not allowed' to accompany her on her next film, *Je t'Aime*. This was shot in the Canadian hinterlands for director Pierre Duceppe. After a long engagement her relationship with Cardin had finally foundered.

'I don't remember precisely why we parted – it came little by little, but what we lived together was an extraordinary relationship and it was such fun. We really enjoyed ourselves. We had a marvellous relationship that was both spiritual and physical. I have great admiration for him but frankly I don't even remember why we parted. I think much of the problem was that we wanted a child very badly and if we had had a child, we'd still be together. I'm responsible for that – I was unable to bear a child. But it takes two to tango. If we had had a child . . . Oh, it's so long ago now.'

Their lives had clearly drifted apart. She spent less and less time in Paris, while he was increasingly in demand there as his business grew. Perhaps she was moving herself away from her life in Paris to soften the blow of the end of the relationship. Veering from sweltering Brazil to snow-bound Quebec seems a radical way to do this, but it must have been appropriately distracting. Possibly, for somebody who says her idea of a travel as in 'holiday' would be two or three days alone on a luxury yacht (complete with crew, *bien sûr*), these drastic hauls must have been practically cold turkey treatments for her.

In the Canadian film she once again plays the older woman to a younger man, this time to her pregnant daughter's husband-to-be, but with the double clinch of being a mother as well. Everybody thought this Oedipus-complex angle would make it interesting, but in the end the film was poorly received and distributed hardly anywhere. Hers might have been another brilliant performance for a gifted director, but the film itself was deeply flawed.

The hard core of Moreau fans must have thanked God for Bertrand Blier, who saved her from being the big star in pictures that were getting smaller and performing valiantly in movies that did her no credit. In the 1970s Blier, son of the actor Bernard Blier, was a young director eager to write something reflective of the changing times. He needed to mark the progression from the New Wave to the permissive and disturbed seventies. By now many of the New Wave directors had developed middle-age spread, and like many others, Blier criticised the fact that they had often neglected to address current French issues by stressing their own visions of reality rather than a socio-political one.

His first book, *Les Valseuses*, translated into English under the title *Making It* (Jonathan Cape), was published in 1972. A big success among those wanting change, it offended all the niceties of the bourgeoisie, toppled taboos and spiked all the sacred cows in Pompidou's tightly buttoned France. The bourgeoisie, particularly the female of the species, was horrified. The book was published at a time when French society was on the point of a little lid-blowing. In the US the Nixon corruption scandal was about to break with Watergate; in Britain there were heady strikes, the three-day week and equality was being promised for women workers.

Jeanne Moreau, leading light of the New Wave and a profoundly non-political animal, was not really part of Bertrand Blier's overview of the new France. Even the words in his book, which Depardieu described as being so strong that they sounded 'dirty', were not her kind of words. But they were friendly and Blier knew she was an actress whose particular strength and delight was to foster the careers of new directors. He had directed two films in the sixties, but not made his mark with them. He still needed to throw his stone through the window of French cinema.

Blier came to her with the script of his book about two 'giggling layabouts, natural grandsons of Rabelais and Guignol'. He had rounded up a cast from the most interesting of the new generation: Gérard Depardieu, now France's one-man film industry, his colleagues from the innovative Café de la Gare theatre company, Patrick Dewaere and Miou-Miou (the former committed suicide in 1982, the latter is still one of France's most popular actresses); plus the young hopefuls Isabelle Huppert and Brigitte Fossey. He had also persuaded jazz violinist Stéphane Grappelli to do the music and an unknown Dutch cameraman, Bruno Nuytten, to film it.

Blier asked Moreau if she would be in *Les Valseuses* ('valseuses' is French slang for testicles), to do a twenty-minute role, a woman called Jeanne who, shortly after her release from prison, shoots herself. She was attracted to the robustly realistic story, presented with none of the usual social fig leaves. When she agreed to join this group of youthful revellers, powered by insolence and edgy insecurities, she could never have envisaged what a *véritable révélation* it would all prove to be.

Les Valseuses is a testosterone-driven story about two rackety, amoral petty criminals, Jean-Claude and Pierrot (Depardieu and Dewaere), who career around France to no apparent end, stealing cars, pulling stick-ups and burglaries, and giving women a hard time. Jean-Claude and Pierrot rob and fornicate with Marie-Ange (Miou-Miou), whom they find too frigid, and consequently decide they fancy a more mature woman. They reckon their answer could come in the form of a newly released female prison inmate, so they hang around outside a woman's jail. In due course Jeanne emerges after a ten-year sentence. She is no longer young, she is no beauty, but she is all they had hoped for. They buy her clothes, give her a wonderful meal and take her to an out-of-season but smart hotel in Le Touquet, where they pass a delirious night of *amour à trois*. A gunshot wakes them at dawn. Jeanne has killed herself.

In her little cardboard suitcase, they find letters from her son, Jacques (Jacques Chailleux), also in prison. Feeling indebted to her, they await his release and take him to the isolated farmhouse where they are now living with Marie-Ange. For Marie-Ange and Jacques, it is love at first sight. Jean-Claude and Pierrot, generously leaving them together, are furious the following morning to hear the frigid Marie-Ange delightedly screaming that she has at last achieved orgasm.

The film does not end there – Blier's story continues to belt life on the head with its flagrant nudity and spontaneous gestures from, in particular, Depardieu and Dewaere, both of whom needed little encouragement.

Moreau's part in this plot was a small but strangely affecting one. At first she is a sort of terminally depressed person, ashen grey and wearing black. By the end, as she lies dead on the bed, half bare in a petticoat with a pool of blood trickling from her, she is as provocative as she was in *The Lovers* fifteen years before, her youth momentarily regained through attention. The scene gave me a shiver down my spine. I thought of something I had read about her saying that an actor has to take care of his life more than anyone else, 'because everything shows'. Everything was showing on that bed: the person who had made *the* film of the generation before, *The Lovers*, had now joined the chorus of this hymn to the next generation.

Depardieu remembers Moreau being like a solid rock to them all during the filming of *Les Valseuses*. While the young actors were nervous and full of tension, constantly feeling that they were being tested as they found their feet at the beginning of their careers, she quietly absorbed herself in her role. 'You have to live the part you're playing, like Jeanne,' Depardieu said. 'You must love the joy of it.' Moreau later introduced Depardieu to Truffaut, which led to the making of *Le Dernier Métro* (*The Last Metro.*)

Les Valseuses was leagues ahead of its time, and set a new trend. In France more people went to see it than saw its box-office rivals *The Sting* and *The Man with the Golden Gun*. At the time it ranked second only to *Emmanuelle* as a financial success.

In Britain, by contrast, it was refused a general certificate by the censors and allowed a limited release only in Greater London. Moreau was chastised by American women for appearing in such an unwholesome movie; Brigitte Fossey was severely criticised for being in a scene involving breastfeeding in public. Hands came up in shock and shame across the nation over France's favourite child star, Isabelle Huppert, then only eighteen, being seen in the film having sex at the side of the road with *both* men. It was all too *monstreux* for words. But everybody saw it. The people who found *Les Valseuses* thoroughly distasteful must have been really galled that same year when Moreau was awarded the national Order of Merit.

While she remained typecast in the older-woman-with-a-younger-man role, Moreau had also embarked on the mother-of-an-adult-child stage of her career. Jacques in *Les Valseuses* was about the same age as her son Jérôme, born in September 1948, who turned twenty-four while they were shooting the film.

In a recent interview, all she would tell me about Jérôme was: 'He's a grown-up. He doesn't want to be spoken about. It is enough just to say he is an artist. He paints. He lives in California. I cannot allow myself to speak about a grown-up person.'

Friends say that the two of them reached a comfortable rapprochement in the early eighties after quite a difficult, diffused and at times painful mother-son relationship. In the days when she did talk openly about him, she always stressed that she hadn't been a typical mother. 'I just did the best I could. He does not call me Mother, he calls me Jeanne. I was never a possessive mother.'

Her most emotional experience was, however, concerned with mother-love: the time when Jérôme nearly died after the crash in Bordeaux with Jean-Paul Belmondo in 1960. His father, who acts as his agent (for exhibitions) in France, told me that his life had been a bit *à droit, à gauche; une vie assez bousculée* – that is, unsettled – living with his mother, his father, his grandparents. When his parents had lived about ten kilometres apart, he would stay with whichever one he felt closest to at the time. He was an unenthusiastic scholar, first as a boarder in France and when older at the American French School in Lausanne. He had left college during the student unrest, studied photography, worked as a film usher and a bookbinder, and was an assistant to his father when he made *Diana*. Pictures of Jérôme as a boy show he has his mother's strong brow and his father's wavy hair.

He finally left France to live in Canada and for the past four years Jérôme Richard has lived alone in Corona del Mar in California. While I was in Paris in November 1993, I went to view the one-man exhibition of his abstract oils at the Galerie Brigitte Schehadi. His paintings were dramatic and modern, bright with Californian light, bold with incandescent tropical tones. In the puff for the exhibition in *Le Nouvel Observateur*, he is merely described as the son of an immensely famous actress and a well-known actor-director.

13

M

'I loved Peter Handke's writing, his poetry, and if I loved it, I was ready to love him.'

When Jeanne Moreau fell in love with Austrian writer and poet Peter Handke, it came as a surprise to most. Even her close friends had no clue that it was happening. He was in his early thirties, she was approaching her fifties. She usually chose younger men, and at forty-six she had the pleasure of discovering that they still chose her.

Moreau and Handke had been introduced in the early seventies by the German film director Wim Wenders. Wenders had been making a film based on a Handke novel, *Die Angst des Tormanns beim Elfmeter* (*The Goalkeeper's Fear of the Penalty Kick*). The two men had met in Düsseldorf in 1966 when Handke was first making a name for himself with avant-garde theatre pieces. They started working together on shorts, Handke writing, Wenders directing, before making several feature films as leading insiders in the emerging New Wave of German arts.

In the New Year of 1974, urged by Handke, Moreau returned to the stage for the first time since Félicien Marceau's hit comedy *La Bonne Soupe* in 1958. She was to appear in the Austrian's play, *La Chevauchée sur le Lac de Constance* (*The Crossing of Lake Constance*) at

L'Espace Cardin. 'The title, which comes from the Goethe poem, suggests we do not feel events until we're past them,' explains Moreau.

Handke, a man obsessed with 'the essence of prose', writes essentially about the more abstract aspects of life, like anguish, solitude and the inability to communicate. *The Crossing of Lake Constance*, which takes place during a house party, had all that but was without plot. Each night the production appears to have been a moveable feast of words, emotions and actions.

Moreau was drawn to the play by the idea of being able to make every performance totally different by having no rigid structural form to which to adhere. It was good to work again with friends like Gérard Depardieu, Delphine Seyrig, Michael Lonsdale and Sami Frey, and she found Claude Régy, a man who was leading theatrical circles in breaking new ground, an interesting director with whom to be involved.

Nobody could really understand why this obscure, rather violent piece was ever put on in Paris. The production certainly garnered plenty of column inches in the press as regards the audience participation – hurling things at the players to protest at the absence of plot.

Moreau, who can suffer from acute stage-fright, found this sort of behaviour at first daunting, later amusing. 'The only reason they came was to participate and give us things to eat, like rotten tomatoes,' joked Depardieu. 'The stage was covered with a whole meal at the end of each performance. We never had to go out to dinner after the show!' One night a man bought six seats and came in with dogs.

On stage Moreau's relationship with Handke was one of complicity – she served as a filter for his words. Their off-stage relationship, however, was provocative enough for the press to keep a sharp eye on the couple. Pictures of them appeared in their columns and 'old' Moreau quotes, like 'Age does not protect you from love, but love, to some extent, protects you from age', were resuscitated.

Although she has often given the press controversial quotes on the subject of love in general, she is actually very discreet about her own love life. She has always believed in lots of great loves rather than just one, and has never been afraid to try another, in case a new love is going to be one of the great ones. (I found a delicious quote where she said that it had happened that she had gone to bed in love with a man and woken up beside a stranger. 'The English, who are not people inclined to hysteria, explain this phenomenon with a saying that goes, "One morning the tea doesn't have the same taste." I think that explains what I found!')

She never uses the word 'lover' in the interviews she gives, preferring to describe with infinite discretion the men she has loved and been loved by as men she 'admires and respects'. Almost without exception – Pierre Cardin broke the rule – her men seem to 'love' her forever as she does them.

I asked her in Paris to be frank about Handke. 'I loved his writing, his poetry, and if I loved it, I was ready to love him. Peter [she pronounces it 'Payder'] and I have stayed very close since *Lake Constance*. I have a profound admiration for him. Friendship is very important to me.'

While many other public figures make similar gestures towards a civilised approach to love and lovers, Moreau genuinely seems to live by what she professes about private and lasting affinities. She and Handke still speak regularly and they hope to work together again soon.

Their affair was partly transposed on to the screen by her in *Lumière* a year later.

Fifteen years later he asked her to appear in his film *Die Abwesenheit* (The Absence) for a fifteen-minute monologue at the end. 'There's no real script in Peter's film but it was exciting to do.'

Just before being pelted nightly on stage in *Lake Constance*, Moreau had made a film based on a Félicien Marceau novel called *Creezy*. A story about politics being a dirty business, the film, directed by Pierre Granier-Deferre, was called *La Race des Seigneurs* (*Jet Set*). Alain Delon starred as a dashing left-wing politician destined for high things, hampered by wife and mistress trouble and a son desperately seeking a father figure. Moreau played a sort of political Lady Macbeth, a respected dark-haired widow, intent on priming her late husband's youthful deputy, the man played by Delon. Delon was an actor she had always admired. The film was by no means an earth-shatterer, but finally the two idols of their generation were together on screen.

Most of the rest of that year Moreau spent doing three films by new young directors, marking time until the autumn, when the San Francisco Film Festival was to pay her its lengthiest-ever tribute, a homage perfectly timed for her to relaunch herself in America.

The festival screened *The Lovers, Jules et Jim, Bay of Angels* and *The Diary of a Chambermaid*, followed by two hours of clips spanning twenty-five years of films. Finally, at midnight, there was an appearance by Mademoiselle Moreau herself. The event was a sell-out. They gave her a rapturous standing ovation. She cried. She wanted to kiss them all, 'But of course, that would have been too much!' They went crazy for her. Photographs of her acknowledging their accolades show her utterly, completely radiant.

It had been five years since she had gone to Hollywood for *Monte Walsh*. Apart from revivals of old films, only the 'shocking' *Going Places* (the US title for *Les Valseuses*) had made it across the Atlantic. The trip for her was lined with the golden thread of King Vidor, the veteran Hollywood director, who flew her from San Francisco in his private plane to spend a weekend in his mansion in Paso Robles. She had met him in a Paris screening-room only weeks before, when he had been with his great friend, silent star and flapper Colleen Moore, and he had promised to show Moreau the true style of old-fashioned Hollywood. She told the *Los Angeles Times* that the luxury of being flown in Vidor's plane was 'the high point of my life in the past three years'.

From there she moved on to Los Angeles, where she appeared on the Johnny Carson and Merv Griffin shows, operating in modern Hollywood style, in which self-promotion is an essential pastime rather than something the studio publicist lines up for you. It was exactly what she needed: expensive mainstream exposure as a star. After all, being a star is part of the job. 'It's something wonderful being known. I don't sulk if I'm recognised, I feel nourished. I make phone calls and people react! It has never been a problem. I have always gone shopping as myself. I've never concealed myself behind hats and glasses. I don't object to people recognising me – I'd worry if they forgot me. I think it's a privilege. I never resent it and I walk freely and speak to people. It's great because you make friends immediately and you learn so much.

'It's very easy to have a private life if you really want it. You only get publicity if that is what you are after. When I was driving in Italy, for instance, the press were after me. So I got out of the car and faced them. They took a lot of pictures, and then click . . . click . . . they went away.'

The Californian trip came as a nourisher after she had carried the can for three new young directors whom her name – and generosity – were helping to launch. She has always been profoundly dedicated to directors and I can understand her desire to nurture talent. But Moreau's eagerness and appetite for work, it must be said, sometimes outstrip the ability of her protégés. Maybe she does not care. Maybe it is the cash – although with the early films of unknown directors there is seldom much of that around. Maybe to be occupied is better than to do nothing. But it strikes me as surprising that a woman who professes to have too little time to do her own thing has allowed herself to be involved in so many undistinguished films which have slipped off the screen almost as soon as they arrived. Yet perhaps I misjudge how difficult it is to anticipate the result of a proposed film project.

The first of these three was *Hu-Man*, in which Terence Stamp and Frédérick (of Nina and Frédérick) van Pallandt also starred. Written by the director, former documentary-maker Jérôme Laperrousaz, it is a loosely paced science-fiction tale about an actor called Terence Stamp, who is a voyager in time, and his old flame Jeanne, who helps him to travel. The film travelled light at the box office but it did win the Golden Asteroid at the 1975 Trieste Science Fiction Film Festival.

Moreau must have been deeply disappointed not to be able to take a greater part in the second film, *Le Jardin qui Bascule* (*The Tilting Garden*), for her protégé, director Guy Gilles, had written the main role for her. Owing to Moreau's other commitments, Delphine Seyrig took the part, but 'for good luck' she wrote and sang a song at the end of the film, accompanied by friend Stéphane Grappelli on the violin.

The third film she nurtured, *Souvenirs d'en France* (*Memories of France*), she was able to watch grow and flourish. One of Moreau's fledglings at the time was André Téchiné. Now one of France's most successful mainstream directors, then he had only made one film, *Paulina s'en Va* (Pauline Flees), shot when he was twenty-one. He had been talking to Moreau for some time about a controversial film he wanted to make about the class situation. With her help, he managed to raise the money to shoot it.

Souvenirs d'en France is a strong, stylised political film that even now, two decades later, is cited as one of the most significant studies of the liberal Gaullist bourgeoisie. Shot near Toulouse, the film is an account of a family in south-west France from the beginning of the century, through two wars and into the seventies. The family, originally Spanish immigrants fleeing the Civil War, climbs the ladder from blacksmith level to owning a forge and finally running a huge factory which earns them a fortune. Moreau plays Berthe, the laundress with a brain and a spine of steel, married off by the father of the dynasty to his son, Hector (Michel Auclair), to be the force behind their new capitalist empire.

During the Second World War Berthe becomes a Resistance heroine, which both alarms the family and benefits it. When a different sort of approach is needed for both factory and family in post-war upheavals and in the battle for power, she becomes the driven industrialist who gets them through.

Says Téchiné: 'Introducing the class struggle into a family story seemed necessary, but completely insufficient for this film. What basically attracted me was the conflicting goals of the characters and the conflict of the sexes.'

The French, not normally a self-critical race, found the sharp screen portraits of his film a revelation. The way it cast a harsh light on the rigidity of many aspects of French life was unprecedented. Even more offensively, it also provided a devastating peep into the deadliness and boredom of French provincial life.

After a brief drawing in of breath, the critics began to think of the film as reflecting a new and healthy trend in French movie-making. Says Moreau: 'We tried to show how the world had changed through this woman I play, through this family and through the industry itself. It's one of the first times an attempt had been made in French cinema to recreate the passing of time over a long period, which gives novelistic and yet violent flavour to the film. All the characters, however long or short their part in the film, are absolutely accurate and true, although Berthe is certainly the one who changes most obviously. At first she is not wanted in the family, particularly by the mother, because she is too proletarian. When Berthe gets into the family, she finally gets everything.'

Here is Moreau once again in a *Diary of a Chambermaid*-type role, a bright woman in a class and society where brains are not required but where, used the right way, they enable her to dictate the rules. She ages slowly, beautifully, from the provincialism of the twenties through the terrors of the German Occupation and then the modernisation of the sixties and beyond. This is certainly one of Moreau's finest performances, and she still thinks of her role of the Resistance woman as one she particularly loved. 'Maybe if I'd been older in the war, maybe I would have been like her but, when you're a young girl still at school . . .' She shrugs as she puffs on a long, slim cigarette. 'It was not in my character. Maybe if I'd been older, maybe . . .'

The film should have gone into competition at the 1975 festival at Cannes, but as Moreau was president of the jury that year it was not allowed to compete. Instead, it was shown in the Directors' Fortnight section, to great acclaim.

Moreau was the fifth woman president of the festival, following Olivia de Havilland, Sophia Loren, Michèle Morgan and Ingrid Bergman. Since then, the only woman to be president has been Françoise Sagan. 'It came as a surprise to me because I hardly ever go to the movies. I'm not a viewer of my own films and virtually never go to premières. Occasionally I go to the theatre to see a friend on stage but I am very shy and avoid galas and first nights. Naturally I took the Cannes job very seriously. I quickly found out there was enough paperwork to choke a horse.'

Apart from the paperwork there was the constant round of films to be seen and the rigid protocol that goes with being president. Moreau, who invariably stays at the Carlton, the gloriously elegant nineteenth-century hotel on the palm-lined Croisette, felt totally at ease, not having to promote a film, but still being able to dress up and be toasted as a celebrity. Her friend and La Garde-Freinet neighbour, BBC producer Peter Adam, who has often been there with her during the film festival, delights in telling how she would sometimes change her clothes six or seven times a day, switching from one designer outfit to the next from a wardrobe of up to sixty dresses lent to her by the great couture houses. 'When she's there she's being a star and doing her job,' he says. 'She has great physical confidence in herself and can sweep people off their feet with her style.'

In 1993, when she was at the Cannes Festival doing a masterclass with a group of directors (which included Téchiné, whose film *Ma Saison Préférée* (*My Favourite Season*), starring Catherine Deneuve and Daniel Auteuil, was there in competition), her presence reminded Cannes regulars of 'the good old days' when style was everything. Chauffeured slowly down the Croisette in an open sports car driven by a handsome young man, she waved graciously at the breathless crowds lining the pavement, her jewels sparkling, silk *foulard* blowing in the wind, the embodiment of Hollywood-sur-Mer.

The nineteenth-century resort of Cannes was selected as the haven for this kind of showbiz in 1938. Disgruntled at seeing most of the Venice Film Festival awards being scooped by rigid pictures from Mussolini's Italy and Hitler's Germany, delegates from the democratic countries decided to start their own international festival here. This *Belle Epoque* resort had been more or less founded to serve as the most ample of the Riviera waterholes for British aristocrats unable to winter in pestilential Nice. It seemed like the perfect place to develop the queen of film festivals.

After a delay caused by the war, the festival got underway in 1946. Ever since then the same faces, frequently with more new teeth, more hair, better tans and tighter tucks behind their ears, swan into town in the latest gear for twelve days every May. Maybe this year the proverbial bread they throw on the waters will come back as smoked salmon sandwiches (the miracle is that it does happen).

It is without doubt the most prestigious of the 600-odd film festivals held in the world annually. At Cannes now about sixty countries send up to 500 films to be viewed by about 40,000 people each year. Even though Hollywood box-office phenomena like Arnold Schwarzenegger and Sylvester Stallone have, in their day, upstaged the normal festival, it has always been the 'old-school' stars – Moreau, Dirk Bogarde, Yves Montand, Elizabeth Taylor – who have made the festival what it is.

In January 1975, Jeanne's father, Anatole Désiré, died. He had continued to live at Le Préverger, where his daughters nursed him through his last years. Jeanne wrote a piece about her father's last year and his death which she has put aside. One day, she says, it will appear in her autobiography. 'He had a long illness,' she says. 'I knew he had cancer but nobody told him so; for him, he died of old age. He went to the clinic only at the very end and died when he was seventy-seven years old.

'I had made him promise me not to die before my birthday because I was away shooting Téchiné's film. Before I left I said: "Please don't do that to me, don't die before my birthday." He looked at me very hard. We had a very aggressive relationship to the end. He died on the twenty-second, the day before my birthday. Of course I left the set and flew in, arriving at his birthplace, Mazirat, where his body had been taken, on my birthday.'

She was joined there by Jean-Louis Richard and their son for the funeral. 'When we walked into the church I saw that the men were all arranged on one side, the women on the other. I sat with my husband and son but the women all stared at me. It was embarrassing, so I moved over to join them.' She shrugs. She has moved so far away from those rural folk of her childhood, although somewhere in her you can feel a root still nourished from that soil. Perhaps it is the way she tends her plants and talks to her flowers; maybe it is her passion for cooking. Somewhere deep inside still lurks Cardin's 'country girl'.

Moreau spent most of 1975 in Paris, in her beautiful high-ceilinged apartment in the Rue du Cirque, just off the Champs Elysées. She had let Jérôme Laperrousaz use the flat, with its heavy wooden doors and muted pinkish and beige tones, as a location for Hu-Man. Filming at home had been fun, and she had enjoyed a deeper involvement in the production side of filming, which she had always found absorbing. This particular movie came at the right time in her life because she was on the verge of taking a new direction.

She had not talked much about her plans to friends. In fact, Orson Welles was the only person with whom she had really discussed them. She knew that the actor's instinct in her was about to coincide with that of the director.

After wrapping on *Souvenirs d'en France* in September 1974, on and off for nearly a year Jeanne Moreau stayed home with only Quick for company. Hunched over her desk behind the pale orange muslin curtains in her big sitting-room, she wrote her first film script.

14

M

'One's soul is like a vast unexplored country.'

'When someone who has eaten only the best food becomes a cook, there is really no excuse for her dishes to be poor,' said Moreau. 'It was because I had worked with so many great film-makers that I was encouraged to direct a film of my own.'

Moreau's very own film, written, directed and interpreted by her, had a long history before it was completed in 1976. From that evening with Welles in the Hotel Meurice when she first voiced her desire to direct, it took, she estimated, nine years, hundreds of note-books and a further seventy kilos of paper to reach a final script.

At first the words did not come easily. Only when she persuaded her novelist friend Madeleine Chapsal to take a week's holiday with her to help with the writing did the words start to flow. 'She put me to bed at night,' recalls Moreau, 'but I'd slide my handwritten pages under her door, and then the next morning they were all crisp and typed. It was a liberation. As if my writing had started to exist.

'After forty, an artist cannot live on the past, like a farmer with the grain stored,' she declared at the time of her first draft. 'One must continue to work, keep growing like a bud that blooms and not dry up on one's feet.'

Over the three years that followed another five versions were written. The film was eventually called *Lumière*. French for light, but also the French equivalent of the director's cue 'Lights, camera, action'.

An old hand at generating funds, Moreau raised half the budget (a minuscule $600,000) from television sources and from a French government grant, and then made a distribution deal with France's powerful Gaumont company to complete the financing. *Lumière* was to acquit itself financially. 'I found a producer, Claire Duval, who, with her husband, had produced *Emmanuelle* and then went on to do the story of Madame Claude, the woman who had all the call-girls. I was sort of a Legion of Decency for her!'

On 18 August 1975, Moreau officially went round the back of the camera for the first time and joined the ranks of actor-directors. *Lumière* was released eight months later.

The film is about actresses in and out of the limelight – certainly the subject she knows most about. This was her way of actually doing something in particular for actresses *d'un certain âge* as well as for herself. What she wrote was an intimate, rather private film that chronicles a week in the life of four actresses of different ages and their complex relationships with one another, their families, other women, men, their careers. The plot, rather like one of Duras', is relatively insignificant; the essence is in the images and the words.

'There are so few good parts for women in films,' Moreau said at the time. 'That is because the men who write the scripts no longer know their women. The ones they know and sleep with and work with are no longer representative of all women, as once they were. Women's Lib has changed everything. I think, more and more now, men are afraid to write about women. I think it's a reaction that is very truthful. Now, with sexual mores in transition, script-writers seem unable to deal with the difficulties of relationships between human beings in love. At least the women in my film will be real.'

The crucial action happens at a party held one evening to celebrate an acting award. A dying doctor, played brilliantly by François Simon, in an act of thoughtlessness, kills himself. The individual decisions the four actresses have to make as a result become the body of the film.

Moreau wanted Audrey Hepburn to head up the cast but she was making *Robin and Marian* for Richard Lester at the time. She approached Bibi Andersson in Sweden, but she was rehearsing *Twelfth Night* with Ingmar Bergman. She also asked two of her closest friends, Silvana Mangano and Anouk Aimée, but when they too were unavailable she reluctantly decided to play the role of Sarah herself.

Sarah, the award-winning actress, has a genius for friendship and warmth, but also has a certain central egomania. She is Moreau, and then again not Moreau. 'Every situation is surely built of your own experience, don't you think?'

Moreau's co-stars are Lucia Bosè, as Sarah's closest friend Laura, Francine Racette, as the ambitious young actress, and Caroline Carter, who completes the quartet as the starlet. Because she had always been interested in what was going on with young talents, Moreau cast emerging French actors Jacques Spiesser, from *The Trout*, Francis Huster, now one of France's most popular performers, and Niels Arestrup, also now a successful screen star. She wanted Harold Pinter to play the writer figure but he was 'in the midst of his scandal over Lady Antonia Fraser'. She next called German actor Bruno Ganz, whom she knew through Peter Handke and Wim Wenders, to play the writer with whom Sarah falls passionately in love – commonly acknowledged as a case of art imitating the life of Moreau and Handke themselves.

Moreau had just turned down the big nurse role in the film version of *One Flew Over the Cuckoo's Nest* and at first had wanted *Cuckoo* star Jack Nicholson to play the young American in Paris. In the end Keith Carradine was cast. I asked her why.

'I decided I wanted a very tall, lovely young man, the sort of guy I think the French film industry is lacking – it has only small, tiny, dark creatures. I wanted a great, tall guy who has that purely American quality, that innocence. I'd been dreaming over an early photograph of Gary Cooper, then I saw Keith in a film, I can't remember which. I later saw a picture of him in a copy of *Woman's Wear Daily* I happened to be glancing through when having dinner with the designer Marc Bohan. I knew he was the actor for me. I called him from Paris and he postponed a recording session to appear in my picture.' Through Moreau, Louis Malle in turn noticed

Carradine and was to cast him as the photographer in *Pretty Baby* a year later.

Lumière is a wry, insider's look at film life and film people. Even more so, it is about women and the way women talk, feel, see things. At heart it is a very personal film in which themes of friendship, love, death, indifference, desire and the cinema are carefully intertwined. An American (male) friend of mine dismissed it as a 'whole lotta spoiled French chicks sitting round a table talking'. I thought it imperfect but very interesting, with some marvellously effective scenes of the backbiting and jealousies of the backstage world.

Lumière certainly gives a sharp idea of what it must be like to be an actress. The presentation of female friendship from a feminine point of view is refreshingly frank. Frank, because these characters *look* like normal women, sitting around at ease, braless, without obvious make-up, nattering about affairs, looking for adventures or longing for a new identity. Moreau lets her actresses reveal themselves barefaced with the supreme assurance of a woman who sometimes dares to meet a stranger without a hint of make-up on. This naked quality in itself is refreshing because women on screen invariably comply to the required audience stereotype of 'a look' that probably took the make-up department several hours to create.

Although not designed as one, *Lumière* was publicised as 'a woman's film'. This categorisation must have chafed the anti-feminist, liberated Moreau, who has always rooted for equality and an end to what she calls the 'war between the two types of human beings'.

'Equality is a most difficult thing to achieve. But it is easier to achieve than happiness. It is specific. Happiness is vague and unobtainable, like the carrot you hold in front of a donkey. I have an admiration for women. I have tried to show women as they are, as they are not usually shown by men.

'There are some great male directors, like Ingmar Bergman, who makes films about women, and uses the feminine part of himself. All men have a feminine part. Women have a masculine part too, of course. All of us have both. It's just a matter of letting that part show,' said Moreau.

Filming took place in Moreau's Rue du Cirque apartment and at

Le Préverger with its simple beauty, her objects, her dogs, the poppies, the fruit trees. In a way, here she celebrates her private world just as Colette celebrated her home, Treille Muscate at St Tropez, in *La Naissance du Jour*. The result is intimate and somehow touching in an almost childlike way, as if Jeanne Moreau wanted to share her 'toys' with you.

When the six-week shoot finished, and having pruned the result from 40,000 metres of negative down to a manageable length, she flew off to Los Angeles to take up a role in Elia Kazan's *The Last Tycoon*. While there she continued working on her own film, doing some of the editing by cable from Hollywood to her editor in Paris.

For Moreau, being both actress and director was not such a dramatic change. 'I can walk and speak at the same time,' she joked sassily. 'It's quite normal if you're an actress with a passion and a curiosity about what you're doing and not just an actress waiting in the middle of the light for directions. If you're creative and you listen and watch, and you've worked with fascinating directors as I have, it's quite normal to want to direct and play in a film you have written. I felt the need to direct. Any difficulties I had were in myself. It was not because of the attitude of the crew, who were very supportive. It was because I was absolutely paranoiac. I was so used to being the one who had been given orders for so many years, the situation was absolutely incredible to me. I had to overcome my paranoia. But I never had any problems. I never had to shout. I never had to scream.

'You start to direct in your head when you write the script. The preparation is exciting: all the casting, the technicians, the fascinating relationships that build up. Then you start shooting and relationships change completely. It's exhilarating and sometimes frustrating. Then when your work is done, you have to go away and let others look at it.'

Lumière is dedicated to Dr Elia (Grisha) Shevitch. 'It's not Grisha in the script, but the film is for him. He was a dear friend, the physician who saw me through the operation for uterine cancer. He was also Alain Resnais' doctor, and doctor to all sorts of artistes. We would sometimes gather at his place to have a drink with him at the end of the day. He spent his last months before he died at Le Préverger.'

The film premièred in Washington DC and later played at the Women's International Film Festival in New York. She went to Washington with it, as part of a delegation from the French film industry, to open a French week at the Kennedy Center and to talk to American film people on the east and west coasts.

As in the mid-seventies there were not many female film directors around, her film aroused enormous interest. *The New York Times* found it 'an extraordinarily good movie', the *Christian Science Monitor* found it 'fascinating'. However, according to the film trade newspaper *Variety*, at the women's festival Moreau became irked by the trivial remarks about women and films made by some of the panel – which included Warren Beatty, who drew a comparison between *Shampoo* and *Lumière* – and she put on her cape and decamped from New York. She probably would have stayed longer in America, but the news of the death of André Malraux prompted her to hasten back home and give moral support to her friend Florence, his daughter.

That same year *Lumière* was invited to the festival at Cannes where it duly made its mark and went round the world on the festival circuit. Some loved it; others, disappointed that the eternal *femme fatale* had made something so banally female, lambasted it as narcissistic. Many felt that if she had been a male director she would have been applauded for having made an '*auteur*' film.

She retorted that she could always have made a film about restaurateurs in the Massif Central just before the beginning of the Second World War, but that she was a woman and an actress and was addressing the subject she knew best. One soul, vast country.

Moreau also used the subject of being an actress to the good in the Sam Spiegel production of *The Last Tycoon*.

'I had met so many people when I was working on stage in Paris. They came to see me. Very quickly I met a lot of people. That's how I knew Walter Wonger, who wanted me to do a film with Joan Bennett. Unfortunately there was a shooting scandal and the film was cancelled. I also knew Sam Spiegel very well. He was the one who asked me to be in *Tycoon*, made at Paramount Studios.'

The Last Tycoon, with a screenplay by Harold Pinter, is based on F. Scott Fitzgerald's last (unfinished) novel about Hollywood in its heyday. It was also to be the last film of one of the giants of old Hollywood, the Constantinople-born Elia Kazan.

'We quickly found we had a rapport, I think he's like me – he likes to be vague,' she is reported to have said during shooting. '"Sadge" adores actors. He never bullies them. And when the camera rolls you feel that he's fascinated. When somebody is like that you are ready to climb Everest to please them.'

She discounts speculation that there are similarities between her and the character she plays, Didi – an impossible temperamental thirties star who battles with directors, complaining about everything down to the studio shampoo. As Didi Moreau is in fact the leading lady in a film within a film, playing opposite Tony Curtis as a matinée idol who has reached the age where he is worried about his inability to keep living up to his sex-symbol status.

'Tony was adorable. He was so unpredictable. He has an incredibly profound sense of humour. From his image and the way he carries himself you wouldn't think so!' she told the *Los Angeles Times*.

Robert De Niro, who had just made *Taxi Driver* and *1900*, played the hot, boyish head of production and Jack Nicholson the Communist union organiser whose ideas threaten the status quo of the Hollywood power structure. Robert Mitchum played the old-guard studio chief. This was a real Hollywood production, not the sort of team Moreau was used to at all. 'You know how it works, making big-budget, studio films in the States. All call-sheets and cars. You don't stay on the [sound] stage between takes – everybody goes back to their trailers. I stayed on stage. In France I always stay on stage and watch. People don't like that in America. So I got very friendly with the chief electrician. When I was told very abruptly to go to my room and I said, "No, I want to watch," he allowed me to stay. He put me on his crane when they were rehearsing the movements. I loved it.'

The film received mixed notices. Watching it now, *The Last Tycoon* is rather like a yearbook of the class of '76. Theresa Russell and Anjelica Huston appear, looking like schoolgirls, and Peter Strauss is like a baseball jock. I don't know what happened to the film's 'discovery', a young model called Ingrid Boulting, but I did interview her at the time and remember her being terrified of Jeanne Moreau.

What seemed to have put her most in awe was the fact that Moreau not only performed, but also sang the song written for her by Maurice Jarre, called 'You Have the Choice'.

Between finishing the *Lumière* shoot and starting on *Tycoon*, Moreau also put in five days on Joseph Losey's rich, Kafkaesque *Mr Klein*. Although the film was a big hit when it came out, and is generally considered one of the classics of twentieth-century cinema, it is not one of her favourites. She says it is too complicated to explain why, yet her role in it as an elegant Jewess in Nazi-occupied Paris is emphatically one of her best.

The making of *Mr Klein* brought Moreau together again with Alain Delon, whose company, Adel Productions, co-produced it. Delon takes the part of a prosperous antique-dealer, Robert Klein, who is mistaken for a mysterious Jewish doppelgänger of the same name. Klein is a sort of Rothschild type, a man who has musical gatherings and glamorous companions.

'I was supposed to do *A la Recherche du Temps Perdu* (*Swann's Way*) when the project was once again put off,' Losey said in *Conversations with Losey*. 'I went to Italy for a rest. Two people who had originally worked with Constantin Costa-Gavras on the *Mr Klein* project told me about the screenplay and said that Delon was interested in it. I liked the idea of working with Alain, so I phoned him.'

The resultant film is handsome and haunting, full of the intangible complexity of Paris in 1942, when indifference and collaboration were everywhere although not spoken about. To a surprising extent the French can be sensitive about the skeletons in their wartime cupboard, and *Mr Klein* tackled the issue of anti-Semitism during the Occupation all too directly for some.

Now at last Moreau also went back to the stage to play in a French translation of Frank Wedekind's *Lulu* in the eponymous role that had fascinated her for so long. The production was directed by Claude Régy at the Théâtre de l'Athénée-Louis Jouvet. She had waited all of fifteen years to play Lulu, but little did she suspect what a rough ride the part would give her.

The *Lulu* project might have gone down better at the Royal Court in London, as she and Richardson had discussed earlier. But by the mid-seventies in Paris it seems it was no longer the right vehicle for her. The Parisians hated *Lulu*. Although the huge central role is notoriously difficult and many thought she handled it beautifully, it seems the production did not gel around her. It must have come as a shattering blow to her self-esteem when the nightly performance was greeted with howls of derision. *Lulu* ran only for a month.

Peter Adam first met Moreau when he went backstage one night to tell her how ashamed he was of her countrymen for whistling and shouting at her during the performance. 'I found her alone, wearing a red dressing-gown and washing her feet in the basin,' he told me. 'I asked her if she'd like to make an *Omnibus* programme with me for the BBC and she immediately replied, "Let's do it." Her relief at the suggestion was obvious.'

During the brief season in 1976 Moreau had the inspiration for a film she thought would be called *La Mise à Mort*, given in English as Moment of Truth – her own interpretation of the meaning is a cross between 'death wish' and 'death blow'. The story was to concern the son of Lulu's lover, who also becomes her lover, when he talks about how he felt about her at fourteen. She did not do anything with the idea but, as she says, one's soul is like 'a vast, unexplored country'. It's probably somewhere in that complex, rather precise and patently vulnerable mind of Moreau's, waiting for the right place and the right time.

15

ℳ

**'Life is just a lot of interesting landscapes and one makes
one's own geography.'**

On 8 February 1977, Jeanne Moreau married her second husband,
the Hollywood director William Friedkin, in a municipal ceremony
in Paris. Florence Malraux and her husband, Alain Resnais, were the
witnesses. After the formalities, the four of them lunched at Le
Grand Vefour in the garden of the Palais Royale.

'We had been living in New York and knew and liked Bill,' says
Malraux. 'When he went to Paris on business we naturally gave him
an introduction to Jeanne. It all happened very quickly.'

Her friends had been amazed two months previously when
Moreau announced the event. It came completely out of the blue.
She had always said 'never again' to marriage. She told Joan Buck in
Paris that she was the first to be surprised by this development. 'We
married because he proposed to me. I was impressed by his courage,
and terrified.'

The two had first met briefly in 1974 when Friedkin was scout-
ing for locations in France for *The French Connection*. His friends say
that he is a boyish chap, with a way of coming across as 'bigger than
life'. He had started in the industry as a mail-room boy in television
in Chicago, where he had grown up, the son of a cigar-roller. He

had just won an Oscar for directing *The French Connection* and made a multi-million-dollar fortune from *The Exorcist*, which at one stage Moreau was going to dub into French. 'I could have made a lot of money dubbing *The Exorcist*, but it would have meant being tied up for six weeks of hard work,' she explained. 'And that's a long time.'

He had already completed the sequel to *The Exorcist*, a remake of *The Wages of Fear* called *Sorcerer*, when they married. 'I never thought I'd have anything to do with that man,' she told me merrily. 'But I don't regret it. When he proposed there was some sort of magic thread between us. Perhaps we should have stayed lovers. Being lovers permits you greater freedom.

'I feel the institution of marriage has lost all its sacred meaning. That's desecration. The freedom of sex has desecrated the sensual and sexual relationship. You read about the sexual revolution, do whatever you please, don't suppress your desires, and you know it's true and you also know that it's not true. Everything has its reverse side, the dark and the light, the heat and the cold. Marriage is a symbol. Now it's a stamp at the town hall or it's sworn in front of priests who belong to a church that is desecrated. It has lost its sacred meaning. We need symbols to live by. You don't have to go in front of somebody from the church or the town hall.'

People were titillated by the fact that, at (reportedly) thirty-six, Friedkin was a dozen years Moreau's junior. Much was made of this younger man coup. The eternal goddess, they said, had struck another young admirer with her arrow of love.

After the wedding ceremony, Moreau packed up in Paris and went for the duration to live with her new husband, mainly in Los Angeles, sometimes in New York, where he had a Park Avenue apartment. In California they had a typical 'star'-type Beverly Hills mansion, complete with electronic gates and silently shuffling servants. Few people knew she was in residence there and they socialised only with Friedkin's friends. Like her, she told me, he did not particularly enjoy the social round and was dedicated to working hard.

For her to be Mrs William Friedkin rather than Jeanne Moreau was strange. Previously when she had visited the States, she had gone as herself. Now it was quite different. Friedkin in fact wanted her to take his name, but she could not see herself in lights as 'Jeanne Friedkin' and in the end refused.

He also wanted his wife to stop work. For the best part of the ensuing year she busied herself staying at home, visiting Warner Brothers Studios to take out various films from the archives, going over them for hours to study how films are made. She also worked on her autobiography for the Paris publisher Grasset, but this remains unfinished.

'I only got as far as the age of fifteen and then left off writing it. I'd written six hundred pages, and maybe three hundred of those were good. I put it on ice because after all I am still living my auto-biography. I started it too early. I'll return to it later,' said Moreau, aged sixty-five. 'Or maybe I'll write a cookbook – that could be just as revealing!'

The Friedkin-Moreau marriage should have become the profes-sional collaboration that was projected when they first met. 'We had planned to do films together, but got so involved in our dramatic relationship that we didn't have time for them,' she said. Then she added: 'It was the most passionate relationship of my life. And you know I have had many.'

One example of what they planned together was a ninety-minute television special featuring singer Neil Diamond at various stops on his European tour of the time. Friedkin was to handle the perfor-mance sequences, while Moreau was to direct the dramatic material. She would also appear in it, directed by her husband, with Bardot, Jacques Tati, Catherine Deneuve and Belmondo thrown in for good measure. The project was eventually shelved due to what she has described as 'friendly disagreements'.

Other projects were also mooted and dropped before the two of them finally managed to work together on a TV show. This was when the Academy of Motion Picture Arts and Sciences asked Friedkin to return to television to produce their forty-ninth Oscars ceremony, with Moreau as part of the live telecast.

What seems to have been their 'magic thread' in due course began to fray. Once they were separated by their careers – he was making a film, *The Brinks Job*, in Chicago and she was on an important film of her own – they just seemed to drift apart, abruptly and with heartache.

'I think Bill resented that I was away working. It was as if I had deserted him,' says Moreau, still almost surprised. 'But, after all, I am a film-maker too.'

While back in France researching this film of hers, she took time off to make that *Omnibus* programme with Peter Adam. Back home at Le Préverger, clad in a white floral dress and coming over as sharply intelligent, capricious, obstinate and discreet, there was certainly nothing newly Californian about her. Chain-smoking, talking with natural electricity, she piled image upon image of her buoyant life in the film industry. She paused only to giggle as she galloped through the undergrowth of her film world. It is difficult to imagine her a Beverly Hills housewife, then, or indeed, ever.

Adam, who was to become her neighbour and do other TV and magazine projects with Moreau, says that despite her air of the sophisticated star, during the *Omnibus* filming she was already deeply sad about her unworkable marriage. She was also grieved about having sold her Rue du Cirque apartment in Paris.

According to Nat Segaloff's book Friedkin – *Hurricane Billy* – 30 March 1978 is the date her husband filed for divorce, stating that he and Moreau had separated. Moreau's response to his divorce petition disputes the date, setting it a year later – 3 March 1979. In any event, the marriage was formally dissolved on 11 December that year. From the divorce papers Moreau learned that her ex-husband was in fact only six years her junior.

She returned to Paris, rather broke and looking 'neglected', to pick up the fabric of her French life once again. Friedkin, it would seem on the rebound, then married Hollywood-based British actress Lesley-Anne Down. He has since divorced her, and is now married to the present chairwoman of Paramount Pictures, Sherry Lansing.

'That marriage with Bill was an extraordinary experience, extremely painful and violent, but it has been so important in my life that I'm happy I went through it,' Moreau told me. 'I went through some moments in that life that were so painful you think you're doomed, but when you come out of it, you feel fortunate to have been able to live through it.

'It had nothing to do with America. I love America. I love their attitude to success, which is palpable and instant. I was in America long before that marriage and very happy to be there. But when I lived there it was a disastrous time, because my marriage went wrong. It could have happened anywhere. It was a problem between a man and a woman.

'I haven't yet solved what attracted us or what went wrong, or what provoked such violent antagonism. But you have to be two to tango. I think we were predestined to go through it. I don't think Bill has a bad memory of me and I don't have a bad memory of him. We don't often see each other. He has his own life, I have mine.'

When I asked William Friedkin to talk to me about this ex-wife of his, his office in Los Angeles replied that he would only do so if she said it was in order. She told me she would fax him her agreement, but in the end she never did. On reflection it struck me as undignified to attempt to annotate in any detail this brief marriage that ended so long ago. I did not pursue the episode. There is a saying in France that you cannot know about anybody's intimate relationship unless you've held the candle. I haven't and do not wish to do so, but going through the press clippings around that time, I found this curiously insightful comment on Moreau: 'Jeanne's heart is like an enormous room that is always cold. A man comes in, lights a fire, the flames swallow everything and then die down. When there are only ashes left, she shivers. She knows you cannot bring cinders back to life. You have to light another fire. This makes her sad. So she is always looking for the man who will not let the flames die down.'

This quote seems sensitive and apt.

The film she was working on with great passion while married to Friedkin was *L'Adolescente* (*The Adolescent Girl*). This is a story about a twelve-year-old girl (Laetitia Chauveau) in 1939 on holiday with her parents in a village in the Aveyron. Watched over by her grandmother (Simone Signoret), she falls in love with a Jewish doctor (Francis Huster). The doctor in turn prefers her mother (Edith Clever).

Essentially the film is about the perils of passing from girlhood to womanhood through first love, first rejection. I asked Moreau the obvious question: 'Who was your first love?'

'Oh, I must have been six years old when I fell in love with my father's hairdresser!' she replied with her throaty laugh. 'There was something about his voice. I know I was fascinated by this man for at least a week!'

The idea for her second film, as for the unrealised *La Mise à Mort*, first came to her when she was on stage in the disastrous *Lulu* production.

'I was struck by a phrase of Wedekind's when Lulu expresses surprise at no longer enjoying the same closeness with one of the characters as she did when he was a child. He replies to Lulu, "The most painful moment in my life was the day I realised the truth about relationships." Sometimes at puberty the moment of realisation is a devastating experience. We feel that we've been cheated for twelve or thirteen years, that we've been misunderstood, that we've been missing serious and important things, without thinking that we've also lived through a period of innocence which we can never again recapture. The loss of *la douceur de vivre*.

'As a counterpoint I chose the summer of 1939, between 14 July and the declaration of war on 2 September, that year when people unconsciously *knew* that war would come but consciously rejected the idea. That time of false, decaying peace, when the enormous black cloud hovering over Europe would change the world for everyone and nothing would ever be the same again. It seemed appropriate to me to use that to define the general meaning of the film.' She wanted, and still wants, to make films to express her urgent feelings about such matters of life and living.

L'Adolescente was co-written with novelist Henriette Jelinek. Some time before, after reading one of her books, Moreau had invited her round to her old apartment in Rue du Cirque. With her background in the Landes region of south-west France, Jelinek was closer than Moreau to the country life and indeed was the right person to collaborate on the screenplay.

Although it was not until April 1979 that Moreau returned to France for good, she started to direct *L'Adolescente* there in August 1978. It was on the first day of shooting on location in the Aveyron that Friedkin called Moreau to say he was asking for a divorce. One may make of this detail what one will.

L'Adolescente came across as a lyrical film with a touching story and, for Moreau, a strong vein of political comment. Although she denies it is at all autobiographical, like *Lumière* it is about her own experiences to an extent – in this case, what she went through as a child. In 1939 she was eleven and, like her heroine, Marie, was also experiencing the strangeness of village life in the country when living near Vichy with grandparents, aunts and uncles in Mazirat. She must have had much the same problems as the girl in the film in relating to puberty, and certainly they were both only too aware of the threat of war, listening with their parents to the news on their crackly wireless about Hitler's soldiers invading Poland. There are striking similarities between little Marie's parents (a butcher father and beautiful Dutch mother) and Moreau's own (the bistro-keeper and the English dancer). The doctor character, she admits, was loosely based on Grisha (Elia Shevitch). The only missing element is the village priest, which she said was due to the fact that the actual priest in the village on location was away on holiday, and they could not afford another actor.

She was thrilled to be behind the camera once again. Signoret described her at the time as a director of 'rare sensitivity'. 'She gives actors intelligent explanations and that's something directors who have never been actors can rarely do,' she said.

Like Clever and Huster, with the rest of the large cast and crew, Signoret made the film on a co-operative basis. Moreau's application for an advance from the state had been rejected because the movie was considered too commercial to deserve that kind of support. She had had to raise the minimum $100,000 needed to finance it independently from German and French television. 'We're going through a bad period,' she complained. 'There are no real producers in France, and foreign countries are reluctant to buy our films.' On completion, however, the film was bought by most countries and its finances were successfully resolved.

Moreau did not act in *L'Adolescente*, there being no suitable role for her, and as a second-time director she went in full of qualms. As the director-cameraman relationship is probably the most crucial in any film production, she used the brilliant Pierre Gautard, who meticulously put right every detail on screen. Her old friend, Philippe Sarde, did the music; he also wrote the theme song, which she sang as a duet with Yves Duteil. The cast itself included many of her friends. If Friedkin was the epitome of American film, his wife at this time could not have been more quintessentially French!

'The first day on set you think you've forgotten everything,' she said. 'Even if I can speak very frankly and precisely with actors, being one myself, I still found I had nothing to go on but some notes I'd taken, my preparation and my understanding with the crew. You're stepping into a completely new world fraught with surprises. With this film the little girl was the problem, because she was just a schoolgirl who had never acted before. I had to be particularly atten- tive with her, since she rebelled against my demands. I was forcing her to go beyond emotions which she not only did not want to express, but did not even want to experience.' (Chauveau in fact went on to pursue a legal career.)

'When directing films, no matter how much you've planned in advance, you always have to cope with the unexpected, as in a war. And then, working on location with no budget for trailers, you spend half your time trying to find comfortable shoes' – Moreau has bunions – 'somewhere to sit and a place to pee!'

As Moreau and her entourage packed up in the Aveyron, the Festival of Paris began to run a retrospective of her films. This must have been nectar for her jaded soul, still shaken by the breaking marriage.

She had had to cut her losses, announcing her return to the capital. But the Paris in which she sought to re-establish herself had changed. She was older, the film industry was altered, the style of life had changed. The eighties were about to happen, after all. She bought herself a new home, a small but sunny apartment on Rue de l'Université in the seventh *arrondissement*, almost in the shadow of the Eiffel Tower. This overlooked a little courtyard filled with trees and had a view of the Seine. Florence Malraux lived in the same build- ing. Moreau moved there, in an almost chrysalis state, and slipped into another long spell of withdrawal. If something does not work out, her reaction is usually physical: the closing of shutters, the lock- ing of doors and the creation of a secure oblivion in which to fold herself.

'It was like a religious retreat,' she told Joan Buck, 'a time to draw back. It lasted a long time. I was astonished.'

Buck in turn recalls: 'When you went to see her in those days, she would wear a kaftan, cook lunch, burn scented candles that smelled magically of moss and tea, explain your life to you, and then, quite abruptly, say: "I'm tired now. You must go." You would be shown to the door, usually with a gift in your hand.'

She worked quietly on the post-production of *L'Adolescente*, which was not released until the New Year of 1979, and did little else. Friends say she was detached and anxious, but it must have pleased her to be awarded the prestigious Prix de l'ACIC (Association des Cadres de l'Industrie Cinématographique) at that time for her work in the industry. The fact that some of her films were presented in various festivals – in Moscow, Salonica and Chicago – must have come as an additional consolation.

However, she did not do much for most of the last year of the decade. When the taxes needed to be paid she did go to Montreal to be in George Kaczender's *Your Ticket is No Longer Valid*, a forgettable film shot in English with Richard Harris and George Peppard. There she looks tired and a bit chubby – almost coarse – playing a brothel madame called Lili Marlene who helps Harris out with his impotence problem. Based on a Romain Gary work about the *anxiety* of impotence, *Au-delà de Cette Limite, Votre Ticket n'est Plus Valable*, it is a dog of a film and nothing like the book.

'It must have been my agent at the time who asked me to do it,' she said with a sigh. 'I wasn't very happy with it. Maybe I needed some quick money for tax or something.'

I do not imagine there was much money for her in *Plein Sud*, made with Luc Béraud, whom she described as her 'godson', directing his second film. As Aunt Hélène to the heroine (played by Clio Goldsmith, daughter of renaissance-man financier Sir James), her role is hardly more than a cameo. Patrick Dewaere of *Les Valseuses* fame, here balding and unprepossessing, plays the professor who falls for the Goldsmith character. This is unbalanced comedy, dotted with some absurd bedroom farce. In flowing scarf and black mules, Moreau ambles through it all eccentrically, when not holding sway in an arty attic. This was not one of her greater screen outings.

Better in the following year was *Mille Milliards de Dollars* made for Henri Verneuil. Again she is with Dewaere, who plays a journalist uncovering political corruption in a huge multinational company. Moreau is cast as the sunken-eyed wife of the general director, a woman with middle-age spread, brought out only for official functions. It is a small but strong role which she plays acutely well, looking saggy and sad. But like the previous couple of films, this is not one that stands out in her filmography. The years 1979 to 1981 do not go down as great ones for her.

Inevitably the time had come for her to quit doing the famous face in the pieces of emerging directors. She needed to survey her career from a more dignified standpoint. There was a gritty choice to be made, between the small project done with friends that could be fun, and kept her occupied doing what she loved most, and turning her energies inwards, alone, to develop new, bigger projects of her own.

'I have no regrets,' she comments. 'Negative things that happen to you are not important. A life is made of everything, ups and downs. An actor is a human being with ups and downs and the downs are sometimes more fruitful for the human being and the artistic expression than the ups.

'When you become an adult you have to face every day a different decision, and if you say yes to something it leads you one way, if you say yes to something else you go another. I just think that maybe there's a way over there, but I chose this way. Life is just a lot of interesting landscapes and one makes one's own geography.'

She must have seen some sort of sign on the horizon of her life, though, for now she began to be much more of a *présence illustrieuse*, representing her country and industry abroad and at film festivals, rather more off screen than on. It was the right move. She was used to living her life as an *artiste* and had no intention of packing it in. Already a legend, unlike most legends she was anything but dead.

Once when asked if she wanted to continue with her career forever, she spikily replied, 'I've no career, I'm not a worker. I do not work in an office or in a company. I am an *artiste* and you are an *artiste* until you die. You don't ask a painter, when are you going to stop painting? Nor a writer. Inspiration doesn't just stop like that. It's God's gift and God is too generous to take it back – unless you really make a mess of it.'

She had not made a mess of it. If the industry could not really cope with the older actress, least of all the unabatedly enthusiastic one, that was hardly her fault. Whether she believed in God or not, He was certainly not about to take back the gift He had given her. She was simply going to have to use it differently. As she says, a role is always a role. It was now important for her to find herself the right ones to play.

16

M

'Homosexuality and heterosexuality mean nothing. Either
you're sexual or you're not.'

The eighties dawned at first as lean years for Moreau. Although she
was feeling run-down, she had to stay abreast of the overheads that
continued to run up in the background, what with Le Préverger, in
the hands of Anna Pradella and her husband Louis, and a new life to
stitch together in Paris. Somebody had to keep it all going, and
throughout Moreau's life the only hand that has ever signed the
cheques has been her own. She had to keep working.

She has also said that it was a time in her life when she needed to
withdraw for a period of interior work, concentrating on cultivating
herself, as she puts it, 'like a patch of land'. Her health had been critical for some time, since in the mid-seventies she had discovered she
was acutely allergic to most pills and other medicines. One gets the
impression that this was a period when one could hear her calling for
help, although one could not hear the words.

'I hadn't really felt as fit as I should. The year before my father
died [1974] I must tell you I had had a very bad accident caused by
an allergy and nearly died. I started to use alternative medicine.
Since then I only use homeopathy and acupuncture. I had tried
everything to cure my allergies. Then one day, for no particular reason, the allergies disappeared and never returned.

'I cut out meat and became macrobiotic, but that became so boring. You see all these shops filled with food and you think, "I'm the one who can live just with my *riz complet* and my little infusions and tea." But it's one of those things you can't do forever if you love food, eating, cooking.'

She still takes tisanes to sleep and infusions of boiled flowers which are good for the nerves. When friends happen to mention complaints like fatigue or depression, she will slip a little ampoule of some magic herbal mix into their hand to help them over it.

'I stopped drinking alcohol, except occasionally maybe a little very good Bordeaux wine.' (Joan Buck describes Moreau's 1967 macrobiotic version of champagne punch as 'Dom Perignon with slices of fresh peaches in it'.) 'Now I haven't drunk a drop of alcohol since 1986. I knew I had to stop and I stopped completely. I won't even eat a cake with rum in it.'

But it seems as if at any suggestion of the world not being right, Moreau, with her essence of cosmic insecurity, goes to ground in her private world only to rebuild, and then dives unquestioningly back into work. Loss, grief, failure, frustration, illness, death are all there in her life, but often her sense of gaiety and joy overrides the unforgivingness of reality. I don't know where she hides her fears, nor how she finds and cherishes herself. It is difficult for an outsider to know how much of her recovery is thanks to intelligence and how much to simply not caring. There seems to be no element of self-pity in her character. She says it is 'the English bit' of her make-up. She finds self-pity 'disgusting'.

'When one knows how to be happy, one knows how to be unhappy. My response to emotional pain is to try to find out why it is so painful and how I am responsible for that pain. In this way I discover a lot.'

This built-in quality of perseverance somehow ignites the devotion of her colleagues, who invariably rally to work on projects with her. Nor should we discount the enduring love of her public, which welcomes her back each time, awarding her all the more accolades for standing up to be counted.

For her, being an actress feeds the woman and being a woman feeds the actress. She needs to keep the one fuelling the other. In common with many people seriously dedicated to their work,

Moreau has had (and still has) little social life. Her work – God forbid you call it 'work' to her face – is her life, and she gladly takes whatever work may still stir a flicker of interest. At the start of the eighties it was to be another record, television shows, more 'famous face' roles that illuminated films which otherwise remained unknown and, at the end of 1980, a play called *L'Intoxe* (The Addict) at the Boulevard Theatre in Paris.

All the forces were moving in the right direction for *L'Intoxe* to be a success. The playwright, Françoise Dorin, was not just a woman after Moreau's own heart, but as it happens she was also born on the same day in the same year as the actress – an important omen for anybody believing in astrology. The play was an outspoken contemporary piece about a headlining radio announcer prone to haranguing those close to her as she worked off her living angst. Jean-Laurent Cochet, a very 'happening' director, was handling the production and Moreau's current favourite couturier, the Norwegian Per Spook, was designing her outfits. It seemed a hand-made vehicle in which to present herself afresh to Parisian audiences.

Fairly quickly, however, Moreau discovered that to plunge nightly (and at matinées in the afternoon too) into such a professional fury of aggression and anger had to take its toll on her private life. 'I did it when I came back from the States after my separation from Friedkin. I thought why not do a boulevard play? My co-star, Jacques Dufilho, is an extraordinary actor. We had a good cast and I enjoyed working with Cochet.

'But there was something in that play I can't explain. I lost my voice, so I went to the American Hospital in Paris for a total check-up. Everybody was very worried. My voice returned and I went back to the theatre. On the third night my voice had gone again. I couldn't do it. I think I had an allergy to that play. It's a difficult play. The first thing when she enters the stage is that she is insulted by everybody. Very demoralising, but an actor doesn't take things like that seriously. I can play La Célestine, a much harder role, for three hours, and everything will be all right with my voice. It was very strange.'

Moreau adds with a naughty gleam in her eye: 'I used the excuse of exhaustion not to do the Coco Chanel film [George Kaczender's *Chanel Solitaire*], even though it would only have meant one day's shoot in Maxim's in Paris. It was total shit. I said I was too tired. One has to be polite.' (That role, Emilienne D'Alençon, was quickly rewritten for Karen Black, who took it over at four days' notice.)

The attrition of her role in *L'Intoxe* continued to wear her down, even more so when audiences found the play depressing. Eight months into the run she dropped out. This was an honourable defeat, however, as she won the Prix Brigadier for her performance. Dorin stepped into the role herself until Danielle Darrieux was ready to take over.

Her co-star, Anne Parillaud, then a young dancer-turned-actress, recalls how deeply she was influenced by Moreau, particularly by her professionalism when things were not going well. 'Jeanne taught me everything about working on stage, about being professional,' she told me, 'and she never gave up, even when she was dropping. You can't imagine the strengths she found.' Parillaud and her mentor were to co-star again in the films *Nikita* and *Map of the Human Heart* a decade later.

Moreau now stepped back from acting. Even though her body was worn out, her voice still had that stimulatingly caressing rasp which curled syllables into submission. For some time she had had a *coup de coeur* over the work of the Belgian poet Norge (real name Georges Mogin), now deceased, whom she had first encountered with his portrait artist wife, Denise Perrier, in Saint Paul de Vence.

'I met him only because of his poetry and it was an extraordinary encounter. I loved his poems and decided I had to sing them. I contacted my friend, the composer Philippe Gérard, who had collaborated with poets like Boris Vian, Louis Aragon and Paul Eluard.'

They took the project to her music producer, Jacques Canetti, who brought out a double album of her singing Norge's poems. It won her the Charles Cros prize.

'It's not obligatory to like Jeanne's voice,' says the elderly Canetti in his Corbusier-designed apartment on the edge of Paris in Saint Cloud. 'But there are not many women's voice discs that sell a hundred thousand copies. She was selling that years ago. It's a very interesting voice. You know it's her immediately you hear it. Somehow it is so personal, as you listen you hear this almost one-to-one extension of her character, exclusively from her to you.

'I first heard her sing in *Jules et Jim*. I rang Truffaut and asked him to give me the rights to "*Le Tourbillon*". At the time I was working as a director for Phillips and we made the record. It was an overnight success.

'When I went freelance, Jeanne stayed with me and our relationship became very profitable, both for her and for me. Her album *Jeanne Moreau* is still immensely popular. It has sold much more than a hundred thousand which, even today, is exceptional.'

Meanwhile, across the ocean on Broadway, an actress called Elinor Jones was performing nightly in her play entitled *What Would Jeanne Moreau Do?*. In this work Moreau is the idol of a fictitious character who always asks herself the title question before she attempts anything. Her hopes are of making herself as 'worldly-wise', 'profound' and 'intelligent' as her idol.

I do not know how Jeanne Moreau answers that particular question in her own life, but the following quote is quite illuminating: 'I've always thought of life as work. You have a certain amount of time given to you and you have to find dedication, passion, concentration. You have to cultivate yourself and be fruitful. I sometimes feel like someone who owns a piece of land and does not use the seasons properly.'

Whichever way her metaphorical crops were growing at the time of that quote, they had not escaped the notice of Bavarian-born director Rainer Werner Fassbinder of the German New Wave. One of the best of the *wunderkind* 'garage' film-makers, he was a prolific director. He could shoot a film in two weeks and then have it taken seriously enough to provoke barbed responses, while luring big audiences as well. Part of the Wenders-Handke set, he was also the first German director with whom Moreau would work. She was very taken by the German New Wave and knew several of the main activists as friends.

'As soon as there's a New Wave somewhere my doorbell rings and there they are,' she laughs. 'I'd feed them, read their scripts and send them down to my country place to work. I had some young German film-makers at Le Préverger for about six months once.'

Fassbinder and Moreau had met at the Berlin Film Festival when he was presenting his *Veronika Voss*. He had invited her to a party in a smoky brasserie where everybody was speaking German, which she did not follow. When he disappeared into the crowd, Moreau left, going back to her hotel. A few weeks later he rang and asked her to be in his next film, *Querelle*. She said yes, and Fassbinder had to put his project on hold while he waited for Moreau to complete her third film with Joseph Losey, *La Truite* (*The Trout*), based on Roger Vailland's novel.

Losey had wanted to make it in English, with Bardot, and as early as in the sixties. Instead he was to make it in French with Isabelle Huppert, and in the eighties. For him Moreau played the rejected wife of the businessman (Jean-Pierre Cassel) in thrall to '*la truite*' (Huppert – an actress Moreau remarks always seems to be 'naked, half-naked or almost naked' on the screen).

A curious film, *The Trout* is set mainly in the Jura where Huppert's character, Frédérique, is the daughter of a trout-breeder. Some scenes are set in Japan where she ultimately sets up the most advanced trout hatchery. The film has little to do with fish, however, and plenty to do with the ambiguous games of seduction. Frédérique herself is somewhat asexual, being married to a homosexual, but she lures herself a heterosexual lover whose wife protects her.

A typically dark Losey film, *The Trout* has not been treated kindly by time and now seems to have lost some of its sexual poignancy. However, when it first came out it did cause something of a flurry. When it was presented at the 1982 Venice Film Festival, some members of the audience were offended, particularly by one of Moreau's lines: 'Homosexuality and heterosexuality mean nothing. Either you're sexual or you're not.' It seems amazing only a decade on, now that human sexuality is more of an open book, that something so straightforward should have caused such upset.

'It's not by accident that this line was given to me. It was floating over the film and Joe didn't know what to do with it,' Moreau told the American magazine, *Interview*, while she was there on a promotional trip. 'He asked me if I could say it in the film and I said yes. It is something that I deeply feel. It's so true and so lucid that I'm surprised people might be offended by it.'

If the Losey film was one that dealt with confused middle-class heterosexuality, Moreau's next project dealt in strong strokes with defined, intense homosexuality. If the Venice audiences found her words in *The Trout* shocking, then heaven help their shock-absorbers if they crossed the road to see *Querelle*, the 'other' Jeanne Moreau film presented at that year's festival. Even the *vaporetti*, it seems, were stunned into silence by *Querelle*.

A supremely stylised, hypnotically sordid dockside drama of homosexual lust and death, *Querelle* was the film which jolted her supporters back to the memory of the fiery, piquant, ground-breaking Moreau. Based on the 1947 novel *Querelle de Brest*, this was Moreau's second Jean Genet film, and also the last film to be made by Fassbinder, who died of an overdose of cocaine and sleeping pills, aged thirty-six, a few weeks after finishing it. With his untimely death, it fell to Moreau, rather than to any of the other actors, to promote the film.

Brad Davis (of *Midnight Express*) plays Querelle, the sailor who steals, smuggles, prostitutes himself and finally commits murder. Franco Nero plays his chief, Seblon, a lieutenant on his ship who yearns for him to submit. In the single female role, Moreau is Madame Lysiane, the ageing and insatiable proprietress of the La Feria brothel overlooking the harbour.

She sees Lysiane as a Utopian definition of 'the woman', the ultimate 'Virgin Mary'. 'On the first day of shooting, they told me on the phone that I was in fact the Virgin Mary. That wasn't in the script and, as I hadn't had any fittings, I didn't know what my costume was. When I arrived at the studio there was a beautiful white dress with white lace and, on the top of that, all the jewels of the woman that owns the brothel. That was quite a surprise to me.'

I see her as a woman still hungry for sexual appreciation at a meal where tastes are sated by homosexual confection. In the grand scheme of things, however, any man who wants Madame Lysiane must first roll the dice with her giant black husband, Nono (Günther Kaufmann). If he wins, he gets Lysiane; if he loses, Nono gets *him*. In the story, Querelle loses – yet he also wins.

As Lysiane, Moreau is sultry, sexy and as gravelly as ground granite. When she closes in on Querelle, she is empress and she is victim, as tough as she is frail, once again the flashing span of emotion that first so attracted Louis Malle moving across her face with split-second timing.

She says the world of Querelle was not one she knew about. She

has known many gay men, but they were mainly writers and artists –
none of them were sailors. 'I used to know a lot of gay writers published by Gallimard. They used to meet in my dressing-room when
I was doing *Pygmalion* and the Cocteau play [*La Machine Infernale*]. I
got to know André Gide in the last months of his life. Genet lived
very close to where I lived; he'd come and pick me up and we'd have
supper together. Later I made *Mademoiselle*, based on his script.'
Moreau also narrated a TV documentary, called *Jean Genet, Saint,
Martyr and Poet*, directed by Guy Gilles, in 1975.

When asked by Duncan Fallowell of *Time Out* if she had ever had
an affair with a homosexual, she replied: 'Well, I lived five years with
Pierre Cardin . . . he wasn't exclusively homosexual, because he lived
with me. I'm not interested in people's sexuality. I don't give a damn
which way they enter the world of sexuality. One is either sexual or
one is not. But it is better to be homosexual than to have dead sexuality.

'If you transformed Querelle into a woman and told the story
from the viewpoint of another heterosexual relationship, it would
work equally well,' reckoned Moreau. 'Because when you speak of
sexuality most people expect physical sex, but sexuality starts in the
mind with the imagination, and that is what Fassbinder, for the first
time in *Querelle*, served by consolidating an already existing artistic
bond.'

Querelle's subject – the homosexual outcast and monster living on
the margins of society – obsessed both Genet and Fassbinder in
turn. Although for Moreau it must have been a fragile matter being
part of the realisation by a German director of a fantasy by a French
writer, she never felt that the film was designed to be particularly
revolutionary, or even about sex.

'I think Fassbinder just wanted to talk about his obsession and that
obsession happened to coincide with Genet's. The idea of being a
thief, a murderer, a traitor – as an outcast, a homosexual – is seen as
an intellectual way of dealing with the situation.

'Like all directors he was totally obsessed by his work. It was fan-
tastic to work with him, because there was no hesitation, no fooling
around. Of course everybody knew he was leading a crazy life,' she
said loyally. 'Working like mad with only two or three hours' sleep
at night, he used to drink and take drugs, I don't know which, and

he was burning out his life. He was found dead one morning in front of his television and amongst all his pieces of paper. He was holding a pen because he was getting ready to start shooting another film.

'I was attracted to working with him because of his films and because of his violent point of view. To me he seemed like a person torn apart by many conflicts. When he called me for *Querelle*, I said yes immediately. I'd read the book but didn't remember a thing about it and didn't have time to read the script before I arrived in Berlin to film. When I saw the drawings for the costumes, I realised that I was to be Dietrich-like. I also sang the theme song. ['Everybody Kills the Thing He Loves'].

'I had a mysterious and fascinating experience with him, but without words. Why not? That can be the ideal relationship. While we were shooting he did not talk to me very often. The only time I ever asked what he wanted of me in a scene, he said, "Be excellent." I thought that was fair enough. We had a very intimate feeling between us. A complicity. From the start he knew I could give him something that he wanted. He didn't know exactly what, and nor did I, but it happened. Fassbinder knew very well what he was doing when he cast me in this film.

'I called him my "unknown dancer". Let's compare it to being in a dance hall, waiting to be asked to dance, and a stranger, a foreigner, comes up and asks you. You start and he's marvellous. To work in this film was for me like dancing. I enjoyed the dance, I enjoyed the film!'

With her provocative smile, she adds: 'Britain was the last country to give *Querelle* a certificate. It even had to be cut before they'd screen it.'

As soon as she had finished work on *Querelle*, Moreau came to London for a live *Guardian* question-and-answer session on the stage of the National Film Theatre, at the time *L'Adolescente* was showing. She arrived from Paris *sans entourage*, with Brad Davis in tow, and stayed at Claridges, where she was apparently thrown out of the bar for wearing trousers!

The *Guardian* interview was chaired by Don Allen, the broadcaster and author of *Finally Truffaut*. Moreau was in a flirty mood, *that* voice in full husk. In the audience was her sister Michelle and her nephew and niece, Michael and Danielle.

'I found her really quite hot to handle,' says Allen. 'The good interviewer knows his role is to press the right button and let the star take over. With Jeanne Moreau the right note was one of flirtatious banter, with lots of opportunities for her to take over, score points and "direct" the interview. The audience had fun and so did we. The John Freeman or Anthony Clare approach would be left for another time.'

He asked if she saw herself, as she had been typecast in many of her films, as a *femme fatale*. She laughed seductively, rolling her eyes. 'Of course I don't see myself as a *femme fatale*. It's difficult for me to share that impression. You want to provoke me?'

When Allen paused briefly, after starting a question with: 'Can I ask you . . .?', with a quick, seductive giggle Moreau chipped in: 'Please do – nothing will stop him!'

They talked about her long, varied career. Clearly for her the cinema was still what Truffaut called 'a magical industry', something to bring a little pleasure to life. 'Let's not talk about changing the world or packing a message in films. Let's try to help people to feel good, entertain them.

'I've never been unhappy with my films or the way my performance has gone, because I don't go and see my films. An actress shouldn't see her films. When you create a character you have your own world. It's something else, it's dream life. I like to embody other people's dreams.'

When asked if she had become jaded from so long in the business, she declared robustly: 'No, I'm not jaded. Of course not, can you imagine! I can't imagine that any people in the industry could be jaded.' Then she paused and repeated the word. '"Jaded" – what does that mean?'

Throughout the session she flirted blatantly, laughing her throaty, smoked-roughened laugh and feeding outrageous come-on lines. Despite generally giving Allen a hard time when he made references to her being a female director or a female actor ('Oh come on, I'm a human being, aren't I?') she never ducked a question. She just defused the ones that did not interest her by delivering a brief, unpremeditated lecture on some intangible subject, like the subconscious or the meaning of life.

Allen was to find this a frequent pattern in future interviews.

'Jeanne Moreau is someone I admire and respect. She's been there, done everything, usually in the fast lane and *jusqu'au bout*. Her views on life may not be wildly original, but at least they are hers, and she certainly takes them and herself seriously enough to ensure that they receive attention. Never an airhead bimbo – the phrase didn't exist when she was in her prime – Moreau is perhaps the French version of the thinking man's mature crumpet.'

With Moreau there are no indiscreet questions, only indiscreet answers. She loves provocative lines and knows how to deliver them. She may not be trying to change society, but *sans doute* she enjoys shaking it up a little, her head tilted coquettishly, eyebrow raised in a question-mark.

17

℀

**'I see life as a voyage and death as a natural accident in the
whole life of the universe.'**

After *Querelle* in 1982 Jeanne Moreau did not make another feature
film for four years.

It is difficult to find a hook on which to hang this off-screen
period, for she remained active with many things, but there is not
that much to show for it. As regards acting, more projects fell
through – like playing Sarah Bernhardt on Broadway, for example –
than came to fruition.

'This was a nice idea, based on the correspondence between
Bernhardt and Françoise Sagan. The original director wanted it done
as two ladies sitting on stage on chairs, reading the letters,' explains
Moreau. 'I said that I loved being on stage, but I'd hate to sit on a chair
and read a letter. I love movement. Then they didn't have a script.
Florence Malraux and Françoise were working on one. By the time the
project was ready I was not free any more. I might still do it. Why not?'

Meanwhile, she travelled extensively for the first time, simply
being herself, living the part of the star. She graced many occasions
where crowds of acolytes floated in and out of her orbit. Michael
York recalls sharing a stage with her at one such occasion, a tribute
to the Palace Theatre in 1983 in New York.

'We were part of a variety show called *Parade of Stars*, staged by Alex Cohen, who used to do the Emmy Awards and knew everybody. I think Jeanne and I did our sketch before George Burns, but after Raquel Welch. We did an excerpt from *Phèdre* in French. I was playing Hippolyte or somebody – I forget now exactly who I was – and Jeanne was playing the divine Sarah playing Phèdre. She was basically just playing the divine Jeanne! Although I only had this tiny connection with her, we had a brief but pertinent time together. As far as I was concerned, it was a dream that came out of the blue.'

She attended plenty of film festivals: New York, where she had two films in 1982, *L'Adolescente* and *The Trout*; the French Film Festival in Sarasota and then Tokyo and Vancouver. In Berlin she was president of the jury as she was at the festival in New Delhi and in Toronto. She toured some of the universities of the US and of Japan, giving courses, and, on the invitation of Italian leading man Vittorio Gassman, taught theatre and Pirandello to the drama students of Florence.

She also started to consolidate herself on the small screen. She was head of the TV festival held in Monte Carlo, having just devised and presented a huge series on the great Hollywood stars for Radio Monte Carlo. These Hollywood star programmes helped to push her towards forming her own production company.

Moreau had written a script of Drieu de la Rochelle's novel about men, *Beloukia*. This she wanted to direct in Morocco. She had another script on the stocks, called *Desires*, co-written with the American author Jim Harrison. It was also about men, and the intrigues of male society, and she wanted to direct it in Australia, which she had recently visited for a film that never came off. She hoped the lead role of this one might suit Robert De Niro. Nothing came of either project, but nevertheless her own Capella Films was founded in mid-1982.

She formed Capella with producer and friend Klaus Hellwig. Their first project was to make seven 16-millimetre TV profiles on actresses, called *Seven Stars Plus One*. (It is obvious who the 'plus one' would be.) The first and only one they completed was a fifty-six-minute TV film on Moreau's heroine of old, Lillian Gish.

'I am very drawn to the destiny of women film stars,' she told me.

'I'm fascinated by the cinema and I want to discover more about the American film industry and its history. I went all over the country for tributes on Gish. Bette Davis had agreed to make a film with me, and so had Ava Gardner. I also managed to approach Greta Garbo, who wouldn't have appeared but would have spoken over the film.'

Other actresses on whom she wanted to focus were Liz Taylor, Faye Dunaway, Meryl Streep, Jane Fonda and Jessica Lange, but Capella collapsed when Hellwig died unexpectedly.

'He had a tumour on the brain. It was a terrible shock. He was an extraordinary man, who'd produced Resnais' *Providence*, and was a wonderful partner. Sadly our series was no more.'

For many years after Capella Moreau had no company of her own, until she formed Spica Productions in 1992. Spica is a star in the constellation of Virgo which, she says, is represented by a sheaf of wheat and symbolises fertility. She drew the logo on the company's letterhead, a simple wheatsheaf encircled by an 'S'. Today she is agentless and conducts all her business through this company, which she runs with her long-time assistant, Armelle Oberlin, out of a pleasant little office in one of the grand, marble-lined buildings on Boulevard Haussmann.

The Spica office, which I visited recently, adjoins the offices of producer Bruno Pesary's Arena Films (Pesary is chairman of Spica). It has that timeless Moreau touch to it: a balcony full of flowering plants and a view through the mansard window over Paris as Pissarro painted it. My eyes strayed across the desk in search of colourful trivia . . . and spotted a letter to Moreau, dated 1963, from the company of Serge Silberman, the producer of *The Diary of a Chambermaid*. This outlined her contractual details for the film. Not wishing to invade her privacy any further, I forced myself to look away but remained angry with myself for the rest of the day because it looked so fascinating.

But then a deep and awesome sense of history, the sense that comes in the presence of artistes who have stood the course, swept me up. My reaction was gratitude that, unlike many of her colleagues, Jeanne Moreau herself was still around to recount the tales of what had gone before.

★

Moreau's interest in the workings of the cinema was now rekindled by a television series made by Canal Plus about the magic of the cinema. The series was called *Les Ateliers du Rêve* (Dream Studios).

Centring on the major film studios of the world, it also explained some of the secrets of cinematic special effects. For example, surrounded by blobs of polyester, Moreau demonstrates how 'snow' is made; swirled up in flames thrown by gas taps, she stands surrounded by fire; lashed by raindrops from overhead pipes, she emerges undampened by rain.

She made several more films for television during the mid-eighties. All were interesting projects and two were for British television.

Her first BBC film was *Vicious Circle*, based on the play *Huis Clos* written by Jean-Paul Sartre in 1944. She took the role of Inès, the lesbian who will go as far as murder and drives her friend to suicide, because it was a little out of the ordinary for her and because she wanted to work with Omar Sharif. Cherie Lunghi and Nickolas Grace co-starred, with Kenneth Ives directing.

Grace recalls: 'There was a kind of diplomatic hierarchical battle between Omar and Jeanne each night about who would pay for supper. They'd never let me pay. They both were exceedingly generous. Omar loved going out to supper every night because he wanted someone to come back and help him learn his lines, but Jeanne used to go off and do her lines herself.'

Says Moreau of her role: 'Inès was very powerful and very new to me. She's a lesbian and a woman devoured by that destructive drive towards the people she loves. She pushed her husband under a tram and drove her lesbian accomplice to suicide. It's so raw and brutal, as the characters have nothing to lose as they're dead.'

I murmur something about the role being a risqué one. She throws her hands up in the air to admonish me. 'Risky perhaps, but never risqué. My life has never been risqué. It was just the way journalists translate it. My life is too exciting to be risqué.' Those lips pout and she gives another Gallic shrug. 'You see, it takes time to learn to open up to life.'

Back in France for Antenne 2 she made *L'Arbre* (The Tree) for Jacques Doillon, now a major French mainstream director (and husband of Jane Birkin). Then in 1985 she appeared in an episode of Nadine Trintignant's series, *Le Tiroir Secret* (The Secret Drawer), with Michèle Morgan and Marie-France Pisier. Moreau played the 'other' wife of Morgan's disappeared husband. (She and Morgan were both honoured as Commanders of Arts and Letters that year.)

L'Arbre was a sombre little film, really, about death, with Moreau playing a grandmother who, together with her granddaughter (Julie Jézéquel), was exploring the one event that joined them: the death of the one's daughter, the other's mother. Death has always been a subject Moreau has confronted in interviews as a sort of obvious result of life. Not for her the fear of dying or the terror of what may wait when life ends. As a non-practising Catholic, she is not afraid of the end but she does comment that no matter when it comes, it will be a little too soon. She feels that she will always need a few more years to be 'clean enough to go on the other side and to improve myself'. 'I'd like to arrive at my final moment with my little parcel of life neatly packaged, well tied up.'

She finds enthralling reading in the *Tibetan Book of the Dead* about traditional local ceremonies preparing people for death, and has developed her ideas after years of reading philosophical and psychological tomes.

'Nothing starts or stops at one specific moment. The older you get, the more you realise that everything is the fruit of what you are. I'll die, *ageing* – what a word, in French I would never use it – like everybody else, but whether I die at seventy-five or at eighty-five, I know I'll die young.

'I've had great agonies and violent helplessness. I had a period when I lived without opening the curtains, when light was unbearable, and so was the idea of waking up. But I always felt that physical death doesn't stop suffering, and the torments are even greater when you feel that if you die they won't end. It's not true that it's a big sleep.

'With the passing of old friends, like Orson, Luís, François and Joseph, the landscape of my life changed, but I did not mourn for long. [François Truffaut died while she was making *The Last Seance* in 1984. The year before Luís Buñuel and Joseph Losey had died, and the year afterwards the world lost Simone Signoret and Orson Welles.] People are alive as long as you think of them and continue to be influenced by them. They are strongly alive in my daily life.

'I see life as a voyage and death as a natural accident in the whole life of the universe. I think that's why I'm so fascinated by planetaria –

they're the closest thing to eternity, things that go on and on, cosmic movements that are larger than human life.'

Digging deeply into her own feelings about life after death, she made *The Last Seance* for Granada Television. It was shot in the studios in Manchester, directed by June Wyndham-Davies, and was based on an Agatha Christie story. Moreau plays Madame Exe, a woman who would sacrifice anything or anyone to make contact with her dead daughter. Once again she causes a death, this time to the medium involved (played by Norma West).

Moreau took the part, she said, because the story had uncanny links with her own memories of mediums. It was set in 1933, in fact the year Moreau began accompanying her maternal grandmother, Elizabeth Buckley, on a trail of seances held around northern England.

'My uncle, Grandmama's twenty-five-year-old son Jack, had drowned off the coast of Liverpool. She had such grief that she was driven on a long but unsuccessful quest to get in touch with him, to bid him farewell. A medium told her that I had psychic gifts myself, so perhaps she thought that by taking me she would have a better chance. The experiences were vivid, but I was never once frightened.

'I was told that I would be able to have visions, maybe even of Jack, if I concentrated on a bunch of flowers or on a glass of water, but my mother forbade it. She was very against it. I never worked on it and I don't want to. I would say that sometimes I have had premonitions as the years go by. Let's put it this way, I know I have a very sure instinct. I wonder if that doesn't come with a certain knowledge and experience. We know that words mean one thing, but beyond the words people sometimes express something else. I feel that I know in what state people are. They don't even have to speak to me about it. It's intuition.

'I am very superstitious, something I *did* get from my Irish grandmother. I can tell the Tarot cards – with chilling accuracy, according to friends – and I used to worry about omens. When I was young I invented a foretelling game, so that I could worry about the future . . .'

I remember her in Cannes that year, 1985, when she had single-handedly organised a very personal memorial event for Truffaut in the festival's Palais. A tiny woman dressed in brilliant red, she stood just out of the spotlight ('the spotlight belongs to Truffaut'). A documentary *Vivement Truffaut!* (*Deeply Truffaut!*), compiled as a homage by Claude de Givray, Truffaut's co-scriptwriter and old friend from their fifties *Cahiers* days, was shown and then more than two dozen of his performers gathered on stage to share his spotlight and say a few words about the man. In her moments dedicated to Truffaut, Moreau managed to crystallise the New Wave, its passion and the energy that had powered it.

At the end there was a thunderous standing ovation. Everyone on stage posed for a 'family portrait', containing his wife Madeleine, daughters Eva (named after Losey's film) and Laura (named after Otto Preminger's), his lover Fanny Ardant, Deneuve, Depardieu, Brialy, Aznavour, Bisset, Léaud, Fossey and too many others to list.

As Moreau strengthened her English roots she also had to sever some of her very deepest French ones. In 1984 she sold Le Préverger to the designer Laura Ashley. She could no longer cope with the responsibility of maintaining it.

Saddened to the quick of her soul, Moreau closed the Mistral blue doors and shutters on that chapter of her life. She bade Anna and Louis farewell, as they left to start a new life in the Pyrénées. So many of her friends there had died or gone away; so much of the spirit of place there had altered. Regrets, she says, she has none . . . but they were there, flickering like a candle constantly on the point of extinction.

'There comes a time when you realise something is over. I no longer wanted to worry about a *maison secondaire*. For me to rent a flat in Paris and spend my free time travelling abroad, instead of going to my country home, seemed to be the right way to live. I felt the need to go to other countries, back to America or to Japan, to meet the people, to see how they live, hear what they think. I discovered that wherever I went, if I felt I was in the right place at the right moment, doing the right thing with the right people, it didn't matter where I was. It could be in Greece, in a hotel in Tokyo or Russia. It didn't matter. I feel like a citizen of the world. I'm very lucky because wherever I go, people know about me. They've seen things I've done, they invite me, and so I feel really related to the world.'

One of her first odysseys was indeed to the United States, where she was finally to make her stage debut on Broadway in a revival of Tennessee Williams' *The Night of the Iguana*. Originally she had been invited to play Maxine, the role Bette Davis made her own on stage in 1961 and which Ava Gardner played in the John Huston film of 1964. But Maxine was still considered 'too American' for Moreau. Instead she took the other lead role, Hannah Jelkes, the spinster with spiritual aspirations not satisfied by materialism.

The production opened, as Broadway plays do, for a trial run 'in the provinces', in this case in Baltimore at the Morris A. Mechanic Theatre. As Moreau was a huge star in the States, the New York and Washington critics rushed over to review it. They saw it, did not like it and said so. They particularly hated Moreau's accent. She got the worst reviews of her life. It ran from 15 October and closed right there on 9 November 1985.

'What went wrong with *Iguana* was a combination of different things,' she says. 'I don't want to reject any responsibility in it because surely I have responsibility towards it. Basically four weeks' rehearsal was not long enough, and anyway one of those weeks was dedicated to the lights. The director, Arthur Sherman, was not strong enough for that adventure. My co-star, Michael Moriarty, is a very strong actor but not a generous man. It was the first time in my life I rehearsed with an actor who had his earphones on listening to music while rehearsing with fellow actors. Eileen Brennan, who was also in the play, wanted to stop. I felt so frustrated and should have said at the beginning that I thought there was something wrong, but being a foreigner . . .

'The man from the *Washington Post* was right. The production, still cutting its teeth, was raw, unready and with acoustics so bad it was hard to hear what anyone was saying. It was not good. I don't mind talking about *Iguana* because it taught me a lot of things – how to deal with feelings of inadequacy in front of an audience, to work with a sense of frustration during rehearsals, to cope with the feeling that somewhere was the real show and we were not there. It confirmed to me that professionalism is vital. You cannot joke with human emotions. With works of art like writing by Tennessee Williams, you have to go deep, deep, deep.'

Moreau packed her bags and left Baltimore. There is no doubt that she had believed the play would run and transfer to Broadway, for she had arranged an apartment swap with Joan Buck, who wanted to spend some time in Paris.

'She stayed in my flat as planned,' says Buck. 'When I returned I found she had given my life a "deep cleansing". My apartment was perfect, filled with the sort of harmonious, serene atmosphere Jeanne manages to put into a place. She had carefully wrapped all my "wrong" china and put it at the back of the linen cupboard and stacked all my towels intelligently. She'd bought certain things she felt I should have, like a certain sort of cooking pot from Le Creuset, and left that magic Jeanne scent behind. My apartment had never felt so comforting or so serene.

'Staying in her apartment in Rue de l'Université was very poignant. It was a very private place, Jeanne's retreat. Every door was painted a different colour, all in sunset tones. Each door had a thick curtain over it. It was very subtle, very eccentric, very Aquarian. A mysterious number of silent Filipinos would come in and clean. The air was fragrant from scented candles. In the bathroom there were bottles of rare eaux de cologne, left for me to use.

'She had just a few pieces of furniture, small pieces from the sixties, a pouffe, small leather ottomans. There was very little furniture – a kind of luxurious simplicity, but underneath was the suggestion of starkness. The tiny guest-room was the library. The other, tiny, bedroom was her office, with a simple trestle table and high chair. Her bed was in the biggest room, the drawing-room. I'd lie in it thinking of the scope of her talent, her life and soul. Every so often her private line next to the bed would ring and wake me. Orson Welles died that fall while she was in New York. Half the world rang to tell Jeanne, and I answered. Fielding the calls about Welles all through the night was a strange, dislocating experience.'

18

ℳ

**'I decided my glass would always be half full, never
half empty.'**

By 1986, when she was called back to the big screen, Moreau had
become the proverbial legend in her own lifetime. If one watches her
most recent films, one sees how she had also moved into the older
woman fuller figure roles. A woman on the threshold of sixty, she
was now showing the 'metaphysical death' she had experienced after
the Friedkin marriage. There was still that great, blazing joy the
camera catches in her, but there was now a deep Celtic sadness, a
quality of melancholy. It must also be said that many of the Jeanne
Moreau films of that time had slipped through the international
screen's net, as it were, like undersized fish, and her loyal fans had to
make do with revivals of her greatest old films in repertory.

She was there, but not really there.

For all concerned it was a relief when, towards the end of the
eighties, there began to develop a sort of revival of her status and her
name. There were retrospectives at home in Quimper, abroad at
London's French Institute and later in Lausanne. She was invited to
join the Académie des Arts et Techniques du Cinéma (1986–1988),
France's version of America's Academy Awards and the body behind
the Césars. She went to Japan to shoot a documentary on Renoir for

Japanese TV, which she followed up with programmes on Cézanne and Gauguin the following year.

While French TV was in pre-production on their own film, *Jeanne Moreau: Mystère et Beauté* (Jeanne Moreau: Mystery and Beauty), she was at last offered a few solid, well-developed roles in substantial films. Against all odds, the *tourbillon* of her life was gusting up another little New Wave for her, pushing back the grey sea of disconsolation that had recently begun lapping on her shores.

Not all the films were remarkable, breathtaking prize-winners, but they were the sort of creditable films that were right for her, and with major roles for her, not just cameos.

One was *Le Paltoquet*, a surrealist comedy with Buñuelian over-tones. The *paltoquet* (pompous fool) of the title (Michel Piccoli) works in Jeanne Moreau's bar, where a group of gamblers (Daniel Auteuil, Richard Bohringer, Philippe Léotard, Claude Piéplu) and a local prostitute (Fanny Ardant) are called upon to help a detective (Jean Yanne) in a murder enquiry. A million miles from the regular French *policier* genre pictures, this one, as directed by the outrageous Michel Deville, is chic and elegantly playful.

It also shows Moreau at her outrageous best, looking joyfully, eccentrically at home with her new peers – the fresh faces of France's second wave – like Auteuil and Bohringer. A joy to watch, she is once again throbbing with life as the sexy licensee, steeped in cyni-cism, pickled in alcohol but never drunk, with her *je m'en foutisme* – her shoulder-shrugging, devil-may-care attitude – sharply and irrev-erently intact.

'When Michel [Deville] approached me, he made it clear that I could invent my own physical personality for the role, so I did. I thought the cast was absolutely exceptional. I wanted so much to be part of this adventure with them. It is so rare that a film unites the best actors of a country on an equal footing.'

She made the Deville film back-to-back with one directed by Michel Drach, called *Sauve Toi, Lola*. This film too is somewhat surreal, not visually this time, but psychologically. The core subject is cancer and Drach's treatment of it is unexpectedly light. Lola (Carole Laure) is a Parisian lawyer dying of cancer. Moreau, a heavy-drinking ambassador's wife, meets her at the Cancer Club. Her first appearance on screen, gaunt and in a frightful wig, comes as a jolt.

She looks like a parody of Liz Taylor on a bad day at the Grand Guignol. The film is full of *One Flew Over the Cuckoo's Nest* touches, showing Moreau in an unhinged, positively unrecognisable light, not only burping but farting as well. The action that is to become statutory in the later Moreau films – the kiss from the younger man to the older woman – is also firmly in evidence.

Her third role in 1986 was due to be as another alcoholic, but was changed at her request to that of a pious woman believing in miracles. *Le Miraculé*, a comedy directed by Jean-Pierre Mocky, is not only a glorious send-up of the French hospital system, but also a brazen look at French society in general. The story concerns an old chap (Jean Poiret) who simulates paralysis after an accident to claim the insurance. With his dumb friend (Michel Serrault) and Moreau, he then goes on a pilgrimage to Lourdes where he is 'cured' by a miracle, thus not losing his claim money but able to function normally again. It is really the Poiret and Serrault Show, with Moreau as the foil for their jokes, but the film has an old-fashioned charm and irreverence that suits them all.

Moreau's main concern with her films at this time seems to be the plight of older women in their society. 'I don't accept the conventions for women over forty: that they are unkissable and that they all drink too much and are neurotic. In the scenarios of the Drach, the Deville and the Mocky films, all the women I was playing were meant to be alcoholics. I didn't think it brought anything to the roles and I made them get rid of it as a defining characteristic.'

The women-over-forty-not-being-kissable prejudice she sorted out herself. With her history as the older woman to the younger man, it is absolutely right that she should have rooted for it to go. She has never balked at the issue in print – 'She's older now, so she fucks less, is conventional, unconscious attitude towards women,' she pointed out to Mark Ginsburg in *Interview*. She was not going to dodge the issue on screen, either.

When asked if she had indeed had an affair with a much younger man, she replied: 'Oh yes, but I never thought about their ages, nor they about mine. When I was forty-four I lived for three years with a young man, a French boy, whom I met when he was nineteen. Now he's married and has children and his wife is charming. But we had a great love affair. I think of love like the *fin de siècle* heroines of

French literature, who so often exclaimed: *Je me suis donnée!* [I have given myself!] Love is love, you give yourself, you don't carry your ages in front of your eyes. I know we were so involved with ourselves that we didn't think about each other's ages.'

'I decided my glass would always be half full, never half empty,' Moreau has often said. With her sudden second wind, brought on perhaps by the realisation that the half empty is only a *soupçon* the other side of half full, she saw her chance for a real comeback and leaped at it. The rewards were spectacular – they are still talking about it in Paris.

She tells the Tale of the Comeback of Jeanne Moreau: 'I'd heard of a German director, Klaus-Michael Grüber, a genius, considered one of the best in the world. He was from the Schaubühne in Berlin and revolutionised the staging of classics in France. He lives mainly in Paris now but works all over Europe doing plays and operas. One day, the then director of the Festival d'Automne in Paris, the late Michel Guy, told me that Mr Grüber would like to work with me. For ten years he'd had in mind a very special play based on the fifth chapter of a novel called *The Irresponsibles* by the Austrian author Hermann Broch. Broch had lived in the United States since the war and died in Chicago in 1951.

'This fifth chapter starts with a woman, a servant – you can't tell her age but she's not young – coming into a room where a man, a house guest in a château, is lying taking his siesta. It's a Sunday afternoon, warm, drawn curtains, but there's a ray of sunlight. She brings into the room a vase which she puts on the table. The man is half asleep. She gradually begins to tell him the story of the house where he is staying and the family who owned it. The story is her own story. She's a girl from the country who has been a servant since the age of thirteen, and she has never talked about it before.

'As the story continues, an incredible tale of crime and passion emerges, but very gently, very calmly, with no shouting or noise. She is embittered and she confesses. When it's finished, after an hour and twenty-five minutes, she goes out. And that's it.'

As Zerline's story unfurled on stage, Moreau would pick up an apple and start to peel it slowly. The story she told is about a baroness who is cold towards her husband, but who responds to a Don Juan's advances, producing a daughter with him, whom Zerline serves. The end of the monologue divulges that Zerline is in love with the betrayed husband. When Moreau, using little more than her singular voice, had finished speaking, the peeled apple was placed back on its plate.

'When Klaus-Michael asked me to do Zerline, I said yes because I'd heard good things of him and I love the stage. But we weren't expecting what happened. It was both a literary and a popular success. The first night was an incredible triumph. I still wonder why. It may be because it deals with very powerful needs and emotions: greed, sexual attraction, hatred, life and death.'

The play, *Le Récit de la Servante Zerline*, opened at Peter Brook's Théâtre Bouffes du Nord, where Moreau emerged like a phoenix from the ashes in her greatest stage triumph since the days of *Cat on a Hot Tin Roof*. By all accounts she rose magnificently to the challenge of a difficult assignment, holding audiences rapt with her recital, eased only by the odd word from her acting partner, Hans Zischler, who sat on the divan, listening to her life, saying no more than a dozen words in all.

There was a splendour in Moreau's quiet ferocity and drive as she conveyed the pride of a woman cheated of her expectations, still the spiritual superior of her social betters. Her whole body seemed to be charged with electricity, radiating a kind of force. People I know who saw her as Zerline still talk about it. The first thing they say is how much they cried, how she moved them.

Her last agent, Georges Beaume — actually the grand master of Parisian agents — says that, as Zerline, Moreau had the quality of Sarah Bernhardt at the turn of the century: 'all voice, presence and charisma'.

'It's something you can't ever learn to acquire. You have it or you don't. Jeanne has,' he said to me, in his office a few minutes' walk from Moreau's apartment. 'In the ten years I was her agent, before she took responsibility for her own affairs, I never saw that "something" leave her. She is like Katharine Hepburn, she lives in a small kingdom of which she is queen. She has what the others don't have.'

From 1986 to 1989 Moreau went on to play Zerline no fewer than 330 times, around France, reviving it in Paris at the Théâtre de l'Atelier, and in eleven countries, including the USSR, Italy, Canada and Germany. In 1988 a sixtieth birthday present to her came in the guise of the Molière Award for Best Actress and the equivalent of an Oscar in Germany as well.

Moreau's chrysalis period was well and truly over.

The Zerline part came at a time when friends say her private life really was in the pits. She was having a sort of delayed and grand menopause. When she started rehearsals, she was apparently a nervous wreck. Things did not go well during the early days, either. Grüber, very particular and very imaginative, is a specific sort of director, and at first she did not understand what he meant. He was a magician and she was one too, but it took a while for their different types of magic to gel. She had an endless cold. She was overweight. She cried easily during rehearsals and just about gave up. So anxious was she, her food would not stay down. She had not yet given up alcohol and was drinking a lot. The character of Zerline was not the character of Jeanne; as other stage characters had done, Zerline, in the rehearsal stage, was dragging her down.

'I think the main problem was that it was difficult for her to play an old woman for the first time,' comments Francis Biras, the designer of the set and of her spartan costume, one that he describes as rather like a nun's outfit – the uniform of an 1890s female domestic. 'She was actually playing a woman older than she was. She dyed her hair very pale yellow rather than have white hair.

'It was a difficult time in her life as well. She was tired, almost ill, and it was an epoch when her career as an international film star was on the slide. Lots of changes were happening in her life. She lost fifteen kilos. I had to alter her costume, take it in by twelve centimetres in the first six months. But it completely revitalised her.'

Says Moreau, well known for her exuberant comment: 'C'est jamais trop tard pour un lifting' [it's never too late for a face-lift] 'Zerline came after the menopause. I lost so much weight playing her that I had un lifting. This lifting was made because of the weight loss. I had a lifting of the eyes a few months after the face one. I didn't want to have everything done at the same time. I can't remember but I think I had an eyelid lifting at the time of Great Catherine, but this one was because of the weight loss. It was an extraordinary time for me. I was very grateful to Klaus-Michael.

'Klaus-Michael is the only person in the world I'd like to work with again, in anything, on stage, on film, whatever. He's an exceptional person. He never gives interviews, doesn't speak to journalists. He never came on tour. The only time I saw him was in Milan, in the Piccolo Teatro, when because of the disposition of the theatre we had to redo the set.'

Unlike the world of film, the theatre still has great roles to offer mature actresses. I asked her how working on stage compares with performances given in front of the camera.

'Well, you use the same devices, but in different ways. In the cinema, you may start with a scene at the end of the story and then the second day you may be involved with a sequence at the beginning. So you have to be very close to your character yet still instinctive. You should never be surprised if a director like Orson Welles comes up with a new scene that isn't even in the script, which is why I don't attach a lot of importance to the script.

'Apart from the script being fragmented, during the six or twelve weeks of shooting a film you are in another world. You make new, very close friends. The outside world doesn't exist. Making a film is like being aboard a ship, except that every day is an emergency. And then there is the aloneness afterwards, the loneliness and the being alone, without the friends you were travelling with.

'Making a film you have to concentrate in a different way. In the cinema you cannot cheat because the camera takes in everything. Your face has to stand up to the constant search and probe of the camera. If you feel you've been weak in one scene showing your character in the future, you can make up for it with another scene shot two days later but relating to something that happens earlier in the film. It sounds very complicated but you have to preserve a very delicate balance all the time. I feel it is best to make a film just for the pleasure of being needed by somebody you admire.

'On the stage, you start and then go on to the end. But the performance grows, it's never the same. Some actors and directors think that rehearsals exist to pinpoint exactly what has to be shown on stage to the audience regularly every night. True, you have to hang on to that, but each time you start, you have to move on, you have to grow with the audience, you have to submit yourself to them. Their attitude may produce in you new feelings and emotions. But ultimately, acting for me is to communicate with people, not to please them.

'So, from the blueprint spread out in front of you at rehearsal, the building grows. You can add a tower, you can add a window, you can shut a window, you can destroy a door, you can build another room. That's how it moves on and on and stays alive. Every night you know you are true to yourself, true to the audience and giving of your best.

'The pleasure of giving life to characters increases. You have to make the most of the extra power you were given at birth to hold the attention of others. The more facets there are to the part you're playing, the more chances you have of existing in their eyes. At first you think about the effect you're having, and then all you have to do is be there. But ultimately success is absolutely important. You must not compromise yourself but if you are not a success, you are not hired again.'

Between seasons as Zerline, in 1987 Moreau made another film. It was for a young director called Antoine Perset and called *La Nuit de l'Océan*. Moreau had herself arranged much of this low-budget Swiss-Spanish production. Jean-Louis Richard had a role in it and the subject matter was close to her heart – a variation on that older woman and younger man story. After all, women over sixty *are* still kissable. The plot also peripherally involved incest.

Moreau plays a bereaved mother of fifty who lives out the realisation of her unconsummated love for her son, lost at sea, with his twenty-five-year-old best friend (played by Pierre-Loup Rajot).

Perset traces his original idea back to an unrelated incident when a friend of his was drowned at sea. Moreau must have had a slight quiver of *déjà vu* from her early days going round with her Irish grandmother trying to make peace with her own drowned boy.

'Jeanne helped me go all the way to deal with and expose the particular taboo of incest between mother and son,' says Perset. 'She brought to the character a powerful sensuality and a depth of feeling in her interpretation which is beyond anything I could have imagined possible.'

Talking to her sister Michelle, by then a freelance writer doing an article for the *Guardian* on location with them in Brittany, Moreau explained her involvement: 'When the film was proposed to me back in 1983, I turned it down flat. Then I went on to try to analyse why my reaction had been quite so violent. It finally came to me that the role was then simply known as "the mother".

'I accepted finally, for the very reasons for which I had refused. I had to confront for myself what it means to be a mother, and the fact of incest in that context. The incestuous situation in the film attracted me very strongly. We read quite frequently in our newspapers reports of fathers abusing their daughters. There is never an inordinate amount of coverage of the fact, and the sentences are usually light. It's more tolerated than condoned. But there is a total refusal, a complete taboo, over a possible act of passion between a mother and a son. In this film there's no direct incest, though. She makes love with her son's best friend.'

This situation linked her frequent point that, if it is considered all right for an older man to have a younger woman as a lover, why is it considered rather distasteful the other way round?

'It is still not an acceptable fact. When the potential distributors saw this film, they were shocked. No distributor wanted to show it. It was too shocking. Can you imagine?

'Women are recognised as sexual creatures only from puberty until menopause, when they can no longer bear children. This attitude has to change and is slowly changing. The realisation is gradually dawning that women in their forties, fifties, sixties, even seventies, live their sexuality, sensuality; pursue their inner lives, their spirituality. There are no limits.'

207

19

℘

'Like every human being I have everything in me – the best and the worst.'

Jeanne Moreau was not free to accept when British director John Schlesinger called to ask her to be in *Madame Sousatzka* (he gave the role to Shirley MacLaine instead). *Zerline* had done Moreau proud, and now she was preparing for another triumph as the extraordinary ancient procuress in a mammoth production of *La Célestine* (*Celestina*).

In the summer of 1989 she began her run as Celestina, the Spanish she-devil in Fernando Rojas' Renaissance tragedy. It was at the Avignon Festival, where she had started in 1951. On stage in the Court of Honour in the Palace of the Popes – apart from the fact that the festival had expanded enormously and some old presences, like Gérard Philipe and Jean Vilar, were sorely missing – not a lot had changed. It felt good for her to be back, especially in a Comédie Française production.

'I still particularly love working on stage. I love rehearsals, I love all the preparation, I love that special time, before going on stage. That time is mine. Nobody disturbs me then. I do my own make-up when I work in the theatre. It takes me about ten minutes. I don't like people I don't know to touch my face and I like to create my own

209

chosen look when I work on stage. Of course it's different working on camera – you need a different kind of making up for that.'

Directed by Antoine Vitez, the production transferred to Paris for the Autumn Festival where, at the Odéon, Moreau as the embodiment of evil in voluminous clothes and with lipstick-gashed mouth continued to get raves. Michael Billington in the *Guardian* wrote: 'She gives off electric sparks; she is predatory, vain, voyeuristic, lewd and earthy;' John Peter in *The Sunday Times*: 'A regal bag-lady who is both mother hen and vulture, dowdy, vigorous and shrewd . . . who triggers off dormant, powerful forces in people.'

When asked if she recognised herself in these descriptions, she said that she recognised the character. 'Like every human being I have everything in me – the best and the worst,' she added enigmatically.

In November 1989, Moreau's mother Kathleen died.

'She was living with my stepfather in a little flat in a retirement home in Brighton, near my sister, who lives there. I had always felt very close to her. She helped me a lot and I think she was proud of me. She used to feel good when I did well and when I was active and doing things, it seemed to give her strength. It came as a great loss to me.'

Life after sixty, is seemed, was accelerating Moreau back into the fast lane.

First she appeared in the title role of a series of six television films based on Jean Giorno's *Ennemonde*, as a wife and mother of nine who falls for a fairground wrestler, finding the real meaning of love. There was an appearance in *Jour Après Jour* for new young director Alain Attal. Then she narrated the Klaus Barbie story, *Hotel Terminus*, for Marcel Ophüls, whom she had known for years.

She put herself briefly back on the international map with her provocative cameo role in Luc Besson's engrossing thriller about a female government assassin, *Nikita* – the film which also introduced Anne Parillaud to a wide audience. Moreau plays the officer of social etiquette and feminine wiles who grooms Nikita, the ex-junkie, into an elegant woman. (Hollywood built up Moreau's role into a much more substantial one in their version of Besson's film, *The Assassin*, in which Anne Bancroft took the Moreau part.)

'There aren't "small roles" for someone like Jeanne, because she is always great,' says Georges Beaume, her agent for this film. 'But Luc didn't dare offer it to her because he felt it was too small a role for her and she'd feel insulted. So I spoke to her on his behalf and found out she was a big Besson fan. "If he wants me, he's got me!" she said without hesitating, and I told him to take it from there.'

Continues Moreau: 'I was on holiday in the Seychelles with my sister when Luc faxed me some drawings and asked me if I wanted him to tell me the story, which he didn't want to do. So I said, "If you don't want to, don't, as long as you explain exactly what you want from me." He replied, "Enjoy your holiday and we'll decide that when we meet," and that's what we did. I think his best quality is his obstinacy. It will take him a long way.

'I didn't know at all who Nikita was, but I could figure out from her appearance in her scenes with me that she had a lot to learn, so I just played it by ear.' (Whether or not Moreau is happy with her performance remains unknown, as she has not seen the film.)

There was another cameo, with her togged up like Mata Hari's grandmother as an exotic woman on a train in a lightweight comedy called *Alberto Express* (directed by Arthur Joffe, son of director Alexandre). As with so many other 'small' films, her name has 'big' billing – and she does get to be kissed by the young hero. It's not a milestone movie, but has a certain curiosity value.

She is kissed in abundance by the younger man in *La Femme Fardée* (The Made-Up Woman), in which she plays a famous cantatrice with whom the novice gigolo, played by Delon's handsome son Anthony, learns his trade during a cruise.

'I liked the novel it was based on [by Françoise Sagan] and the director, José Pinheiro, was my friend. Anthony [Delon] still had a lot to learn but it was a pleasant film to make,' she says, not taking the bait I lay about cross-generational romancing.

Now Moreau was very definitely back on the *premier plan*, magazines rushed again to print stories on her, extolling anew her beauty, her glamour, her talent. There were even features on the places she shops ('*J'adore le Marks et Spencer de Londres*'), the *salons de thé* where she takes the odd *éclair* or *marrons glacés*, the boutiques she favours, now Saint-Laurent Rive Gauche rather than Cardin.

At an age when other women treading the edge of time from the forties through to the nineties might have perhaps assumed a slightly subdued style, she was out there cheering – an extraordinary survivor, looking great, her life back on course. Her joy at having found her footing once again rejuvenated her. She told Joan Buck, who visited her in Paris around that time, that she now felt as she had when she was nineteen or twenty.

'"I have a very juvenile feeling of change and new life," she said. She looked absolutely beautiful, with a fresh, smooth face, as if reborn, and an eager smile like a child on the first day of school holidays,' says Buck.

The '*lifting*' she had had probably helped, but it is remarkable, seeing Moreau's films made at the time, how she truly does seem to have shed decades rather than just years. Unlike her Hollywood sisters, she does not seem to give a damn about these '*liftings*', a subject I had passed sleepless nights over in anticipation of asking the question. She chatted on, unprompted, about going grey and how she loathes wasting time going to the hairdresser's.

'I only go to check the roots. My grey hair grows in a very funny way,' explained Moreau, tilting her head to show me. 'They grow here at the back and, like with men, on the sides – rather like an orthodox priest!'

To mark her revived fortunes, Moreau moved to a new apartment, a large one with windows on all sides and balconies holding a jungle of flowers, roses to the east (the drawing-room), hydrangeas to the west (the kitchen), smelling warmly of musk and wood. In a long square off Rue du Faubourg St Honoré, a stone's throw from the Arc de Triomphe, it is in the old Russian quarter of the sixteenth *arrondissement*. When the wind blows a certain way, she can hear the bells from the Russian Orthodox Church.

I visited her there in her safe, quiet haven filled with vases of exotic flowers. With its wheaty-coloured walls, sky blue ceilings and soft, rough fabrics (mainly from England), there is almost a country feel about it. Most of her collections have been given away, except for the decorative eggs which she no longer collects but which friends still bring her. She has a vast assortment of shoes, packed neatly in stacked shoeboxes. When I first called the entrance hall was piled with film scripts that she had to read for her new job, and her large study was lined with books. She has some lovely paintings and there are a few *objets* from much-loved films, like the clapperboard from *Je m'Appelle Victor* (*My Name is Victor*) and an Aboriginal screen, brought back from filming in Australia. But the general feel is spacious and uncluttered.

The Australian film, *Until the End of the World*, she made for Wim Wenders in 1990. A contemporary of Fassbinder, Wenders is one of the group of German film-makers Moreau has known for some time. All born at the end of the Third Reich and part of the sixties underground circuit, they set up the *Filmverlag der Autoren*, the backbone of the German New Wave. Their collaborations with her have been dotted throughout the second half of her career. Wenders she had known for all of sixteen years before this opportunity arose.

'In *Until the End of the World* I had written a part,' says Wenders, 'for a blind woman who, at the end of her life, was finally able to see. That was a very difficult part to cast, by any standards. I wanted her to be beautiful, and gentle, and wise, and strong, someone of whom you'd believe that she had been in love with her husband (played by Max von Sydow) for a whole lifetime. It wasn't a question of choosing Jeanne for the role. I couldn't have made the film *without* her.'

Her section of this futuristic feature was shot in Australia, where the two main characters – a Parisian (Solveig Dommartin) and the stranger she meets, Sam (William Hurt) – venture on a peculiar pilgrimage. He goes to his mother (Moreau), who lives in the middle of the Australian desert. She goes too, but in search of a new destiny.

Moreau seems to have had problems both with Dommartin, who was trying to find her feet, and with Wenders, Dommartin's boyfriend, who Moreau felt sometimes could not get to grips with problems. Nevertheless, Moreau loved Australia and the Australians loved her back.

One of her co-stars, the Aboriginal actor Ernie Dingo (who plays Burt in the film) told me: 'At the Gold Coast Studios in Brisbane, where they did some production work on the film, people would queue up outside her dressing-room, just to get her autograph.'

Moreau's sixty-second birthday occurred at the other end of the world – at Mosfilm, Moscow's state film studios constructed in a park beside the 'castle' where Stalin once lived. During the Perestroika period, when she was on tour with *Zerline*, a man in the audience had sent her a film script. The author turned out to be Roustam Khamdamov, the long-neglected director originally from Uzbekistan, who had not been permitted to practise film-making in sixteen years.

'He'd written the script and I was the only person he wanted for his film,' explains Moreau. 'The script was translated into French and I read it. I thought it sounded a crazy story but I had some free time and said I was willing to do it. Of course, they couldn't pay me, but I said it didn't matter, we'd see about that in the future. They really and truly didn't have money, not even enough to house and feed me. So we had to find a co-producer. I discussed it with a great many people but they all turned it down. They said I was being unreasonable.'

Eventually the man who had backed her in *Chambermaid* so many years before, Serge Silberman, then seventy-three years old, guaranteed twenty-five per cent of the budget (about £600,000), some technical help and 16,000 metres of film in return for distributing the completed work in Europe. Originally a civil engineer, he turned producer after the Second World War. Moreau says he is a man who is ready to take risks.

'After Jeanne told me about the film and about Roustam, I saw a short film he'd made, read a synopsis of the new story and saw several shots made of it earlier in black and white,' said Silberman. 'I decided to take a minority share in the production with Mosfilm.'

Moreau took the job as 'the star' and was received as a star indeed. Danièle Heymann of *Le Monde* described her arrival: 'At the airport in Moscow a whale on wheels with tinted windows came to fetch her. She was assured that this doddering limo once transported Stalin himself.'

Like everybody else, Moreau worked for 200 roubles a month (then about £195), and thus became an official co-producer with a share of the hypothetical profits as her salary. Her dressing-room was a canvas shack thrown up in a corner and her costume included laddered silk stockings and, from her own collection, the shoes she had worn in *Jules et Jim*.

Peter Adam, who was in Moscow to write a story on Moreau for German *Vogue*, used to spend the long evenings with her in that 'old

Russian' bastion, the Hotel Sovietskaya, cooped up in the suite which had once been occupied by President Mitterrand. 'We hadn't seen each other for a year or two since she was last in London at BAFTA to receive a BFI fellowship. I was also supposed to make a documentary on the making of the Russian film, but things didn't work out, so we mainly spent our time talking, playing cards, eating together. I think we both felt very lonely there.

'Jeanne always takes suitcases of her own cooking utensils and the food she likes. In Russia then it was still very chaotic and there was nothing to eat except gristle and *borscht*, and she would cook us dinners on her little stove in her room. At Christmas the local church organised her a goose and a really fine red cabbage, so she made us a feast. It was rather primitive at the Sovietskaya and Jeanne doesn't ever submit to something not up to scratch. She had them running around and made sure I had the best, down to good bath salts in my bathroom!'

The film was called *Anna Karamazov*, a title that came from a joke in a Nabokov book – when Nabokov once asked one of his American students why she wanted to learn Russian, he was told, 'So that I can read *Anna Karamazov* in the original.' Thus were Tolstoy and Dostoyevsky, Anna Karenina and the Brothers Karamazov linked forever.

The story is set in the forties and is about a woman who returns to Leningrad after twenty years in a Stalinist labour camp. Released but finding no place for herself in the post-war world, she turns to killing and stealing hoarded wealth to spread it among the destitute. The film is designed as both comedy and tragedy.

It made it to Cannes for the festival of 1991, but it seems that the timing was unfortunate. In the new heady days of Mikhail Gorbachev's reforms, the film came across as worthwhile only to the avant-garde faithful; otherwise, it was construed as wildly out of date.

'Jeanne had a romanticism about this venture,' recollects Georges Beaume, who was also with her in Moscow. 'She thought it would be something very special and worked incredibly hard on her character. But the film didn't correspond with its promise, didn't live up to her expectations. The build-up was much better than the result. Mosfilm paid out nothing.'

The director, who has never made another film, does not even have a copy of *Anna Karamazov*, which remains with Silberman and Moreau in France.

Everybody awaited Moreau's next film, *Le Pas Suspendu de la Cigogne* (The Suspended Step of the Stork), with baited breath. Thirty years after Antonioni's *La Notte*, it was to bring Moreau and Mastroianni together once again.

Directed by the left-wing Greek director Theo Angelopoulos, whom Moreau had met at Cannes while talking about *Anna Karamazov*, the script had been written with the two of them in mind. Spica's chairman, Bruno Pesary of Arena Films, produced it.

A tale of displaced people, shot in a wintry, bleak part of Greece, it seems worlds apart from the carefree sunshine Greece of the tourist postcard. About the border problem, a subject many people do not want to highlight, the film is set in a small Greek town just across from the then Yugoslav border – one of the last 'protected' towns, where there is no 'barrier bashing'.

The story is about what happens when a young journalist (Gregory Karr) believes he has spotted a missing Greek politician from the days of the colonels (Mastroianni) among the crowds of Albanian, Turkish and Kurdish refugees. Moreau, who plays Mastroianni's wife, is brought there by the journalist to identify him after thirty years of separation. They have a clandestine meeting on the bridge across the river that divides the two countries.

As Moreau describes it: 'We were shooting very close to the actual Yugoslav border, in a little town called Florina, and were violently attacked by the pro-nationalist Orthodox Greek Archibishop Avgoustinos, who basically excommunicated us because the story was about opening up such borders. He was so against us he'd ring the church bells when we were shooting so that we couldn't do sound. We were also attacked for being pro-Common Market, because they felt that Britain had sold them down the river. What with the cold and the snow, it was real agony. It was only because Theo is so brilliant that Marcello and I stayed.'

According to Aliki Roussin-Croney, the consultant on the film, they stayed on with extreme reluctance: 'The conditions were atrocious. It was twenty-five degrees below and the place was a tip.

Mastroianni had pneumonia and flew back to Italy as soon as he could. Moreau was very off-colour as well and extremely uncommunicative. They were staying in separate hotels, she in the better one, he in the tatty one in the middle of town with Theo, and didn't see much of each other. Mastroianni had brought his housekeeper with him, along with his saucepans and spaghetti, so they used to eat together. Moreau stayed apart, on her own, I think. But they were real professionals when the cameras rolled. The scene when they meet on the bridge, after a thirty-year gap in their marriage, is beautiful, *touching*.'

Afterwards Moreau went to thaw out from the Angelopoulos experience in glorious, warm Guadaloupe.

While Moreau was in New Delhi heading up the festival in 1985, she met the venerable Belgian-born author Marguerite Yourcenar. Still vigorous, although in her eighties, Yourcenar immediately suggested that the two of them travel to Rajasthan together. Moreau had to decline because of previous commitments, but in August, 1991, she took to the stage in the mediaeval Cour de la Charité at Carpentras in Provence to honour Yourcenar as the first woman ever to be elected to the Académie Française by reading extracts from her *L'Oeuvre au Noir*. Translated into English as *The Abyss*, the novel concerns one Zeno, a mediaeval heretic on the brink of making discoveries crucial to the beginning of the modern world.

'I could see behind that old woman the incredible youthfulness of her literary creativity. I did three evenings of reading at Carpentras, in that lovely old convent, under open skies, the stars moving overhead. It was one of those perfect events that leave no trace,' says Moreau. 'It was an instant of incredible beauty, like poetry. People think poetry means boring, but I find poetry incredible. I've read poetry since I was a child. Poetry feeds my soul.'

Moreau had first tried acupuncture as part of her holistic approach to health as far back as 1967, so when the young director Didier Martini asked her to play an acupuncturist in his film, *A Demain*, she was intrigued.

'Although the film is autobiographical of Didier and his family, it seemed the part was a bit autobiographical for me too, because I had become really interested in this fascinating craft. The hero of the film is a little boy, Didier, son of a family of doctors, whose grandmother is the first woman in Europe to use acupuncture. I play that grandmother and I learned much about the art of working with pins.'

She then came out in support of yet another new young director for her next film, taking the role of the formidable nun in Vincent Ward's *Map of the Human Heart*.

Map is a bizarre and beautiful love story, this time between a detribalised Canadian Eskimo called Avik (Jason Scott Lee) and Albertine (Anne Parillaud), a half-caste Indian girl he has met in a sanatorium (run by Moreau). They have both been sent there on a TB cure. When they are wrenched apart and returned to their homes, Avik finds he is ostracised by his own people. He joins the RAF when war breaks out, only to run into the beautiful Albertine again.

'Like everybody else, I'd seen *Jules et Jim*,' says Ward, a New Zealander. 'I'd met Jeanne when she was in Australia a few years before and with my co-writer, Louis Nowra, wrote the character of this harsh French-Canadian Catholic nun with her in mind. We thought she could be tough and bring that dimension to the character. I particularly wanted her also because she and Anne (Parillaud) are very close.

'But Jeanne said no when I sent her the script. I kept contacting her. I just felt, particularly as she had been excommunicated in the Angelopoulos film, that she would be drawn to play Sister Banville, who runs the TB sanatorium like an army camp and virtually prises the two orphans apart.

'Eventually she said I could come and see her. By this time I was so anxious, I'd bought some flowers for her and took a taxi to her apartment, but I was so nervous that I left the slip of paper with her apartment number on it in the taxi. There were no names on the doorbells and the taxi had driven off, so I had to go back to my hotel, find her number and ring her to explain. When we finally met she said, "I know what you want and you know what I'm going to say," and then she said yes. It is a sort of game she plays with charm and grace. I was scared of her at first, but she became very supportive of the project.'

Even though she does not like using her voice without her face being there, her next two jobs were voice only. Nor could they have been further apart. For her friend Claude Berri (who produced the remake of *Queen Margot* with Isabelle Adjani) and for Jean-Jacques Annaud, the director, she narrated the film of Duras' best-selling autobiographical novel of East-West romance in twenties Saigon, the hugely successful *L'Amant* (*The Lover*). This she did in both French and English, her voice giving the film a sensual tone that soars leagues above the beautiful, bare bodies of the principal actors, Jane Marsh and Tony Leung.

'Right away I accepted to be the voice, because I wasn't going to let by the opportunity to speak the text of such a beautiful novel,' says Moreau. 'It is very flattering to think that my voice might carry all that it implies to express oneself in place of the author – in both English and French.'

Her second voice part came about through her friend Bruno Ganz, who was doing the German voice to Peter Cohan's documentary, *L'Architecture du Chaos*. Moreau was used in the French version.

'The film was about Hitler's fascination with the arts and I personally found Cohan's approach, of National Socialism through Hitler's fascination with paintings, architecture and so on, was very, very interesting,' says Moreau. 'Even though I don't speak German, I find many absorbing things in German history and I was pleased to be able to pass some of them on.

'Before the Wall fell, I seriously planned to rent a flat and live for a year in Berlin. I don't think speaking German would be a problem. I have a good ear so I can very easily *sound* like I speak German even if it's not true!'

20

M

'In a five-minute conversation with her one afternoon in
Normandy I unlearned a lot of rigid rubbish which had been
imparted to me over the decades.'

Alec Guinness

Like Alec Guinness, Jeanne Moreau is now one of the most distinguished veterans of the world film industry. Her skill at articulating
herself and her zest for her chosen lifestyle has not faded with the
years. If anything, she is more passionate about her work than ever
and will fight very fiercely for the industry's future. While spending
time with her I have searched for glimpses of the possibly dry and
faded air of the moth that has courted the flame of such a career for
too many seasons, but I have caught none. She still loves the spotlight
and is happy to give her all when it is on her.

During the actor–film-maker masterclass she gave with eight other
directors at Cannes in 1993, she walked in – a volcano in a
hydrangea pink suit, dwarfed by Robert Altman – and for more than
two hours led the panel in a tough, gritty and useful class. She dismissed young hecklers with a flick of the wrist, encouraged others to
pose pointed questions. She might be small and still petite, but she
can make fully grown men quake. Wasting time is not her thing and
while she has a knack for cajoling people into her slipstream, if they
do not flow with her one feels that the weight of her disapproval will
clamp their souls forever somewhere in purgatory. I observed her at

a press conference in Paris to promote one of France's newest film festivals, Equinox, a week-long gathering of scriptwriters each September in Bordeaux. When a reporter asked a pointless personal question, she blasted him to kingdom come without so much as drawing breath.

In 1993 she was on the jury at Cannes, which was presided over by Louis Malle. She was also representing ARP (Auteurs-Réalisateurs-Producteurs), a European association of writers, directors and producers which defends cinematographic creation and authors' rights. On the last night, when she compèred the awards ceremony, she announced herself simply: '*Je suis Jeanne Moreau, je suis actrice*' [I'm Jeanne Moreau, I'm an actress] and got on with it.

That year she was also head of the Commission d'Avances sur Recettes, the state-supported panel that takes a percentage of the French box office and ploughs it back into helping script development and film-making in general, a role in which she was mercilessly efficient.

When I interviewed her then, she told me: 'I read four hundred scripts in the first nine months, and made decisions about which to fund and which not to. Jack Lang [France's Minister of Culture] said I should do it because there are many ways to make films and my knowledge of cinema goes beyond the acting. He gave me the freedom to choose the people who surround me at CAR and my group includes producers, scriptwriters, directors, a lady cameraman, an executive producer – all sides of the business.'

She succeeded philosopher-writer Bernard Henry Levy there for 1993. Talking about the job, behind her big, solid, wooden desk, she was pure, tough businesswoman. 'We get scores of scripts, all from people who have already at least made their first film,' she said, puffing on a long cigarette, vaguely indicating the hall, where further piles of scripts blocked the parquet. 'It has meant giving up acting for months and months to read them all.

'It is because of my job with CAR that I was asked to be part of the Equinox project. Robert Redford's Sundance Film Festival helped by sending us some scriptwriters. It is quite difficult to get scriptwriters in France who are willing to share their knowledge and spend a week away from their desks, so it has been quite hard to set up.

'Both CAR and Equinox are there to incarnate – to incarnate characters, stories, new films.' She looked across at me with those eyes full of experience and shrugged. 'Isn't life all about incarnation?'

I asked her if she felt she has nine lives, like a cat. 'Yes,' she replied with a slanted glance, 'I may even have more'.

One of my favourite Moreau movies is *La Vieille qui Marchait dans la Mer* (*The Old Lady who Walked in the Sea*). For it she was paid a top-ranking fee (about FFR 2 million, £250,000), her highest in years, and her spellbinding portrayal of 'Lady M.' won her her first César in 1992.

In Laurent Heynemann's daring and cutting comedy, based on the novel by San Antonio, Moreau plays a fading society beauty, now a gross con-artist. She uses her former lover, an ancient and debauched diplomat called Pompilius (the inimitable Michel Serrault), and the personable young Lambert (Luc Thullier) as partners in money-making scams. It could have been a profoundly vulgar film if someone else had played the old lady, but somehow she managed to carry it off.

The film opens in gorgeous Guadaloupe, where young Lambert's job is to walk the arthritic Lady M. in the sea while she grooms him for greater things, not necessarily as her lover but certainly as her toy-boy. The action moves to the Côte d'Azur to her stylish villa where Moreau and Serrault (last seen together in *Le Miraculé*) keep up a running stream of bitingly vile and mutual insults ('Go and put your decalcified bones under the sheets, you look like a dummy whose wax is melting' is about the most printable) while Lambert is drawn in as desirable young blood to the ageing couple.

This is a deep and dark character study of moral tyranny, with Moreau looking at times more raddled than the late Bette Davis. Serrault, both sclerotic and senile, eggs her on to be as foul as she can.

'I think it is one of my best roles!' she exclaims. 'I could not walk normally after the film, because of using that cane, and I could not speak French correctly because of all her swearing. But I was fascinated by her and I rang the author, Frédéric Dard, one Sunday morning, to ask him to write a continuation of the story for me.'

Apart from being one of the most politically incorrect, brazen, blatantly (but deliciously) distasteful feature movies ever made, it is the film that will always remain as an example of the difference between the French- and the English-speaking world. I saw it first in South Africa, where many people left the cinema tsk-tsking in shock and distress, and then a second time in England, where exactly the same reaction occurred. At the Everyman, a cinema which could hardly have an audience more devoted to supporting foreign films, this was the one that sustained the shortest run in its history. Then I saw it in France, where a packed audience was convulsed with joy and applauded every dastardly move; it ran for ages, too. When Moreau collected her César for it, the gathered dignitaries nearly expired in ecstasy. *Vive la différence!*

One might ask why an elegant, fabulously well-established actress like Jeanne Moreau does not allow herself to 'grow old gracefully' – in other words, to retire.

Part of the answer is undoubtedly that French cinema has always had a tradition of maintaining disgraceful old ladies. Part of the answer is also that Moreau does not give much of a damn. A lot of the answer is that Moreau has not yet made much provision for her old age.

'Oh, I will work till I die,' she growls. 'I have no pension. I have never saved my money. Pensions? I don't know what they are. I thought of starting one but I haven't yet. Why can't I still be on screen when I'm ninety? I may be doing something totally different by then. I may be a producer. Paf! Without any doubt, I'll work till I die.'

Her next choice of role was certainly as adventurous as any she had made before. Waris Hussein's film *The Clothes in the Wardrobe*, made for BBC Television, was adapted from Alice Thomas Ellis's stridently anti-establishment novel about ex-colonials in late-fifties surburban Britain. The story is woven around the planned but unwanted wedding of a pretty teenager (Lena Headley) and the dreary man next door (David Threlfall). Julie Walters plays the girl's divorced mother and Joan Plowright the groom's mother, but it is Moreau who steals the show as the alluring Lili. An exotic flame-haired free spirit, Lili is an old Anglo-Egyptian friend from Cairo, sent to deliver them all from terminal dowdiness and the poor bespoke girl from a hopeless marriage. The outcome is Lili sexually straddling the groom, riding him in the greenhouse, to the horror and shock of his mother, bride and in-laws-to-be. At the triumphant moment, she looks around at the gaping assembly in close-up and smiles that archaic smile Truffaut once caught so memorably in *Jules et Jim*.

'I did that deliberately, as a tribute to *Jules et Jim*,' says Hussein. 'I wanted to encompass everybody with her presence. But I had to be careful not to make it look like I was being sycophantic. Jeanne hates grovellers or fakes. From a director she doesn't want adoration, she wants direction.'

For Moreau Lili was another 'grow old disgracefully' role. 'Whoever thought of me for this role, I thank from the bottom of my heart,' she joyously faxed producer Norma Heyman in her acceptance.

'But I am not like Lili,' she says, excusing herself. 'She is too much for me. I couldn't stand the proximity of a woman like that, good God! I am a quiet person. I don't intrude in other people's lives. But I think that sometimes in our lives we'd like to meet somebody like that, who would come and provoke a mess and take over and bring things out that have been lying dormant.'

The film, a resounding favourite of mine, was picked up for cinematic distribution in the US under the title *The Summer House*. At the time of writing Moreau was being tipped for an Oscar nomination.

After *The Clothes in the Wardrobe*, with her British links renewed, she accepted the office of patron, with Claude Sautet, of the UK's only French film festival, held every October in Edinburgh and Glasgow.

She had also made another British film, *A Foreign Field* (after the line in Rupert Brooke's poem), this time playing a wartime whore. A BBC film set in Normandy, it is about a small group of veterans who make a pilgrimage to pay their respects to their friends left behind in the war cemetery there. It soon becomes obvious that two of the old boys (Leo McKern and John Randolph) were in their day rivals for what they thought were the romantic affections of Angélique (Moreau). They rendezvous with her in the village in which they were once billeted, where she still lives but in a retirement home.

Directed by Charles Sturridge, it is an ensemble piece also starring Alec Guinness, Lauren Bacall and Geraldine Chaplin. Moreau apparently picked her unflattering costumes herself, clothes that most actresses of her vintage would not be seen dead in. When they were commented on, she retorted that she wanted to make sure they were right for the part, to the surprise of everybody there who expected her to be more caring about her image and less professional.

Guinness plays the role of Amos, a soldier mentally affected by being hit by shrapnel during the Battle of Normany. He told me how he wished he had met Moreau earlier. 'If only I had met her twenty years ago she would have made a great and happy difference to my own performing,' he said. 'In a five-minute conversation with her one afternoon in Normandy I unlearned a lot of rigid rubbish which had been imparted to me over the decades. She is delightful and exciting to be with, not only as an actress but as a person. I want to know her a lot better.'

In 1993 at Cannes I saw Moreau in the appealing *My Name is Victor*. In this first feature by yet another new young director, this time Guy Jacques, she plays Victor's Great Aunt Rose, a cantankerous old lady who has lived in seclusion upstairs in her wheelchair since the war. The neighbours believe she must be dead, but Victor and Rose share a whimsical and charming complicity.

I bring the film up with Moreau, mainly to ask her how she feels about ageing.

'Oh, but I started that when I was hardly twenty, when in *Caves of the Vatican* I had to age into an old, worn-out woman with a heavy past. As a woman of my age I can see many things. I see the earth ageing around me. The trees I knew as saplings have grown tall and old. I feel a synthesis. The privilege of age is that I have more confidence and I am calmer. I know more about myself, I feel less egocentric. Anyway, in France you can still be a woman when you're sixty or sixty-five. We replace youth with charm and *savoir faire*. We have a literary tradition of passionate older women, as in Balzac, Stendhal, Colette, Choderlos de Laclos. Their works are full of older women. Glamour can be very constraining, you know.'

How about playing the grandmother role, then?

'I might be a grandmother on screen but you don't play a grand-mother, you play a character. It just happens she's a grandmother.'

Point taken.

I think Moreau would probably make a very good grandmother in real life. She would school the infant in discipline and teach it to love books, value tradition and be aware of destiny. She would have time possibly to be much more involved with a grandchild than – as a star and erotic symbol – she had as mother to Jérôme.

In New York there is a homeopath called Dominique Richard, who claims that he is Jeanne Moreau's authentic son. Rather like the character in John Guare's play *Six Degrees of Separation*, based on a true story, who claims to be Sidney Poitier's son and gets away with it, this Richard has also pulled off the bogus identification with some success.

'Sometimes I meet people in the street in New York who say to me, "Oh, your son saved my life," or "He was so good for my daughter's back,"' says Moreau. 'I've never met him, I don't know him, he doesn't know me, he's never met me. At first I was quite angry, because it's a lie and I don't like liars. But then I thought maybe it was an honour. There was another one, too, a musician in an American pop group, who also said he was my son. But I only have one son, Jérôme.'

Their mother-son relationship has clearly been emotionally deli-cate on both sides. She once met me at her door, blanched and shaken. Jérôme had been run over in California, where he lives. His leg had been broken in two places. No mother could have been more concerned. Her anguish hovered around her like a cape.

'My son is in hospital, his father is sick with a fever, my whole family is in bed,' she said in a tiny, crumpled voice. I was taken aback to see such vulnerability in this steel-spined woman who I knew could be as imperious as the president of France. But I was also pleased – relieved – to see that chink in her armour.

Moreau has always had her own screen family, with planty of 'god-sons' like Luc Beraud and 'goddaughters' like Anne Parillaud, the new generation who are building the French film's future.

'Anne is one of our great actors,' she says, when asked who the industry's 'young hopes' are. 'She has character as a person. Beyond

God's gift of talent, there is an extraordinary personality. So has Juliette Binoche and Sandrine Bonnaire. I'd love to direct them. They have the whole panorama. They will still be there in forty, fifty years. Of the new girls there is Judith Godrèche, Irène Jacob and Fanny Bastien. They are definitely our future stars.

'At sixty-five I no longer think, "Oh, I would like to work with so-and-so. I'm not a debutante, I don't wait by the phone; it's the opposite. People want to work with me now and I'm the one who provokes things. If I want to work with someone, I provoke it. I produce. I pick up the phone and ring them.

In 1995 she will direct her third film, *Adieu, Bonjour*, with a cast that includes Anouk Aimée, from a script she is co-writing with Emmanuel List, who wrote *My Name is Victor*.

'I don't have problems with inspiration for writing. I have all the fairytales in the world, all the mythology there is. If I have a problem with a character I try to figure out where the character belongs in this incredible family of gods, semi-gods and humans. You have all aspects of human nature, with its violence, its duels, its love, its everything, in mythology. My books on mythology carry me. I read so much – of mythology, of everything, Shakespeare, philosophy, Sufi poetry, Japanese poetry, I *need* to read.

'Between working on this film I will be directing a documentary on Cannes, to be ready by 1997 in time for the film festival's fiftieth anniversary. I might also be shooting *Richard III* with Ian McKellen.'

Set in London in the 1930s, their version of *Richard III* is based on the Royal Shakespeare Company's stage production which starred McKellen, who has written the screenplay and will co-produce the film, directed by Alex Cox, to a $7 million budget.

'A crucial figure in the play is Queen Margaret,' McKellen told me. 'She actually came from Anjou and we thought it would be wonderful to have the greatest French screen actress alive, so we asked Jeanne and she said yes. It's Shakespeare's most popular play; I think it will make a very popular film.'

Moreau is also writing a book, a *dictionnaire subjectif* (a personalised view of the world, annotated alphabetically, as first done by Alexandre Dumas). She jokes that this will probably never get beyond the letter 'A'.

'With two of my films opening in America (*Old Lady* and *The*

Summer House) and the big retrospective of my work at the Museum of Modern Art in New York, much of my year will be spent travelling. If I have any spare time I will make another record with Jacques [Canetti] of Jacques Prévert poems and perhaps one of new songs written by Jean-Louis Murat.'

She talks with an air of being careful, yet at the same time careless. It's deceptive. She makes it seem easy, as if her rich life has come naturally, but one is aware all the time that there's something – a certain dismay, perhaps, that she has not enough time to do justice to all life has to offer. Beneath the fabric on the outside, there's a feeling that if things slip out of synch in the smooth train of Jeanne Moreau, the one that arrives on time at the right platform will get derailed, crash down the banks, its wheels spinning in the air.

'I suppose the side of me I like least is my natural disposition to profundity. Aquarius is a fixed sign and there's something fixed in me. Maybe it's the presence of Saturn, but there's a sort of something strict that I always have to fight against. It's not that I'm humourless. I love to have fun. But I'm not *ludique* enough. It's a philosophical word. It means "playful". I am not able to play games to get to an end. I haven't a developed sense of game. I wish I could ease up more. I'm very strict. Obviously I deal with it, but let's say it's one of my problems, my strictness. For people close to me it's probably hard. I expect a lot from my friends but they must have fun with me otherwise they wouldn't still be there after all these years!

'Because I am so strict with myself, I need to organise myself properly. I don't get exhausted, upset, as long as I'm organised. For that I need to be alone. I need the luxury of solitude. In any event, I am a very shy person. I don't mind going out to the shops but I don't like social evenings, parties and dinners where it is all small talk. I like to have real conversation, with one or two friends, over a good meal that I've cooked for them.

'I have no partner now and I'm not excluding anything from the point of view of relationships – it is very moving to be loved and very hard to resist – but I have work to do and I need to be alone for a certain time. You never live alone, even if solitude is your field. You are part of a community and the community is the world.

'I have had so many wonderful relationships – some with people who are unknown, some with people who are known – like Louis and Pierre – some with very young men. So many great loves. Sometimes I think to myself, "What a strange person you are."

Appendix

Theatre Work

1948–51 Member of the Comédie Française
1951–52 Member of the Théâtre Nationale Populaire

Other Theatres

1953 *L'Heure Eblouissante* Anna Bonacci
1954 *La Machine Infernale (The Infernal Machine)* Jean Cocteau
1955 *Pygmalion* George Bernard Shaw
1956 *La Chatte sur un Toit Brûlant (Cat on a Hot Tin Roof)* Tennessee Williams
1958 *La Bonne Soupe* Félicien Marceau
1974 *La Chevauchée Sur Le Lac De Constance (The Crossing of Lake Constance)* Peter Handke
1976 *Lulu* Frank Wedekind
1980 *L'Intoxe* Françoise Dorin
1985 *The Night of the Iguana* Tennessee Williams
1986 *Le Récit de la Servante Zerline* Hermann Broch
1989 *La Célestine (Celestina)* Fernando de Rojas

Filmography
(with directors)

1949	*Dernier Amour* Jean Stelli
1950	*Meurtres* Richard Pottier
	Pigalle-Saint-Germain-des-Prés André Berthomieu
1952	*L'Homme de ma Vie* Guy Lefranc
	Il est Minuit, Docteur Schweitzer André Haguet
1953	*Dortoir des Grandes* Henri Decoin
	Julietta Marc Allégret
1954	*Touchez Pas au Grisbi* (*Honour Among Thieves*, aka *Hands Off the Loot*) Jacques Becker
	Secrets D'Alcôve Henri Decoin
	(Episode: *Le Billet de Logement*)
	Les Intrigantes (*The Parasites*) Henri Decoin
	La Reine Margot Jean Dréville
1955	*Les Hommes en Blanc* Ralph Habib
	M'sieur la Caille (*The Pigeon*) André Pergament
	Gas-Oil Gilles Grangier
1956	*Le Salaire du Péché* Denys de la Patellière
1957	*Jusqu'au Dernier* Pierre Billon
	Les Louves Luis Saslavsky
	L'Etrange Monsieur Stève Raymond Bailly
1958	*Trois Jours à Vivre* Gilles Grangier
	Echec au Porteur Gilles Grangier
	Ascenseur pour l'Echafaud (*Lift to the Scaffold*, aka *Frantic*) Louis Malle
	Le Dos au Mur (*Back to the Wall*) Edouard Molinaro
1959	*Les Amants* (*The Lovers*) Louis Malle
	Les Quatre Cents Coups (*The Four Hundred Blows*) François Truffaut
	Les Liaisons Dangereuses Roger Vadim
1960	*Five Branded Women* Martin Ritt
	Dialogue des Carmélites R.P. Bruckberger & Philippe Agostini
	Moderato Cantabile (*Seven Days, Seven Nights*) Peter Brook

1961	*La Notte* Michelangelo Antonioni
	Une Femme est une Femme Jean-Luc Godard
1962	*Jules et Jim* François Truffaut
	Eva Joseph Losey
1963	*The Trial* Orson Welles
	La Baie des Anges (*Bay of Angels*) Jacques Demy
	Peau de Banane (*Banana Peel*) Marcel Ophüls
	Le Feu Follet (*A Time to Live and a Time to Die*, aka *Will o' the Wisp*) Louis Malle
1964	*The Victors* Carl Foreman
	Le Journal d'une Femme de Chambre (*The Diary of a Chambermaid*) Luís Buñuel
	The Train John Frankenheimer
1965	*Mata Hari, Agent H21* Jean-Louis Richard
	The Yellow Rolls-Royce Anthony Asquith
	Viva Maria! Louis Malle
1966	*Chimes at Midnight* (aka *Falstaff*) Orson Welles
	Mademoiselle (*Summer Fires*) Tony Richardson
1967	*The Sailor From Gibraltar* Tony Richardson
	The Deep (aka *Direction Towards Death, Dead Reckoning*) Orson Welles (unfinished)
	Le Plus Vieux Métier du Monde (*The Oldest Profession in the World*) Philippe de Broca
	(Episode: *Mademoiselle Mimi*)
1968	*La Mariée était en Noir* (*The Bride Wore Black*) François Truffaut
1969	*Great Catherine* Gordon Flemyng
	Le Corps de Diane (*Diana*) Jean-Louis Richard
1970	*Le Petit Théâtre de Jean Renoir* Jean Renoir
	Monte Walsh William Fraker
	Alex in Wonderland Paul Mazursky
1971	*Comptes à Rebours* Roger Pigaut
	L'Humeur Vagabonde Edouard Luntz
	The Other Side of the Wind Orson Welles (unfinished)
1972	*Chère Louise* (*Dear Louise*) Philippe de Broca
	The Immortal Story Orson Welles
1973	*Nathalie Granger* Marguerite Duras
	Absences Répétées Guy Gilles

M

1974	*Je t'Aime* Pierre Duceppe
	Les Valseuses (*Making It*, aka *Going Places*) Bertrand Blier
	La Race des Seigneurs (*Jet Set*) Pierre Granier-Defferre
1975	*Joanna Francesca* (*Jeanne la Française*) Carlos Diegues
	Le Jardin qui Bascule (*The Tilting Garden*) Guy Gilles
	Hu-Man Jérôme Laperrousaz
	Souvenirs d'en France André Téchiné
1976	*Lumière* Jeanne Moreau
	Mr Klein Joseph Losey
1977	*The Last Tycoon* Elia Kazan
1979	*L'Adolescente* (*The Adolescent Girl*) Jeanne Moreau
1981	*Plein Sud* Luc Béraud
1982	*Your Ticket is no Longer Valid* George Kaczender
	Mille Milliards de Dollars Henri Verneuil
	La Truite (*The Trout*) Joseph Losey
	Querelle Rainer Werner Fassbinder
1984	*L'Arbre* Jacques Doillon (Antenne 2)
1985	*Vicious Circle* Kenneth Ives (BBC)
1986	*The Last Seance* June Wyndham-Davies (Granada TV)
	Le Tiroir Secret Nadine Trintignant (Canal Plus)
	Sauve-Toi, Lola Michel Drach
	Le Paltoquet Michel Deville
1987	*Le Miraculé* Jean-Pierre Mocky
1988	*La Nuit de l'Océan* Antoine Perset
	Ennemonde Claude Santelli
	Jour Après Jour Alain Attal
	Hotel Terminus Max Ophüls (voice only)
1989	*Nikita* Luc Besson
	Alberto Express Arthur Joffe
1990	*Anna Karamazov* Roustam Khamdamov
	La Femme Fardée José Pinheiro
1991	*Until the End of the World* Wim Wenders
	Le Pas Suspendu de la Cigogne Theo Angelopoulos
	La Vieille qui Marchait dans la Mer Laurent Heynemann
	Map of the Human Heart Vincent Ward
	A Demain Didier Martiny
	L'Amant (*The Lover*) Jean-Jacques Annaud (voice only)
	L'Architecture du Chaos Peter Cohan (voice only)

1992	*The Clothes in the Wardrobe* (*The Summer House*) Waris Hussein (BBC)
	L'Absence Peter Handke
1993	*A Foreign Field* Charles Sturridge (BBC)
	Je m'Appelle Victor (*My Name is Victor*) Guy Jacques

Major Awards

1960	Best Actress: Cannes Film Festival (*Moderato Cantabile*)
	Grand Prix de l'Office Catholique Internationale du Cinéma (Dialogue des Carmélites)
	French Film Actress of the Year: *Figaro/Cinémonde* (Le *Dialogue des Carmélites*)
1962	Etoile de Cristal (*Jules et Jim*)
	Best Actress: Melbourne Festival (*La Notte*)
1964	Grand Prix du Disque
	Best Actress: Karlovy-Vary Festival (*Le Journal d'une Femme de Chambre*)
1966	Prix Francis-Carco: Singer of the Year
1967	Best Foreign Actress: British Film Academy (*Viva Maria!*)
1973	Order of Merit
1975	Légion d'honneur
1979	Prix de l'ACIC (Association des Cadres de l'Industrie Cinématographique)
1980	Prix de l'Académie Charles Cros
	Prix Brigadier (*L'Intoxe*)
1985	Commander of French Arts and Letters
1987	Prix de la Critique (*Le Récit de la Servante Zerline*)
1988	Officer of the French National Order of Merit
	Molière (*Le Récit de la Servante Zerline*)
1990	Fellowship of the British Film Institute
1991	Légion d'honneur: Officer of the National Order
1992	César: Best Actress (*La Vieille qui Marchait dans la Mer*)
	Lion d'Or: Venice Film Festival (for her career)

ACKNOWLEDGEMENTS

My thanks go to all the people who took the time and energy to contribute to this book, particularly to my brother Stephen for the huge amount of time he spent involved at every level; Jean-Claude Moireau for his generous assistance; Tony Crawley, Pamela Godfrey, Marcelle Katz and Kevin Wilson for providing me with endless reference material; Judy Olivier and Michael Popham for their comments; Marie-Pierre Moine for her translation; the Everyman Cinema for their well-timed Jeanne Moreau season; Peter Adam, Joan Juliet Buck, Patricia Losey, Louis Malle, Florence Malraux, Madeleine Morgenstern, Michelle Moreau, Armelle Oberlin, Jean-Louis Richard, Micheline Rozan, David Wigg, and the numerous colleagues and associates of Jeanne Moreau who co-operated with me; and, of course, Jeanne Moreau herself.

Some of the factual and quoted matter in this book is based on previously published material. My grateful thanks to the list of publications that follows: *Time, Time Out, The Sunday Times,* the *Observer,* the *New York Times, Vogue US, Interview,* the *Guardian, New Yorker, LA Times, Queen,* the *Daily Mirror, Cosmopolitan,* the *Evening News,* the *Evening Standard, Cinema, Paris Match, Le Monde,* the *Sunday Express, LA Magazine, Look, Variety,* the *Christian Science Monitor* and Jean-Claude Moireau's superb book *Jeanne Moreau* (Editions Ramsay).

Although every effort has been made to contact the present copyright holders of some of the photographs used in this book, we apologise in advance for any unintentional omissions and will be pleased to insert the appropriate acknowledgement to individuals in future editions. The publishers would like to thank the following film distribution and production companies whose film stills and publicity pictures appear in this book:

Nouvelles Editions de Films
Films du Carrosse
Palace Pictures
Warner Bros.
Gala Films
Samuel Goldwyn
Unifrance Films
United Artists Corporation

Translations of film titles not familiar to a British audience are in Roman. Titles of films released in the UK are in italics.

BIBLIOGRAPHY

Jeanne Moreau – Jean-Claude Moireau (Ramsay, 1988)

Long Distance Runner – Tony Richardson (Faber and Faber, 1993)

Vanessa Redgrave –Vanessa Redgrave (Hutchinson, 1991)

The Memoirs of Roger Vadim – Roger Vadim (Weidenfeld & Nicolson, 1986)

The Films in My Life – François Truffaut (Allen Lane, 1980)

My Last Breath – Luís Buñuel (Jonathan Cape, 1983)

The New Wave – Peter Graham (Doubleday, 1968)

Histoire de Ma Vie – Jean Marais (Albin Michel, 1975)

Vivien – the Life of Vivien Leigh – Alexander Walker (Weidenfeld and Nicolson, 1987)

Losey on Losey – Edited by Tom Milne (Cinema One Series No.2, 1967)

Conversations with Losey – Michel Ciment (Methuen, 1985)

Hurricane Billy – Nat Segaloff (William Morrow, 1990)

Vedettes au Microscope – Jacques Baroche (Contact Editions, 1961)

Femmes – José Luis de Villalonga (Stock, 1975)

Limelighters – Orianna Fallaci (Michael Joseph, 1967)

What The Censor Saw – John Trevelyan (Michael Joseph, 1973)

INDEX

*Each film mentioned in which Jeanne Moreau appeared
has its own separate entry*

Absence, The 147
Absences Répétées 132
Abwesenheit, Die 147
Adam, Peter 151, 163, 168, 214–15
A Demain 217–18
Adieu, Bonjour 228
Adolescente, L' 9, 169–72, 173, 190
Adolescent Girl, The 9, 169–72, 173
Aimée, Anouk 228
Albee, Edward 131
Alberto Express 211
Alex in Wonderland 127
Allégret, Marc 29
Allen, Don 185–87
All Over 131
Altman, Robert 221
Amant, L' 219
Amants, Les 29, 37–42
Amour Monstre, L' 65
Andalusian Dog 83
Andersson, Bibi 157
And God Created Woman 38
Angeli, Pier 88
Angelopoulos, Theo 216
Anna Karamazov 215–16
Anouilh, Jean 11
Antigone 11
Antonioni, Michelangelo 53–54, 65
Antony and Cleopatra 70

Arbre, L' 192–93
Architecture du Chaos, L' 219
Ardant, Fanny 200
Arestrup, Niels 157
ARP 222
Ascenseur pour l'Echafaud 22, 27, 35–36
Ashley, Laura 74
Asquith, Anthony 87
Ateliers du Rêve, Les 192
Attal, Alain 210
Auclair, Michel 150
*Au-delà de Cette Limite, Votre Ticket n'est Plus
    Valable* 173
Avgoustinos, Archbishop 216
Avignon, Bastion de la France 20
Avignon Theatre Festival 15, 20
Avventura, L' 53, 65
Aznavour, Charles 116

Bacall, Lauren 226
Back to the Wall 36
Baie des Anges, La 78–79
Baker, Stanley 63
Banana Peel 79, 80–81
Bannen, Ian 106, 107
Bardot, Brigitte 40, 47, 77, 89, 99, 102
Barrault, Jean-Louis 17
Barrymore, Lionel 93
Barsacq, André 43

Bassiak, Cyrus 79
Bastien, Fanny 228
Battle of the Bulge, The 88
Bay of Angels 78–79
Bazin, André 36, 45, 46
BBC 192
Beaume, Georges 203, 211, 215
Beauvoir, Simone de 132–33
Becker, Jacques 29
Beckett, Samuel 20
Bed, The 30
Bell, Marie 19
Belmondo, Jean-Paul 46, 51, 52, 53, 54, 80
Beloukia 190
Béraud, Luc 173, 227
Bergman, Ingmar 65, 132
Berlin Film Festival 32
Berri, Claude 78, 132
Berthomieu, André 28
Besson, Luc 210
Bête Humaine, La 10, 121
Billington, Michael 210
Billon, Pierre 32
Binoche, Juliette 228
Biras, Francis 204
Black, Karen 180
Blakey, Art 47
Blier, Bertrand 139–42
Bob and Carol and Ted and Alice 127
Bogarde, Dirk 127, 153
Bohan, Marc 157
Bonacci, Anna 20
Bonnaire, Sandrine 228
Bonne Chance, Charlie 92
Bonnes, Les 65
Bonne Soupe, La 43, 45
Bory, Jean-Marc 37, 38, 39
Bosè, Lucia 137, 157
Boudet, Micheline 19
Boudu Sauvé des Eaux 121
Boudu Saved From Drowning 121
Boulanger, Daniel 116
Boulting, Ingrid 161
Bouquet, Michel 116, 131
Brennan, Eileen 196
Bresson, Robert 35
Brialy, Jean-Claude 35, 45, 46, 54
Bride Wore Black, The 107, 115
Broca, Philippe de 109
Bron, Eleanor 106
Brook, Peter 22, 51, 52, 62, 70, 203

Brooks, Richard 22
Brossard, Chandler 103
Bruckberger, René-Léopold 48
Bryant, Michael 116, 117
Buck, Joan Juliet 75, 112, 113, 117–18, 165, 172, 197
Buckley, Elizabeth 194
Buñuel, Luís 82–85, 101, 118, 193
Burton, Richard 87

Caine, Michael 113
Calef, Noël 35
Canby, Vincent 137
Canetti, Jacques 180, 229
Cannes Film Festival: 1966 95, 105; 1975 151; 1976 160; 1985 194–95; 1993 152, 222; history of 152–53
Capella Films 190, 191
Cardin, Pierre: meets JM 58–59; relations with JM 67–68, 69, 139; engagement to JM 99; film debut 138
Carradine, Keith 157–58
Carter, Caroline 157
Carrière, Jean-Claude 100, 102
Carter, Caroline 157
Casarès, Maria 11
Cassavetes, John 125
Cassel, Jean-Pierre 182
Cat on a Hot Tin Roof 22, 33
Cavanaugh, Desmond 113
Caves du Vatican 17, 226
Célestine, La 209
Ces Mal Aimés 17
Chailleux, Geraldine 226
Chapsal, Madeleine 155
Charrier, Jacques 89
Chase, James Hadley 61
Chatel, François 101
Chauveau, Laetitia 169, 172
Chère Louise 109, 135–36
Chevauchée sur le Lac de Constance, La 145–47
Cinémathèque 118–19
Citizen Kane 65
Clavel, Maurice 15
Clément, René 82
Clever, Edith 169
Cloche d'Or, La 2, 3
Close, Glenn 47
Clothes in the Wardrobe, The 224
Cluny, Alain 38
Cochet, Jean-Laurent 179
Cocteau, Jean 14, 21, 82

Coeur en Hiver, Un 80
Cohan, Peter 219
Comédie Française viii, 15, 16, 17, 18–19
Commission d'Avances sur Recettes 222, 223
Comptes à Rebours 128
Condemned Man Escapes, A 35
Conservatoire d'Art Dramatique 12
Constantine, Eddie 36
Corneille, Pierre 20
Corps de Diane, Le 119
Costa-Gavras, Constantin 162
Côté Cour Côté Champs 132
Cousteau, Jacques 34
Coutard, Raoul 56, 107
Cox, Alex 228
Creezy 147
Crémieux, Octave 121
Crossing of Lake Constance, The 145–47
Curtis, Tony 161

Dali, Salvador 83
Damned, The 61
Dard, Frédéric 223
Darrieux, Danielle 32
Davies, June Wyndham 194
Davis, Bette 191
Davis, Brad 183, 185
Davis, Miles 35
Dazzling Hour, The 21, 22, 26, 28
Dead Calm 116
Dead Reckoning 116
Dear Louise 109, 135–36
Decaë, Henri 36
Decoin, Henri 29, 30
Deep, The 116–17, 132
Deeply Truffaut 195
Delon, Alain 46, 162
Delon, Nathalie 85
Demoiselles de Rochefort, Les 78
Demy, Jacques 78
Deneuve, Catherine 46, 78, 115, 131
De Niro, Robert 161, 190
Denner, Charles 116
Depardieu, Gérard 137, 140, 141, 142, 146
Dernier Amour 26–27
Dernier Métro, Le 45, 142
De Sica, Vittorio 63
Desires 190
Deville, Michel 200
Devine, George 88
Dewaere, Patrick 141, 173

Dialogue des Carmélites 48, 50
Diamond, Neil 167
Diana 119, 143
Diary of a Chambermaid, The 82–85
Diegues, Carlos 138
Dietrich, Marlene 121
Dindon, Le 17
Dingo, Ernie 213
Direction Towards Death 116
Divan, Le 9
Doillon, Jacques 192
Doisneau, Robert 131
Dommartin, Solveig 213
Don Quixote 132
Dorin, François 179
Dorléac, Françoise 78
Dortoir des Grandes 29
Dos au Mur, Le 36
Douglas, Kirk 49
Down, Lesley-Anne 168
Down and Out in Beverly Hills 121
Drach, Michel 200
Dréville, Jean 31
Drieu, Pierre 81
Duceppe, Pierre 139
Dufilho, Jacques 179
Duras, Marguerite 41, 51, 52, 62, 96, 131, 137
Durrell, Lawrence 126
Duteil, Yves 171
Duval, Claire 156

Eastman, Carol 127
Echec au Porteur 33, 36
Eight and a Half 127
Eisenstein, Sergei 61
Emily Will Know 32
Emmanuelle 93, 94, 156
Equinox project 222
Et Dieu Créa la Femme 37–38
Etrange Monsieur Steve, L' 33
Eva 61–65

Fahrenheit 451 56
Fallaci, Oriana 42, 96
Fallowell, Duncan 184
Falstaff 94–96
Fassbinder, Rainer Werner 74, 181–82, 184–85
Fellini, Federico 65, 127
Femme Fardée, La 211

Fernandel 27, 28
Feu Follet, Le 81–82, 100
Feydeau, Georges-Léon-Jules-Marie 17
55 Days at Peking 80
film industry: support for 27; Quality
    Premium 27; recession 123
Finney, Albert 57, 69
Fitzgerald, F. Scott 160
Five Branded Women 50
Flemyng, Gordon 112
Flon, Suzanne 21, 26
Folies Bergères 2, 3
Fonda, Peter 69
Foreign Field, A 225–26
Foreman, Carl 68, 69
Forman, Milos 120
Fossey, Brigitte 142
Four Hundred Blows, The 45
Fraker, William A. 126
Frankenheimer, John 70
Free Cinema Wave 104
Fresnay, Pierre 28
Frey, Sami 146
Friedkin, William 165–68, 169, 170
Funès, Louis de 30

Gabin, Jean 10, 27, 29–30, 32, 36
Gale, John 96, 113
Gance, Abel 31
Ganz, Bruno 157
Garbo, Greta 92, 191
Gardner, Ava 80, 114, 191
Gary, Romain 173
Gas-Oil 32
Gassman, Vittorio 190
Gautard, Pierre 171
Geddes, Barbara Bel 50
Gelin, Daniel 33
Gémier, Firmin 19
Genet, Jean 65, 103, 183, 184
George, Adrian 77
Gérard, Philippe 180
Gide, André 17, 184
Gielgud, John 94
Gilles, Guy 132, 149, 184
Gilliatt, Penelope 53, 129
Ginsburg, Mark 201
Gion, Christian 132
Gish, Lillian 190
Givray, Claude 195
Godard, Jean-Luc 54, 61, 78, 109

Goddard, Paulette 83
Godrèche, Judith 228
Going Places 148
Golden Age, The 83
Goldsmith, Clio 173
Good Luck, Charlie 92
Good Soup, The 43, 45
Grace, Nickolas 136, 192
Graduate, The 49–50, 111
Grangier, Gilles 33
Granier-Deferre, Pierre 147
Grappelli, Stéphane 149
Great Catherine 112, 114, 204
Greco, Juliet 15
Grenier, Richard 90
Griffith, Hugh 106
Groddeck, Dr George 117
Grüber, Klaus-Michael 202, 203, 204–5
Guers, Paul 22
Guggenheimer, Peggy 63
Guinness, Alec 226
Guy, Michel 202

Haguet, André 28
Hakim, Raymond 63
Hakim, Robert 63
Hamilton, George 69, 99
Handke, Peter 145–47
Hands off the Loot 29
Harris, Richard 173
Harrison, Jim 190
Harrison, Rex 87
Harvey, Laurence 116
Haudepin, Didier 51
Havel, Vaclav 120
Hawkins, Jack 112
Headley, Lena 224
Heart in Winter, A, 80
Hellwig, Klaus 190
Hepburn, Audrey 157
Heston, Charlton 80
Heure Eblouissante, L' 21, 22, 26, 28
Heyman, Norma 225
Heymann, Danièle 82
Heynemann, Laurent 223
Higgins, Anthony 129
Hiroshima Mon Amour 51
Hirsch, Robert 30
Hollywood 61, 80, 125
Homme de Ma Vie, L' 28
Hommes en Blanc, Les 32

Honour Among Thieves 29
Hotel Terminus 210
Hu-Man 149, 153
Human Beast, The 10, 121
Humeur Vagabonde, L' 79, 131
Huppert, Isabelle 4, 142, 182
Hurt, John 106
Hurt, William 213
Hussein, Waris 224, 225
Huster, Francis 157, 169
Huston, Anjelica 161
Huston, John 128

Il est Minuit, Docteur Schweitzer 28
Immortal Story, The 109–10
Inès, Denis d' 12, 14
Infernal Machine, The 21, 32, 61, 184
Intoxe, L' 179–80
Intrigantes, Les 30
Irish, William 115
Irrepressibles, The 202–3
Isherwood, Christopher 105
It's Midnight, Dr Schweitzer 28
Ives, Kenneth 192

Jacques, Guy 226
Jacob, Irène 228
Jardin qui Bascule, Le 132, 149
Jarre, Maurice 162
Jeanne Chante Jeanne 128
Jeanne Moreau: Mystère et Beauté 200
Jelinek, Henriette 170
Je t'Aime 139
Jet Set 147–48
Jézéquel, Julie 193
Joanna Francesca 138
Joffe, Arthur 211
Jones, Elinor 181
Jouffa, François 37
Jour Après Jour 210
Journal d'une Femme de Chambre, Le 82–85
Jouvet, Louis 14, 16
Judas Was a Woman 10, 121
Jules et Jim 55–58
Julietta 29
Jusqu'au Dernier 32–33

Kaczender, George 173, 179
Kafka, Franz 65
Karina, Anna 46, 54, 78, 109
Kaufmann, Günther 183

Kazan, Elia 159, 161
Khamdamov, Roustam 214
Kidder, Margot 127
Kidman, Nicole 116
Knapp, Simone 101
Kubrick, Stanley 49
Kyrou, Ado 85
Lancaster, Burt 69, 70
Lang, Jack 222
Langlois, Henri 118–19
Lansing, Sherry 168
Lanzac, Frédéric 37
Laperrousaz, Jérôme 149, 153
Last Love 26–27
Last Metro, The 45, 142
Last Seance, The 129, 193, 194
Last Tycoon, The 159, 160–62
Laure, Carole 200
Laurençon, Monsieur 11
Léaud, Jean-Pierre 45
Lee, Jason Scott 218
Lefranc, Guy 28
Leigh, Vivien 91
Lemaire, Philippe 31, 32
Leroi, Francis 37
Lester, Richard 121, 157
Levy, Bernard Henry 222
Lévy, Raoul 52, 63
Liaisons Dangereuses, Les 47–48
Lift to the Scaffold 22, 27, 35–36
Limelighters 96
Lisi, Virna 63
List, Emmanuel 228
Lit, Le 30
Lonsdale, Michael 116, 146
Loren, Sophia 41, 65
Losey, Joseph 61–64, 105, 162, 182, 193
Losey, Patricia 64
Louves, Les 33
Lover, The 219
Lovers, The 29, 37–42
Lugagne, Françoise 83
Lulu 88, 162–63, 170
Lumière 156–60
Lunghi, Cherie 192
Luntz, Edouard 131

Machine Infernale, La 21, 32, 61, 184
McKellen, Ian 228–29
McKern, Leo 225
MacLaine, Shirley 100

Mademoiselle 64, 103–5
Made-Up Woman, The 211
Malkovich, John 47
Malle, Louis: sees JM in *Cat on a Hot Tin Roof* 22; on *La Reine Margot* 31–32; relationship with JM 33–36, 41–42; background 34–35; on film-making 71; and *Le Feu Follet* 81–82; and *Viva Maria!* 102 *see also under names of his films*
Malraux, André 40, 44, 160
Malraux, Florence 44, 62, 76, 160, 165, 172
Manchurian Candidate, The 70
Mangano, Silvana 50, 130
Manifeste des 343 131
Mann, Claude 78
Mann, Roderick 88
Map of the Human Heart 218
Marais, Jean 21, 27, 29, 121
Marceau, Félicien 43, 147
Mariée était en Noir, La 115–16
Martini, Didier 217
Mastroianni, Marcello 53, 54, 216, 217
Mata Hari, Agent H21, 91–93
Mata Hari: The Red Dancer 92
Matton, Charles 116
Mazursky, Paul 127
Memories of France 149–51
Men in White 32
Mercouri, Melina 51, 69
Meurtres 28
Meyer, Jean 16, 17
Migraine 29
Mille Milliards de Dollars 173–74
Miller, Henry 1, 2, 126
Miraculé, Le 201
Mirbeau, Octave 82
Mise à Mort, La 163, 170
Mr Klein 162
Mocky, Jean-Pierre 201
Moderato Cantabile 51–53, 137
Moine, Le 85
Molinaro, Edouard 36
Monde du Silence, Le 34
Monk, Thelonius 47
Monsieur Ripois 82
Montand, Yves 111, 119
Montenegro, Fernanda 138
Monte Walsh 126
Month in the Country, A 16
Moore, Colleen 148

Morange, Cyril 112, 125
Moreau, Anatole Désiré (father): early life 1–2; runs café-restaurant 2; origins 3; moves to Vichy 3; returns to Paris 6; called up in Vichy 8; strictness 10; attitude to JM as actress 11, 12, 16, 21; death 12, 153; parts from Kathleen 14; with JM at Le Préverger 76, 78, 117, 124
Moreau, Arsène (uncle) 2, 3
Moreau, Jeanne: real life persona ix; birth ix, 2; childhood ix, 3–6, 9, 19–11, 194; English language ix; career summary ix–x; name 2; at Vichy 3–4; schools 4, 7; parents bickering 5; sister's birth 5; Englishness 6; returns to Paris 6; wartime experience 8–10; desire to be somebody 10; ballet lessons 10, 29; reading 10, 15, 76–77, 228; early acquaintance with films 10; early desire to be an actress 11; awarded Légion d'honneur 12; at Conservatory 13–16; parents separate 14; stays with father 14; endurance and determination 14; joins Comédie Française 15–16; first job 16; offered contract at Française 16; and Richard 17; marriage 17; and Jérôme 17, 18, 142–43, 227; Richard leaves her 18; on love 18, 68–69, 89–91, 146–47; leaves Française 19; radio work 19; joins Théâtre Nationale Populaire 19; TV debut 20; on acting 20; goes free-lance 20; growing confidence 21; and mother's divorce costs 25; appearance 25, 28, 96; first film 26; acting traits 29–30; visits London 30–31; and Louis Malle 33–36, 41–42, 81–82; and nudity 41, 93; break from filming 42; private life 43, 48, 148–49; moves to Versailles 43; and astrology 43–44, 52; and Truffaut 44–46, 57; and the New Wave 46, 123, 140; and taxes 50; German Best Foreign Actress Award 51; Cannes Best Actress Award 51; lives in Blaye 52; lovers kept as friends 54, 113, 147; wins Academy's Crystal Star 57; and Cardin 58–59, 67–68, 69, 184; and Losey 63; on directors and leading ladies 64; and Brigitte Bardot 65, 77, 89, 101–3; and Orson Welles 65, 109–10, 116; first film in England 69; international reputation

69, 70; buys Le Préverger 73; sells Le
Préverger 74, 195; life at Le Préverger
74–75; divorces Richard 75; cooking 76,
125; first album of songs 79; and Tony
Richardson 88, 105, 106, 107; 'clenched
agonised face' 88–89; on Frenchmen
89–90; and on-set 'family' 92, 93;
receives Oscar and BAFTA awards 103;
receives Francis Carco Prize 103; and
Theodore Roubanis 108; records second
album 109; record prize 109; wishes to
direct 110; US reaction to 111; and
Richardson's divorce 114–15; painting
of 116; retrospectives of films 117, 172;
Les Chansons de Clarisse 117; therapy
117, 118; and politics 119, 131;
organisation of life 124–25; goes to
Hollywood 125, 126; relations with
technicians 126–27; leaves Hollywood
127; and money 128–29; and style
129–30; produces *Vogue* 130–31;
abortions 131–32; homage to Proust
132; founds magazine *IN* 132; on age
135–36; relation with Cardin flounders
139; inability to bear a child 139;
awarded Order of Merit 142; relations
with Jérôme 142–43; and Peter Handke
145–47; stage work 145–47, 162–63;
stage-fright 146; and publicity 148–49;
president of Cannes jury 151; father's
death 153; Rue du Cirque apartment
153, 158, 168; and film production 153;
first film script 154–56; as director 156,
159, 170–72; second marriage 165; and
William Friedkin 165–69, 170; returns
to Paris 168; Festival of Paris
retrospective 172; Rue de l'Université
apartment 172; awarded Prix de l'ACIC
173; becomes more *présence illustrieuse*
174; health 177–78, 217; allergies 177;
drinking habits 178, 204; character
178–79; loses voice 179; wins Prix
Brigadier 180; wins Charles Cros prize
180; voice 180–81; *Jeanne Moreau* album
181; on Fassbinder 184–85; *Guardian*
question-and-answer session 185–86;
off-screen in 1980s 189; scripts 190;
forms production company, Capella
films 190; and women film stars 190–91;
forms Spica Productions 191; television
films, 1980s 192; on life and death
193–94; family memories 194;
superstitions 194; memorial for Truffaut
194–95; and travel 195; Broadway debut
196; older women fuller figure roles 199;
revival of status 199; Quimper
retrospectives 199; invited to join
Academie des Arts et Techniques du
Cinéma 199; TV programmes 199–200;
and problems of older women 201;
awarded Molière Award for Best Actress
204; face-life 204; compares stage work
with cinema work 205–6; on the theatre
209–10; mother dies 210; TV films 210;
in USSR 213–16; in Greece 216–17;
and poetry 217; masterclass at Cannes
221; formidable character 221–22; and
Equinox project 222–23; represents
ARP 222; head of Commission
d'avances sur Recettes 222; claims of
maternity 227; *dictionnaire subjectif* 228;
disposition to profundity 229 Moreau,
Jérôme (son): birth 17; injured in car
accident 52–53; and politics 119;
relations with JM 142–43, 227; unsettled
life 143; lives in California 143
Moreau, Kathleen Sarah Buckley (mother):
marriage 2; gives birth to JM 2;
background 3; trips to England 6;
marriage unhappy 7; at sea in war; in
occupied Paris, 9; and JM's wish to be
actress 11–12; death 210
Moreau, Michelle (sister): birth 5; helps JM
with learning lines 13–14; goes to
England with mother 14; and JM and
Cardin 58
Morgan, Michèle 196
Morocco 121
Mosfilm 213–16
Mostel, Zero 112
Moustaki, Georges 128, 132
M'sieur la Caille 32
Murat, Jean-Louis 229
Murat, Prince Napoléon 33
My Name is Victor 226, 228

Nathalie Granger 137
Negulesco, Julian 136
Nero, Franco 183
Never on Sunday 51
Neveux, Georges 11
New Delhi 190, 217

Newman, Paul 50
Newton, Helmut 130
New Wave: Czech 120; French 35, 44, 46, 50, 123; German 145, 181, 213; UK 58; US 125
Nichols, Mike 50, 111
Nicholson, Jack 161
Nikita 210
Nimier, Roger 22, 33, 53
Nin, Anaïs 2, 126
Nolte, Nick 121
Norge 180
Nothing in Her Way 80
Notte, La 53–54
Novarro, Ramón 92–93
Nowra, Louis 218
Noyce, Philip 116
Nuit de l'Océan, La 206–7

Oberlin, Armelle 191
Observer 96, 113
Oeil de Vichy, L' 4
Old Lady who Walked in the Sea, The 223, 228
Olivier, Laurence 91
Omnibus programme 163, 167
Ontkean, Michael 127
Ophüls, Marcel 54, 80, 210
Ophüls, Max 54
Othello 17
Other Side of the Wind, The 132
O'Toole, Peter 85, 88, 112
Ozenne, Jean 83

Page, Anthony 88
Palance, Jack 126
Pallandt, Frédérick van 149
Paltoquet, Le 200
Papatakis, Nico 65
Parade of Stars 190
Parapluies de Cherbourg, Les 78
Parasites, The 30
Parillaud, Anne 180, 210, 218, 227
Passer, Ivan 120
Pas Suspendu de la Cigogne, Le 218
Patellière, Denys de la 32
Paulina s'en Va 150
Pauline Flees 150
Pauwels, Louis 65
Paxinou, Katina 65
Peau de Banane 79
Peau Douce, La 79

Pellegrin, Raymond 32, 33
Penn, Arthur 69–70
Peppard, George 69, 13
Perier, François 33
Perkins, Anthony 65, 67
Perset, Antoine 206
Pesary, Bruno 191, 216
Petit Théâtre de Jean Renoir, Le 121
Philipe, Gérard 20, 47
Piaf, Edith 89–90
Piccoli, Michel 83, 200
Pigalle-Saint-Germain-des-Prés 28
Pigaut, Roger 128
Pigeon, The 32
Pinheiro, José 211
Pinter, Harold 157
Pisier, Marie-France 193
Playboy 93
Plein Sud 173
Plus Vieux Métier du Monde, Le 109
Point de Lendemain 38
Poiret, Jean 201
Pompidou, Georges 123
Pottier, Richard 28
Pradella, Anna 43, 75–76, 101, 112, 177, 195
Pradella, Louis 75, 112, 177, 195
Prévert, Jacques 131, 229
Prince of Hamburg 20
Proust, Marcel 132
Psycho 67
Purdom, Edmund 88
Pygmalion 21, 32, 184

'Quand l'Amour Meurt' 121
Quatre Cents Coups, Les 45, 109
Quayle, Anthony 91
Querelle 74, 79, 182, 183–85

Race des Seigneurs, La 147–48
Racette, Francine 157
Rajot, Pierre-Loup 206
Randolph, John 225
Rear Window 115
Récit de la Servante Zerline, Le 203
Redgrave, Vanessa 103, 105, 108, 115
Reggiani, Serge 128
Règle du Jeu, La 65, 121
Régy, Claude 146, 162
Reichenbach, François 77
Reine Margot, La 31–32
Renoir, Jean 10, 83, 121, 127

Repeated Absences 132
Resnais, Alain 62, 119, 159, 165
Rezvani, Serge *see* Bassiak, Cyrus
Rich, Claude 116
Richard, Dominique 227
Richard, Jean-Louis: and JM at Conservatory
    13; marriage to JM 17; leaves JM 18; and
    Jules et Jim 57; directs JM 91–92, 93;
    screenplay for *La Mariée était en Noir* 115;
    and *IN* 132
Richard III 228
Richardson, Ralph 94
Richardson, Tony 64, 78, 88, 103, 104–5,
    106, 107, 108, 127
Ritt, Martin 50
Rivette, Jacques 127
Robin and Marian 157
Roché, Henri-Pierre 55
Ronet, Maurice 35, 46, 81
Roubanis, Theodore 108
Rousseau, Serge 116
Roussin-Croney, Aliki 216–17
Routledge, Nancy 32
Rozan, Micheline 44, 62, 109
Rudyar, Dane 44
Rules of the Game, The 65, 121
Russell, Theresa 161
Russell, Ken 127
Rutherford, Margaret 94

Sagan, Françoise 131, 132, 151, 189, 211
Sailor From Gibraltar, The 105–9, 115
Salaire du Péché, Le 32
Salkind, Alexander 67
San Francisco Film Festival 148
Sarde, Philippe 171
Sartre, Jean-Paul 15, 192
Saturday Night and Sunday Morning 58
Sautet, Claude 80
Sauve Toi, Lola 200–1
Schlesinger, John 209
Schneider, Romy 65, 69, 105
Scofield, Paul 69, 70
Scorsese, Martin 125
Secret Drawer, The 192
Secrets d'Alcove 30
Segaloff, Nat 168
Serrault, Michel 201, 223
Serre, Henri 55
Seven Days, Seven Nights 51
Seyrig, Delphine 146, 149

Sharif, Omar 85, 192
Sharkey, Ray 127
Shaw, George Bernard 21, 112
Sherman, Arthur 196
Shevitch, Dr Elia 159, 171
She-Wolves, The 33
Shoot the Pianist 116
Signoret, Simone 27, 119, 128, 169, 171, 193
Silberman, Serge 82, 191, 214, 216
Silken Skin 79
Simenon, Georges 65
Simon, François 156
Siren of Mississippi 115
Siritzky, Alain 37, 94
Sommer, Elke 69
Sonja, Magda 92
Souvenirs d'en France 149–51
Spartacus 49
Spiegel, Sam 105, 160
Spiesser, Jacques 157
Spook, Per 179
Stamp, Terence 113, 149
Stelli, Jean 26
Stewart, Alexandra 81
Strauss, Peter 161
Sturridge, Charles 226
Summer Fires 103–5
The Summer House 225, 228–229
Suspended Step of the Stork, The 216
Sutherland, Donald 127
Swingle, Ward 80
Sydow, Max von 213

Tamiroff, Akim 65
Taylor, Elizabeth 22, 87, 128, 153
Téchiné, André 150, 152
Terrasse du Midi, La 15
Three Rooms in Manhattan 65
Threlfall, David 224
Thullier, Luc 223
Tilting Garden, The 132, 149
Time 103
Time to Live and a Time to Die, A 81
Tiroir Secret, Le 192
Todd, Richard 30
Touchard, Pierre-Aimé 16
Touchez Pas au Grisbi 29
Train, The 69–70, 84
Tree, The 192–93
Trevelyan, John 39–40
Trial, The 65–67

Trintignant, Jean-Louis 38, 47, 92, 130, 192
Trois Jours à Vivre 33
Trout, The 64, 157, 182, 190
Truffaut, François: and JM's appearance 26; on *The Lovers* 37; relationship with JM 44–46, 57; background 45; and *Jules et Jim* 56, 57; script for *Mata Hari, Agent H21* 92; screenplay for *La Mariée était en Noir* 115; death 193; memorial for 194–95
Truite, La 64, 157, 182, 190
Tutin, Dorothy 128

Umbrellas of Cherbourg, The 78
Une Femme est Une Femme 54
Unifrance 31
Until the End of the World 213
Until the Last 32–33
Une Vie Privée 100

Vadim, Annette 47
Vadim, Roger 37, 46, 47–48, 63
Valseuses, Les 137, 140–42, 148
Ventura, Lino 27, 29, 35
Very Private Affair, A 100
Vian, Boris 47
Vicious Circle 136, 192
Victors, The 68, 69
Vidor, King 148
Vieille qui Marchait dans la Mer, La 223
Vilmorin, Louise de 29, 38, 40, 109
Vilar, Jean 15, 19, 20
Vitez, Antoine 210
Vitti, Monica 53
Viva Maria! 69, 79, 96, 99–103
Vivant, Dominique 38
Vivement Truffaut! 195
Voyage de Thésée, Le 11

Wages of Sin 32

Walker, Patric 44
Wall, Jean 21, 35
Wallach, Eli 69
Walters, Julie 224
Ward, Vincent 218
Wedekind, Frank 88, 162
Welles, Orson: meets JM 65; support for JM 65; and *Chimes et Midnight* 94–96; stage-fright 95–96; in *The Sailor From Gibraltar* 106; first colour film 109–10; unfinished work 132; death 193, 197 *see also under names of his films*
Wenders, Wim 145, 213
Werner, Oskar 55, 56
West, Norma 194
What Would Jeanne Moreau Do? 181
When Love Dies 121
Whom Glory Still Adores 112
Will Adams Story, The 88
Williams, Charles 80
Williams, Tennessee 22
Willie and Phil 127
Will o' the Wisp 81
Window of Ted Teztlaff, The 115
Wonger, Walter 160
Woolrich, Cornell 115

Yanne, Jean 200
Yellow Rolls-Royce, The 87–88
York, Michael 189–90
Young Girls of Rochefort, The 78
Yourcenar, Marguerite 217
Your Ticket Is No Longer Valid 173

Zaguri, Bob 101
Zane, Billy 117
Zelle, Margarete Gertrude 92
Zischler, Hans 203
Zola, Emile 10